# The Virginia Supreme Court

## An Institutional and Political Analysis

Also published for the Institute of Government, University of Virginia:

Chester W. Bain, *Annexation in Virginia: The Use of the Judicial Process for Readjusting City-County Boundaries.* 1966. xiv, 258 pp.

Chester W. Bain, *"A Body Incorporate": The Evolution of City-County Separation in Virginia.* 1967. xii, 142 pp.

David G. Temple, *Merger Politics: Local Government Consolidation in Tidewater Virginia.* 1972. xii, 225 pp.

# The Virginia Supreme Court
## *An Institutional and Political Analysis*

Thomas R. Morris

Published for
the Institute of Government, University of Virginia

The University Press of Virginia
Charlottesville

THE UNIVERSITY PRESS OF VIRGINIA


Library of Congress Cataloging in Publication Data

Morris, Thomas R.
The Virginia Supreme Court.

Bibliography: p.
Includes index.
1. Virginia. Supreme Court of Appeals.
KFV2912.M67 347'.755'035 75-1158 ISBN 0-8139-0587-7

*First published 1975*

Printed in the United States of America

*To Barbara Lyn*

# *Foreword*

The Institute of Government of the University of Virginia is pleased to present the fourth in a series of monographs on selected aspects of government and politics in Virginia. The leading role played by Virginia jurists in the development of the American constitutional system has long been understood and appreciated, but far less attention has been given to the role of the bench and bar in the governing process at the state and local levels. This study helps to fill a major void by broadening our understanding of the functioning of the Commonwealth's highest court.

Clifton McCleskey, *Director*
Institute of Government

*Charlottesville, Virginia*
*December 1974*

# *Preface*

The judiciary has traditionally been the least known and least understood branch of government. Growing public awareness of the significance of the federal judiciary has not been matched by increased visibility for the state judiciary. Furthermore, research has been confined almost exclusively to the highly visible and prestigious United States Supreme Court. Only during the last decade have political scientists shown interest in the systematic analysis of the state and lower federal courts. The challenge to take the state judiciary seriously was sounded almost one hundred and fifty years ago. Chief Justice John Marshall's reminder to the delegates at the Virginia Constitutional Convention of 1829–30 is inscribed across the facade of the Virginia Supreme Court Building: "The Judicial Department comes home in its effects to every man's fireside: it passes on his property, his reputation, his life, his all."

It is hoped that this study will not contribute unduly to the "upper court bias" by focusing on the state's highest tribunal. The state Supreme Court lends itself to analysis because of the ready availability and manageability of resource materials pertaining to it and because of its frequent involvement in cases with statewide implications. In Virginia there are three major classes of courts: the Supreme Court, standing alone at the apex of the judicial hierarchy; the circuit courts; and the minor courts, or courts not of record. The lower two classes were subjected to a major overhaul under a court reorganization plan that went into effect on July 1, 1973. The morass of special city courts of record—hustings, chancery, law and equity, and corporation—were merged into a uniform circuit court system. The courts not of record were consolidated into a statewide system of general district courts and juvenile and domestic relations district courts. This last class of courts, denoted as minor because of its location in the judicial hierarchy and not because of its importance, handles the bulk of litigation in the Virginia court system. In 1971, for example, when the Supreme Court rendered 218 opinions and the courts of record concluded slightly over 80,000 cases, the courts not of record disposed of over 1.4 million cases.

An institutional and political analysis of the Virginia Supreme Court is justified by the absence of a recent comprehensive survey of that judicial tribunal. Analyses of the court, most of which have been published in law journals, have tended to be either legalistic or biographical in nature and severely limited in scope. The sole book-length treatment of the state's highest court is Margaret V. Nelson's *A Study of Judicial Review in Virginia, 1789–1928* (New York: Columbia University Press, 1947). However, by concerning herself primarily with the function of judicial review, Dr. Nelson significantly narrowed the grounds on which to evaluate the tribunal's role in the political system. Her occasional efforts to place the court's action in the context of the contemporary political scene confirm the reader's suspicion that there is more to the story than the legal facts of each case demonstrate. Furthermore, the book does not deal with the court as participating in the political process and as therefore being acted upon by the other political actors.

The objective of this study is to examine and describe the place of the Virginia Supreme Court in the state's system of government and politics. As a political scientist rather than a lawyer, I view the court, not as simply a legal institution, but as part of Virginia's political system. Although legal values obviously influence the court, past research has tended to emphasize these legal values to the exclusion of political factors. The present study, while acknowledging both legal and political characteristics of the court, will stress the latter without denying the former. In short, the court will be viewed as part of the process by which policies are made and carried out for society—in this case, Virginia society. Emphasis will be placed on governmental actors and public law only for the sake of limiting the scope of the inquiry. The following questions have been singled out for examination: How has the Virginia Supreme Court acquired its place in the political system? Who gets on the court? What are the court's procedures? What type of cases does the court decide? What is the court's relationship with other agencies of government? What decisions does it make and of what significance are they?

From the creation of the Virginia Supreme Court until 1971, the court was constitutionally labeled the Supreme Court of Appeals. The 1971 Constitution refers to the body as simply the Supreme Court. For the sake of uniformity the current title will be used throughout this work. Likewise, before the adoption of the 1928 constitutional amendment increasing the size of the Supreme Court, Virginia justices were called judges, as were all members of the state judiciary. This study will employ the current terminology, and all members of the Supreme Court will be referred to as justices. However, individual members serving prior to 1928 will retain the title of judge.

This study would never have been started without the encouragement and support of several persons. Two teachers were instrumental in fostering my academic career: the late Prof. Ralph Eisenberg of the University of Virginia nurtured my academic interest in Virginia politics, and Alpheus T. Mason, Professor Emeritus of Princeton University, instilled an enduring fascination with the judicial function of government. The faithful support and pride which my parents demonstrated throughout my years of formal education were a source of satisfaction. Finally, my wife, Barbara Lyn, contributed to this study from beginning to end in more ways than she probably cares to remember. She was unfailingly supportive and served as an indispensable typist, researcher, and critic.

The following persons from the University of Virginia read all or part of the manuscript at various stages of completion, and I am deeply grateful for their comments and criticisms: Henry J. Abraham, Weldon Cooper, Robert J. Harris, S. J. Makielski, Jr. (now at Loyola University, New Orleans), and Charles K. Woltz. Prof. Clifton McCleskey and the staff at the Institute of Government provided the necessary support and assistance to ensure the completion of this project. I am also especially indebted to the former governors, justices, and court personnel who graciously submitted to interviews and whose names are listed in the Bibliography. One member of the court, Justice Harry L. Carrico, deserves to be singled out for his cooperation and counsel. Needless to say, any errors that remain are the responsibility of the author.

Thomas R. Morris

*Richmond, Virginia*
*November 1974*

# *Contents*

Appendixes



## Tables

## Figures



## Chart



## Illustrations

# The Virginia Supreme Court

## An Institutional and Political Analysis

# I *Constitutional and Political Development*

THE colonial origins of the Virginia Supreme Court can be traced to 1606, the year in which the constitutional history of Virginia began. On April 10 King James I granted the Virginia Company a charter that provided for a Council, to be composed of thirteen members, "which shall govern and order all matters and causes, which shall arise, grow, or happen" in the colony. The Council was to elect a president annually from among its members, and the opinion of the majority was to prevail in all decisions. Since the charter did not provide for a resident governor, all the functions of government—legislative, executive, and judicial—were entrusted to the Council, which was to act in accordance with the laws of England. The Council possessed substantial power to exercise its judicial functions with respect to both capital and lesser offenses. For itself, the crown specifically reserved only the right of absolute pardon and the power to punish persons convicted of crimes against citizens of friendly states and those guilty of attempting to dissuade any of the people from allegiance to the king or the church. In spite of this immense judicial authority, the councillors never received a commission or took an oath as judges. This omission prompted one writer to evaluate the Council in this manner: "Out of such haphazard beginnings rose an unique political institution, a body involved in the formulation of policy as the upper house of the Assembly and in interpreting this policy as the highest court of the colony."[1]

A second charter was issued in 1609, providing for a governor appointed in England in place of a president selected by the Council. Throughout the earliest years of the colony the governor and Council did not separate their executive and judicial duties. The Council first began to sit separately as a court of justice and as a council of state in the 1620s. Regular quarterly court sessions be-

[1] Hugh F. Rankin, *Criminal Trial Proceedings in the General Court of Colonial Virginia* (Charlottesville: University Press of Virginia, 1965), p. 3.

came the practice, and the governor and Council were known as the Quarter Court when they convened to conduct judicial business. The practice was formalized by a 1632 statute specifying that four quarter courts were to be held yearly, beginning the first of March, June, September, and December, for the purpose of hearing appeals from inferior courts.[2] When the June term was later abolished as unnecessary and inconvenient, the term *quarter court* became a misnomer. The court was renamed the General Court in 1661 as a more appropriate appellation for a place "where all persons and causes have general audience and receive determination."[3]

## The General Assembly as Supreme Court

Virginia's experiment in popular government began with the convening of the first General Assembly at Jamestown, July 30, 1619. The Assembly was composed of twenty-two elected burgesses, the governor, and six councillors. Under this plan of government, the General Assembly was the highest tribunal in the colony. Initially, the legislature assumed original and appellate jurisdiction for both civil and criminal cases. As a matter of practice, the General Assembly was inclined to refer judicial questions, particularly civil matters, to the governor and Council. The judicial function of the legislature was performed by a committee of justice composed of both burgesses and councillors. Although the entire General Assembly was required to confirm the decisions of the committee, the popularly elected burgesses dominated the membership of the committee. The composition of the committee led one writer to comment that in practice "the highest court of appeal in the colony was an elective body, directly responsible to the people."[4]

The pressure of legislative duties forced the General Assembly to devote less and less of its time to judicial matters. As early as 1641 its civil jurisdiction was limited primarily to appellate cases.

[2] William W. Hening, ed., *The Statutes at Large . . . of Virginia,* 13 vols. (reprint; Charlottesville: Published for the Jamestown Foundation by the University Press of Virginia, 1969), 1:174.

[3] Ibid., 2:58.

[4] Oliver P. Chitwood, *Justice in Colonial Virginia* (Baltimore: Johns Hopkins Press, 1905), p. 24.

In 1661 the power to hear criminal cases involving life and limb was vested in the governor and Council sitting as the General Court. By virtue of this power the General Court shared the highest judicial authority in the colony with the General Assembly. At no time, however, did the legislature voluntarily abrogate its judicial authority. As late as 1662, an act of the General Assembly specified the first day of each session to be devoted to receiving presentments of grand juries and to inquiry into the operation of the court system.[5] Furthermore, the Assembly was unequivocal in its assertion that "no act of court or proclamation doe hereafter enjoyne any obedience contrary to an act of Assembly."[6]

In 1683 a royal order divested the legislature of its remaining right to hear appeals, thereby making the General Court the sole colonywide supreme court. The burgesses registered a loud protest when the crown discontinued their right to hear appeals. The authorities in England, on the other hand, having just surveyed the developments related to Bacon's Rebellion, saw the popularly elected branch of the Assembly as a potential threat to the dominant position of the governor and Council. It was feared the burgesses might in time actually dominate the administration of justice in the colony. The burgesses were not easily reconciled to the loss of power. Their representative in England was instructed to urge the appointment to the Council of only those men with proper legal training.[7] Again, at the beginning of the eighteenth century, the burgesses differed with royal authority over the composition of the General Court. Partly in response to the arbitrary conduct of Gov. Francis Nicholson as presiding officer of the General Court, the General Assembly proposed the appointment of five judges with fixed terms and qualifications. However, the Board of Trade in London, which after 1696 served as the primary body for dealing with colonial affairs, altered the legislation so as to allow the governor and Council to continue serving as the supreme court of the colony.[8]

[5] Hening, 2:63, 108.

[6] Ibid., 1:447.

[7] Philip A. Bruce, *Institutional History of Virginia in the Seventeenth Century*, 2 vols. (New York: Putnam's, 1910), 1:694–96.

[8] Rankin, pp. 21–22; *Executive Journals of the Council of Colonial Virginia*, 6 vols. (Richmond: Virginia State Library, 1925–66), 3:106.

## The General Court

Beginning in 1684 the General Court met twice a year, convening in April and October. It exercised original and appellate jurisdiction with regard to both civil and criminal cases. A 1705 act for regulating and settling the proceedings of the General Court defined its broad jurisdictional outlines: "To hear and determine, all causes, matters, and things whatsoever, relating to or concerning any person or persons, ecclesiastic or civil, or to any other persons or things, of what nature soever the same shall be, whether the same be brought before them by original process, or appeal from any other court, or by any other ways or means whatsoever."[9] All criminal cases in which the loss of life or limb was at stake (except in the case of slaves) were heard in the General Court. Its original jurisdiction in certain categories of civil cases was eventually vested in the inferior courts. Appeals to the General Court were primarily from the county courts, formerly called monthly courts.[10]

Any five members of the General Court constituted a quorum, with either the governor or the president of the Council acting as the presiding officer. According to one historian of the court, the members often took turns on the bench so that all could receive an equal share of the compensation that was apportioned on the basis of attendance.[11] The councillors were appointed by the king on the basis of social standing, family ties, and property holdings rather than knowledge of the law. Consequently, few of the councillors possessed any formal legal education. In defense of the councillors it should be noted that they were among the most capable men of the colony, with broad experience in a variety of fields. Many of them had previously served as county justices. In the early years of the colony the councillors could seek legal advice from England, but quite likely they relied "on their own judgments for guidance more than on law and precedents."[12] The inadequacy of the councillors with regard to legal matters was rectified somewhat by the governor's appointment of an attorney general. By

[9] Hening, 3:289.

[10] Rankin, pp. 44–46. Slaves charged with capital crimes were tried by the county justices on the basis of a special commission issued by the governor.

[11] Ibid., p. 52.

[12] Chitwood, p. 123.

1703 the attorney general was required to live in the capital city of Williamsburg and was frequently requested to advise the Council concerning the applicability of pertinent legal principles.[13]

The transfer of the supreme judicial authority from the General Assembly to the General Court transformed the latter into practically a court of last resort. However, the General Court did not review acts of the legislature, since that power was vested in the governor and ultimately in the King in Council. All laws and judicial decisions made by the officials of the colony were to be in accord with the laws and ordinances of England. The British crown never relinquished its prerogative to review the judicial and legislative proceedings of the colony. Appeals of judgments or sentences of the courts could be made to the King in Council. Occasionally the appellant was successful in securing a reversal of the General Court, although as a practical matter the expense and long-distance travel inherent in the procedure rendered it prohibitive in most instances.[14]

The precedent set by the reviewing tribunal in England of deciding whether a colonial statute was in accord with the laws of England was noted by the legal authorities in the colony. In 1776, when a county court in Virginia was confronted with the question of whether the Stamp Act was binding in Virginia, the judges were unanimously of the opinion that the law was of no effect on the inhabitants of the colony "inasmuch as they conceived the said act to be unconstitutional."[15] Nevertheless, the authority of the General Court was severely limited even when compared with that of similar institutions in other colonies. In the beginning none of the colonies had a supreme court; but, of ten of America's oldest states, only Virginia failed to provide for a separate supreme court during the colonial period. A developmental study of those states concluded that the common characteristic of the colonial states was the "impotence of the courts vis-à-vis other governmental

[13] Rankin, pp. 53–55.

[14] Roscoe Pound, *Organization of Courts* (Boston: Little, Brown, 1940), p. 53. For a survey of colonial appeals to the King in Council, see George A. Washburne, *Imperial Control of the Administration of Justice in the Thirteen American Colonies, 1684–1776*, Studies in History, Economics, and Public Law (New York: Columbia University, 1923), chaps. 3, 4.

[15] Charles G. Haines, *The American Doctrine of Judicial Supremacy* (Berkeley: University of California Press, 1932), pp. 60–61.

structures."[16] This characterization was especially pronounced in Virginia because of the lack of separation between the highest court and the Council. The Council, with its aristocratic members, was the most powerful body in the colony; and yet, with the exception of its independence from the lower house of the Assembly regarding judicial matters, it remained virtually indistinguishable from the other branches of government.

## The Virginia Supreme Court

With independence from Great Britain came the necessity of making changes in the form of Virginia government. Since judicial appeals would no longer be made to the King in Council, provision had to be made for a self-contained judiciary. Furthermore, a major concern was to eliminate the unhealthy situation arising from an appellate judiciary made up of an executive and his council. On June 29, 1776, five days prior to the signing of the Declaration of Independence, the delegates to the Virginia Constitutional Convention unanimously adopted a plan for the future form of state government.

According to the Constitution of 1776 the Virginia Supreme Court was to be composed of members elected by the legislature for the purpose of exercising duties solely of a judicial nature. Basic to the design of free government framed for Virginia was the principle that the legislative, executive, and judicial branches of government were to be separate and distinct. Officials who had been chosen by the crown or its agents in the colonial period—such as the governor and Council—were now to be elected by the legislature. The governor was to exercise the executive function of government with the advice of a Council of State, or Privy Council, which, unlike the colonial governor's Council, was to possess no judicial authority. A popularly elected Senate was to replace the colonial Council as the upper chamber of the General Assembly.

The judicial function of government was to be vested in a Su-

[16] In addition to Virginia, the states were Connecticut, Massachusetts, New Hampshire, Rhode Island, New Jersey, New York, Pennsylvania, North Carolina, and South Carolina. Constance R. Crito, "American State Supreme Courts and Judges: A Study in Political Development" (Ph.D. diss., Yale University, 1969), p. 39.

preme Court, in a reconstituted General Court, and in additional superior courts: "The two Houses of Assembly shall by joint ballot, appoint Judges of the Supreme Court of Appeals, and General Court, Judges in Chancery, Judges of Admiralty, Secretary, and Attorney-General to be commissioned by the Governor, and continue in office during good behavior."[17] The constitution did not elaborate on the organization of the colonial court structures beyond these broad outlines; consequently, the General Assembly was given not only the power of appointing the judges but also the responsibility for constituting the court system.

In 1777 the General Assembly acted to discharge its responsibilities by establishing a Court of Admiralty and a High Court of Chancery, each consisting of three judges. The General Court was reestablished to include five judges, three of whom would constitute a quorum. An act of the legislature in May 1779 provided for the first Virginia Supreme Court, to consist of judges of the existing Admiralty, General, and Chancery courts. The jurisdiction of the Supreme Court, which was primarily appellate, extended to those cases "brought before [it] by appeals and writs of errour to reverse decrees of the high court of chancery, judgments of the general court, and sentences of the court of admiralty."[18] The new court was to meet semiannually, sessions beginning on the twenty-ninth of March and August unless the date fell on Sunday, in which case the court was to convene the following day.

On August 30, 1779, Edmund Pendleton and George Wythe of the Court of Chancery, John Blair of the General Court, and Benjamin Waller, Richard Cary, and William R. W. Curle of the Court of Admiralty gathered in Williamsburg for the purpose of organizing the first Supreme Court. Pendleton became the president of the court as a result of being the first judge of the Chancery Court, which had been given precedence over the other two courts in the act constituting the new tribunal. The judges had not been issued commissions for their offices on the Supreme Court. Knowing each other to be members of the judiciary, they decided that the commissions they received for their seats on the lower courts

[17] Va. Constitution (hereafter cited as Con.), 1776. The texts of Virginia's constitutions from 1776 through 1902 may be found in Francis N. Thorpe, comp. and ed., *The Federal and State Constitutions . . . of the United States,* 7 vols. (Washington, D.C.: Government Printing Office, 1907), vol. 7.

[18] Ibid., 10:91.

would suffice. Therefore, in compliance with the stipulations of the enabling legislation, Wythe and Blair administered the oath of office to Pendleton, who proceeded to administer the oath to the other members present.[19] In this manner the Virginia Supreme Court came into existence. The British invasion of Virginia temporarily interrupted the work of the court, but with the end of the war the justices immediately attended to business. After the seat of government was moved to Richmond, in 1779, the court sat in the courthouse of Henrico County.

In 1788, the year in which Virginia ratified the Federal Constitution, the General Assembly made major changes in the court system of the state. On January 2, 1788, the legislature established district courts in an effort to alleviate the overcrowded docket of the General Court. The assignment of the members of the Supreme Court to the various districts, however, imposed a heavy burden on the justices without any increase in pay. In the spring term of the court it was agreed that the new duties threatened the independence of the judiciary, and a remonstrance to the General Assembly was drawn up, read in open court, presented to the governor, and printed in several newspapers.[20]

A special session of the legislature called by the governor in the summer of 1788 to consider the matter suspended the effective date of the act until after the next session of the legislature. The General Assembly attempted to resolve the problem by reconstituting the Supreme Court. The new court was to be entirely separate from the other courts, as it is today, and was to consist of five justices chosen by the joint ballot of both houses of the legislature. However, the General Assembly made no provision for those members of the old Supreme Court not elected to the new tribunal. When the original Supreme Court convened for the last time, in March 1789, the judges resigned their positions only after expressing their disapproval of the Assembly's action in removing constitutional officers from their seats.

Under the new legislation the members of the General Court were allotted to the district courts. Appellate jurisdiction in crim-

[19] *First Case of the Judges*, 4 Call (8 Va.) 1 (1779).

[20] *Case of the Judges*, 4 Call (8 Va.) 135, 141–51 (1788); David J. Mays, *Edmund Pendleton, 1721–1803, A Biography*, 2 vols. (Cambridge: Harvard University Press, 1952), 2:273.

inal matters was eventually vested in the General Court, while the Supreme Court exercised appellate jurisdiction in civil cases. The state therefore had a double-headed court system for hearing appeals in civil and criminal cases until the General Court was abolished, in 1852. Since that time the Supreme Court has been the state's appellate tribunal in both civil and criminal cases.

## Judicial Review

The primary weakness of the Virginia Constitution of 1776 was that it provided for the predominance of the legislature. The prerogatives of the executive were carefully limited: the governor was restricted to three successive one-year terms and could not serve again until he had been out of office for four years, and the exercise of the executive powers of the office was to be tempered by the advice of a Council of State. Moreover, the governor and the Council of State, as well as the judges of Virginia, were to be elected by the legislature. The result was that in spite of the explicit constitutional commitment to separate and distinct branches of government, the legislature exercised such a preponderance of power as to render the principle ineffective. Thomas Jefferson summed up the development in Virginia in these words: "173 despots [the number of Virginia legislators] would surely be as oppressive as one."[21]

The Virginia judiciary was sensitive to the need to establish its independence from the legislative branch. Some historians have suggested that opposition to the preeminent position of the legislature is what encouraged the early acceptance of judicial review of the constitutionality of legislative actions.[22] After 1784, with the popular party in firm control of the Virginia legislature, the Supreme Court provided the conservative elements of the state with a potential check on the General Assembly. Whatever the causes may have been, the principle of judicial review was clearly established by the state judiciary early in Virginia's history.

21 Jefferson, *Notes on the State of Virginia* (Chapel Hill: University of North Carolina Press, 1955), p. 120.

22 Allan Nevins, *The American States during and after the Revolution, 1775–1789* (New York: Kelley, 1924), p. 169.

As early as 1782 the original Supreme Court, dominated by conservative members, asserted its right to declare legislation unconstitutional. Three men had been convicted of treason by the General Court under a 1776 act that had removed the power of pardon from the executive. The House of Delegates had granted the men a pardon, but the Senate had refused to concur in the action. By a vote of six to two, the members of the Supreme Court held the pardons to be invalid without the concurrence of the Senate and thereby avoided a ruling on whether the statute was at variance with the constitution. While contemporary interest in the case focused on the plight of the prisoners, the opinion of George Wythe resulted in the case's being recorded as a landmark in the development of judicial review in Virginia and throughout the nation. Judge Wythe, law teacher of John Marshall, left no doubt as to his view of the Supreme Court's power: "Nay more, if the whole legislature, an event to be deprecated, should attempt to overleap the bounds, prescribed to them by the people, I, in administering the public justice of the country, will meet the united powers, at my seat in this tribunal; and, pointing to the constitution, will say, to them, here is the limit of your authority; and, hither, shall you go, but no further."[23] Although Wythe's pronouncement has often been quoted in defense of the courts, Judge James Mercer actually went one step beyond Wythe and declared the act of the legislature unconstitutional. Regrettably, Mercer's opinion, for some reason not printed by the court reporter, went unnoticed for a century and a half, until it was discovered among the notes of Judge Edmund Pendleton.[24] Pendleton wrote a separate opinion, avoiding the issue of judicial review as "a tremendous question, the decision of which might involve consequences to which gentlemen may not have extended their ideas."[25]

The position of the remaining justices on judicial review is somewhat unclear. According to Pendleton's biographer, two of the members, Richard Cary and Paul Carrington, found no conflict between the act and the constitution, and the others either

[23] *Commonwealth* v. *Caton*, 4 Call (8 Va.) 5, 8 (1782).

[24] Mays, 2:196.

[25] 4 Call (8 Va.) 17.

opposed the concept of judicial review or, like Pendleton, decided the case on other grounds.[26] The court reporter reproduced the separate opinions of Wythe and Pendleton and indicated that the remaining justices "were of the opinion, that the Court had power to declare any resolution or act of the legislature, or either branch of it, to be unconstitutional and void."[27] In any event it is clear that the case, especially Wythe's oft-quoted proclamation and Mercer's overlooked opinion, presaged the establishment of judicial review in Virginia.

The *Case of the Judges*, 1788, continued the development of judicial review by the Virginia courts. In the remonstrance to the General Assembly referred to earlier, the issue was forcefully stated in these words: "When they [the judges] decide between an act of the people, and an act of the legislature, they are within the line of their duty, declaring what the law is, and not making a new law. And ever disposed to maintain harmony with other members of government so necessary to promote the happiness of society, they most sincerely wish, that the present infraction of the constitution may be remedied by the legislature themselves; and thereby all further uneasiness on the occasion be prevented."[28] The court was granted its wish when the legislation in question was revised. And yet when the legislature's solution, including the reconstitution of the Supreme Court as a separate court, failed to provide for the old members, the conservative justices resigned their offices with a minimum of fuss to facilitate "the attainment of so desirable an object as the establishment of courts, which by the expeditious administration of justice, will not only give that relief to suffering creditors, which has already been too long withheld from them, but contribute much to the increase of industry, and improvements of the morals of the people."[29] One factor undoubtedly contributing to the speedy acceptance of judicial review in Virginia was the temperate position assumed by the Supreme Court. The Democratic-Republican legislature was of course

[26] Mays, 2:196–97.

[27] 4 Call (8 Va.) 20.

[28] 4 Call (8 Va.) 146. For a thorough discussion of this case, see Margaret V. Nelson, "The Cases of the Judges, Fact or Fiction," *Virginia Law Review* 31 (1944): 243–55.

[29] 4 Call (8 Va.) 149–50.

not pleased by the action of the court, but the justices' deferential tone played a part in mimimizing the conflict between the two branches of government.

If the *Case of the Judges* laid the cornerstone for the establishment of judicial review in Virginia, *Kamper* v. *Hawkins,* 1793, completed the construction. In the latter decision the General Court elaborated on the earlier opinions of the Supreme Court in declaring an act of the legislature unconstitutional. The case was a continuation of the conflict between the legislature and the judiciary concerning the reorganization of the district courts. Notwithstanding the fact that the district courts had been created by the legislature, the 1788 act extended to judges of those courts the power of granting injunctions to stay proceedings on judgments obtained in the same courts. This injunctive power had formerly been reserved for a constitutional court, the High Court of Chancery. The question before the General Court was whether a district court judge could constitutionally exercise the functions of a judge in chancery. Judge Nelson perceived three alternative courses of action for the General Court: "1st, to Refuse to decide the question at all, which would be a dereliction of duty; or 2dly, To wait for the Legislature to decide whether the act be unconstitutional, which would be contrary [to the separation of powers clause in the Constitution]. 3dly, To decide that the act is void, and therefore that the claimant under it cannot succeed."[30] The court, choosing the third alternative, decided that only judges chosen in accordance with the provisions of the constitution could issue an injunction authorized by the law. Significantly, Judge Nelson noted the *Case of the Judges* in observing that "it has been decided by the judges of the Supreme Court of Appeals (whether judicially or not is another question), that a law contrary to the constitution is 'void.' "[31] *Kamper* was one of the most important state precedents for judicial review before John Marshall enunciated this principle for the United States Supreme Court in *Marbury* v. *Madison,* 1803. The opinions of the Virginia judges in *Kamper,* as well as the earlier remonstrance to the General Assembly by the justices, received considerable attention contemporaneously and were printed in pamphlet form.

[30] *Kamper* v. *Hawkins,* 1 Va. Cases 31 (1793).
[31] 1 Va. Cases 23.

After *Kamper*, the principle of judicial review for state courts was widely accepted in Virginia. Writing in an 1837 opinion for the Virginia Supreme Court, Judge Henry St. George Tucker was able to assert: "The power of the judiciary to decide on the constitutionality of a law is too firmly settled to be questioned."[32] However, the unquestioned acceptance of the principle did not immediately lead to its frequent exercise by the Virginia courts. The second case in which a state law was declared unconstitutional was not until 1828.[33] The period between 1789 and 1861, in which less than 35 cases pertained to the constitutionality of legislative action, was "characterized by both a hesitancy to test the validity of laws and a hesitancy on the part of the courts to declare laws invalid on constitutional grounds."[34] The full flowering of judicial review was not until after the Civil War. From 1861 to 1902 the Virginia Supreme Court heard over 130 cases pertaining to judicial review and declared acts unconstitutional in more than one-third of them.[35] By the end of the nineteenth century the "testing of laws in the court had become an expected procedure awaited alike by the legislature who passed them and the people who were to obey them."[36]

## Spencer Roane

Judge Spencer Roane, one of the early members of the Virginia Supreme Court, merits special attention by virtue of the prominent role he played in the politics both of the nation and of his native state of Virginia. He was easily the dominant figure on the high bench and in state politics during the first two decades of the nineteenth century. Judge Roane was elected to the Virginia Supreme Court on December 2, 1794, and served until his death, on September 4, 1822. He was reputed to have been Jefferson's choice for Chief Justice of the United States had not the timely

[32] *Goddin* v. *Crump*, 8 Leigh (35 Va.) 154 (1837).

[33] *Crenshaw and Crenshaw* v. *The Slate River Co.*, 6 Randolph (27 Va.) 271 (1828).

[34] Margaret V. Nelson, *A Study of Judicial Review in Virginia, 1789–1928* (New York: Columbia University Press, 1947), p. 32.

[35] Ibid., pp. 54, 80.

[36] Ibid., p. 182.

resignation of Oliver Ellsworth allowed President Adams to appoint another Virginian, John Marshall.

When Roane was elected to the high bench in Virginia, the Democratic-Republican party of Jefferson was in firm control of the Old Dominion. The Virginia judge inherited the leadership of the party organization and, from his position on the Supreme Court, wielded extraordinary influence in the political affairs of the state. Roane founded the *Richmond Enquirer*, one of the most influential newspapers in the country, and chose his cousin, Thomas Ritchie, to be editor. With Ritchie as a powerful ally, Roane proceeded to control the nomination and election of members to the General Assembly and, at times, actually drafted bills and resolutions that were passed by the legislature. According to one historian, by 1815 "Roane was the most powerful politician in the state."[37]

The fact that Roane was so active politically while on the court might have been the subject of heated criticism had it not been for his overwhelming support in the legislature. Moreover, he voiced the sentiments of many Virginians in his strident attacks on the nationalizing opinions of the United States Supreme Court, presided over by John Marshall. Just as the Virginia General Assembly had made known its opposition to the action of the national government in the form of the Virginia Resolutions, the state's highest court, with Roane leading the way, expressed its dissent. The opportunity was provided in a case involving the title to large tracts of land lying between the Rappahannock and Potomac rivers. In *Martin* v. *Hunter's Lessee*, the nation's highest court overruled the decision of the Virginia Supreme Court and ordered that state court to enter a judgment reversing its own decision.[38] A unanimous Virginia court denied the authority of the United States Supreme Court to review its decisions and refused to obey the mandate of the federal court. In his opinion Judge Roane chided the appellee's counsel for admonishing the Virginia justices to consider the consequences of their decision in view of the anarchical tendencies of the South. Political consequences were of no concern

[37] William E. Dodd, "Chief Justice Marshall and Virginia, 1813–1821," *American Historical Review* 12 (1907):776–77. See also Albert J. Beveridge, *The Life of John Marshall*, 4 vols. (Boston and New York: Houghton Mifflin, 1916–19), 4:146–47.

[38] 7 Cranch (11 U.S.) 603 (1813).

to the justices, argued Roane, but it would be well to remember "that there is a Charybdis to be avoided, as a Scylla; that a centripetal, as well as a centrifugal principle, exists in the government; and that no calamity would be more to be deplored by the American people, than a vortex in the general government, which should ingulph and sweep away, every vestige of the state constitutions."[39] Spencer Roane and the judicial tribunal on which he sat were thus embroiled in the most heated political controversy of the period.

## Judicial Independence

Although the independence of the courts had, for all intents and purposes, been assured following the early confrontation with the legislature, the debate on this issue continued for many years. The Virginia judicial system operated as a "rigid and self-perpetuating" oligarchy.[40] Justices of the county courts were appointed for life by the governor on the recommendation of the other court members. While reserving his strongest criticism for the county court system, Jefferson observed with disapproval that "the judges of the highest courts are dependent on none but themselves." The former president bemoaned the fact that the judges were "irremovable, but by their own body."[41]

Predictably, the judicial oligarchy of the state was a prime target of the reformers during the Constitutional Convention of 1829–30. One of Jefferson's criticisms was heeded in the constitutional provision that a judge could be removed from a court by a two-thirds vote of each house of the legislature if that judge received a statement of the charges twenty days before the General Assembly acted and if the cause for removal was entered in the journal of each house. The sole power to try impeachments was also removed from the General Court or, in cases where a judge of that court was charged, the Supreme Court, and placed in the Senate.[42]

39 *Hunter* v. *Martin*, 4 Munford (18 Va.) 1, 261 (1815).

40 Beveridge, 4:487.

41 Jefferson to Samuel Kercheval, July 12, 1816, Paul L. Ford, ed., *The Writings of Thomas Jefferson*, 10 vols. (New York: G. P. Putnam's Sons, 1892–99), 10:38.

42 Con., 1830, art. III, sec. 13; art. V, sec. 6. Neither of these methods was ever successfully invoked against a member of the Virginia Supreme Court.

The debate on the tenure of office for the judges has been described as "one of the most brilliant exhibitions of the Convention."[43] The conservatives' great fear was that a majority of the legislature, unable to obtain a two-thirds vote in each house to remove an obnoxious judge, might accomplish the same purpose by abolishing the court and then immediately creating a new court with new judges. (The Supreme Court, being a constitutional court, would not be subject to such manipulation.)

Littleton W. Tazewell of Norfolk proposed that only "one Supreme Court" be provided for in the constitution in conformity with the terms of the Federal Constitution, and that the justices of this court hold office during good behavior, beyond the control of the legislature. The inferior courts, however, would be subject to abolishment or modification by the General Assembly. In this manner the Virginia Supreme Court would become "consecrated as much as the Supreme Court of the United States."[44] The national precedent could be cited to clarify any confusion with respect to the Virginia judicial system. Tazewell argued that an independent judiciary did not require that the inferior courts be independent of the legislature: "Preserve your Supreme Court independent, and you get all you need."[45]

The most prominent defender of the independence of Virginia's judicial system was the chief justice of the United States, John Marshall, who was a member of the Judiciary Committee at the convention. In view of the fact that the Virginia Constitution antedated the Constitution of the United States, Marshall saw no reason to change the name of Virginia's high court or the structure of the state's judiciary to conform to the fixed federal construction. And, unconvinced by Tazewell's argument, the chief justice launched into an eloquent defense of a judge's tenure continuing during good behavior:

Advert, Sir to the duties of a Judge. He has to pass between the Government and the man whom that Government is prosecuting: between the most powerful individual in the community, and the poorest and most

[43] Hugh B. Grigsby, *The Virginia Convention of 1829–30* (Richmond: MacFarlane and Fergusson, 1854), p. 16.

[44] *Proceedings and Debates of the Virginia State Convention of 1829–1830*, 2 vols. (1830; reprint ed., New York: Da Capo Press, 1971), 2:614–15, 617.

[45] Ibid., 2:614.

unpopular. It is of the last importance, that in the exercise of these duties, he should observe the utmost fairness. Need I press the necessity of this? Does not every man feel that his own personal security and the security of his property depends on that fairness? The Judicial Department comes home in its effects to every man's fireside: it passes on his property, his reputation, his life, his all. Is it not, to the last degree important, that he should be rendered perfectly and completely independent, with nothing to influence or control him but God and his conscience? . . . the whole good which may grow out of this convention, be it what it may, will never compensate for the evil of changing the tenure of the Judicial office.[46]

As Marshall's biographer observed, "Seldom in any parliamentary body has an appeal been so fruitful of votes."[47] Tazewell's amendment was defeated by a vote of fifty-six to twenty-nine.[48] Reflecting this vote, article V, section 2, of the new constitution stated: "No law abolishing any court shall be construed to deprive a judge thereof of his office, unless two-thirds of the members of each house present concur in the passing thereof." The independence of the members of the Supreme Court was further protected by the provision that while they were in office, their fixed and adequate salaries could not be reduced.

## Popular Election of Justices

Less than twenty-five years after Marshall's earnest plea for judicial independence, the Reform Convention of 1850–51 not only limited the terms of the justices but also provided for the popular election of the judiciary. The state was divided into five judicial sections with provision that the qualified voters of each section would elect one justice to the Supreme Court for a term of twelve years. One circuit judge for each of twenty-one judicial circuits was also to be elected by the voters for an eight-year term. Whereas the conservatives had been triumphant at the Convention of 1829–30, the western delegates and eastern reformers prevailed at the Reform Convention.

46 Ibid., 2:616.

47 Beveridge, 4:496.

48 *Proceedings and Debates of the Virginia State Convention of 1829–1830* 2:619.

Two basic arguments were advanced against a continuation of legislative selection of justices to serve for unlimited terms: justices would continue to be chosen by a legislative caucus in which a minority of the total membership of the Assembly might prevail, and Supreme Court members could continue to serve at an advanced age. Three modes of judicial selection were before the delegates for consideration: selection by the legislature, by the qualified voters of each section, and by all the qualified voters of the state.[49] The last-named method was overwhelmingly rejected, thus narrowing the convention's choice to selection by the legislature or by the voters of each section. The Judiciary Committee of the convention, which favored legislative election, attempted to quell the criticism directed at the advanced age of some of the justices by recommending a limited term of service as well as an upper age limit of seventy years. The committee also advocated that a justice be elected for each section by the joint vote of the legislature.

The major argument against popular election by sections was that the voters would be uninformed as to the qualifications of the candidates, and that the caucuses of the political parties would therefore in effect be making the selection. Furthermore, it was maintained that since a member of the Supreme Court served the entire state, his political base should be the entire state, not one section of it. In making the case for the report of the Judiciary Committee, John Janney of Loudoun, who had replaced Richard C. L. Moncure as chairman when the latter was elected to the state Supreme Court, pointed out the paucity of complaints against the court and the excellence of the members chosen under the old method: "I am not willing to abandon the system that has given to the Commonwealth a Pendleton, a Roane, a Cabell, the two Tuckers, a Green, a Baldwin, an Allen, and a host of others that I could name, and last, though not least, Richard Moncure."

Daniel H. Hoge of Montgomery submitted the amendment to vest the power of election in the qualified voters of each section.

49 The only record of the debates during this period of the convention are the supplements published in the Richmond newspapers. They have been collected and bound together in two volumes at the Virginia State Library under the title, *Virginia Constitutional Convention, 1850–51: Debates and Proceedings.* All references in this study are to the debates and proceedings on June 18, 19, 20, 21, 1851, preserved in vol. 2.

He based his case on the sovereignty of the voters and their competency to elect the members of the Supreme Court. It was absurd, he maintained, to argue that the voters were competent enough to elect others to make the selection but not competent enough to make the choice themselves. Furthermore, he submitted that his amendment not only conformed to the principles of popular government but also maintained the independence of the judiciary:

I do not mean that nicknamed independence of the judiciary, that is so common in these days, that would elevate the judges above the people, and make them wholly irresponsible to those in whom resides inherently all rightful sovereignty. That is not an independent judiciary; but a despotism—an order of irresponsible agents. But I mean the independence of the judiciary, as it was originally understood by the wise and learned of both England and America. I have never learned that an independent judiciary meant independence of the people, or irresponsibility to those whose trustees and servant they are designed to be; but an independence of the other departments of the government.

By a vote of forty-nine to forty-seven, the delegates decided to strike the Judiciary Committee's proposal for election by the legislature. Hoge's amendment was then passed by a vote of fifty-three to thirty-six.

As is evidenced by the debates of the convention, the decisions of the Supreme Court are not what prompted the change in the selection procedures and the tenure of the justices; since 1789 only two acts of the legislature had been declared unconstitutional.[50] The spirit of Jacksonian Democracy that pervaded the convention proceedings is a more plausible explanation. The convention also innovated the popular election of the governor, the lieutenant governor, and the attorney general. Furthermore, from 1850 to 1859 thirteen states in addition to Virginia provided for the popular election of the appellate judiciary. Popular election of Virginia judges, therefore, can be explained as part of a much broader movement to democratize political recruitment in general.

The effect of popular election by sections was of no noticeable consequence for the political system. No laws were declared unconstitutional during the period the justices were elected by the people. Popular elections for members of the Supreme Court were

[50] Nelson, *Judicial Review in Virginia*, p. 214.

actually held only twice: in 1852, to fill the new court; and in 1859, to fill a vacancy on the court. In the first judicial elections held under the new constitution, on May 27, 1852, three of the justices who had been elected by the legislature to sit on the old court successfully sought reelection. Two of the incumbents, Richard C. L. Moncure and John J. Allen, were unopposed. The third member, Judge William Daniel, received last-minute opposition from a Whig candidate. Green B. Samuels and George H. Lee were elected over their opponents to fill the remaining two seats. In May 1859, William Robertson was elected to the seat left vacant at the death of Judge Samuels. Consequently, although six men were popularly elected to sit on the Supreme Court, only three of them were newcomers to the high bench.

## Election by the Legislature

The Constitution of 1864 was framed by the "restored" government organized in Alexandria and recognized by Presidents Lincoln and Johnson as the official Virginia government. The new constitution retained the provision for limiting the tenure of the justices but reverted to the procedure of having members of the judiciary elected by the General Assembly. It attempted to allay some of the earlier criticisms of the legislative caucus by specifying that the General Assembly was to elect by joint vote one member for each of the three sections from persons nominated by the governor. In 1870 the Underwood Constitution eliminated the provision for separate judicial sections and the nominating prerogative of the governor in returning the full powers of election to the General Assembly.

The judicial career of Judge Richard C. L. Moncure, who was elected four times to the Supreme Court under three different methods of selection, illustrates the development of the judicial selection process in Virginia. Judge Moncure served as a member of the Reform Convention until March 31, 1851, when he was elected by the General Assembly to fill the seat left vacant at the death of Judge Francis T. Brooke. Following the adoption of the Constitution of 1851, Moncure was elected by popular vote. In 1866 he was nominated by Gov. Francis H. Pierpont and elected by the legislature in accordance with the provisions of the 1864 Constitution. With the appointment of a military Court of Appeals in 1869, Judge Moncure returned to private law practice. Under the 1870 Constitution he was elected by the General Assembly to a twelve-year term. Moncure died August 24, 1882, less than six months before that term expired. With the adoption of the 1870 Constitution, the selection procedures were once again in conformity with Virginia's first constitution except that now the tenure of the justices was not during good behavior but for twelve-year terms.

The issue of popular election of Supreme Court members was debated at length by delegates to the Constitutional Convention of 1901–2. The arguments largely paralleled those of the Reform Convention.[51] The advocates of popular election also pointed to the large number of states in which judges were elected by the people and cited the justices elected by the voters of Virginia in the 1850s as evidence of the people's competency in such matters. The practice of logrolling and bargaining among the legislators was continually stressed, with one delegate warning "that the opportunities for the master play in politics are certainly greater in any legislative body than they are among the people at large."[52] The opponents of popular election argued the necessity of an independent judiciary as ground for not making its members dependent on the votes of the people. They rejected the experience of popular election in the 1850s as not being long enough to constitute a valid precedent. Moreover, they argued, the electorate of the 1850s was not comparable to that of 1902, owing to the enfranchisement of the Negro following the close of the Civil War. Three different votes were taken on the question of popular election of the justices, with a vote of twenty-nine for to thirty-eight against the proposition being the closest margin.[53] A strong case was also made for selection by the governor with the advice and consent of the General Assembly. The federal experience, as well as substantial portions of Hamilton's *Federalist Paper* No. 76 on judicial appointments, was cited in support of the proposition. Once again three

[51] Ralph Clipman McDanel, *The Virginia Constitutional Convention of 1901–1902* (Baltimore: Johns Hopkins Press, 1928), pp. 107–10.

[52] *Proceedings and Debates of the Constitutional Convention, 1901–1902*, 2 vols. (Richmond: Hermitage Press, 1906), 1:1373.

[53] Ibid., 1:1425; 2:1721, 3084.

different votes were taken, with the proposal at one point being defeated by the narrow margin of thirty-eight to thirty-two.[54] The Constitution of 1902 therefore provided for the continuance of election of Supreme Court members by the General Assembly for twelve-year terms.

The issue of popular election was raised again by Gov. Westmoreland Davis in his 1918 inaugural address.[55] Governor Davis saw the practice of one coordinate branch of government electing another as an anomaly in government. He further suggested that the fear of Negro domination was no longer well founded. No action was taken by the legislature on this proposal. Subsequent efforts to reform the selection procedure were largely defused by the increased use of interim appointment by the governor for initial elevation to the court. In the years since the appeal for reform by Governor Davis, twenty of the twenty-six men selected to sit on the court have been appointed by Virginia governors in the intervals between legislative sessions. Although interim appointees remain subject to election by the legislature, the practice of gubernatorial appointment has diminished the role of the General Assembly in the selection process. The requirement of formal election of justices by the General Assembly now appears secure for many years, with the continuance of the procedure by the 1971 Constitution.

## Terms of Justices

Under the Constitution of 1870, the terms of the Supreme Court members elected by the General Assembly in March 1870 were to expire simultaneously on January 1, 1883. By this time, the Readjuster party was at the pinnacle of its political power in the state. Its gubernatorial candidate, William E. Cameron, had been victorious in 1881, and the party had gained control of both houses of the legislature in 1879 and 1881. The changed composition of the legislature was dramatically mirrored in the election of the Supreme Court members during the 1882 session of the legisla-

54 Ibid., 1:1533–34, 1543; 2:1721, 1747.

55 Va., General Assembly, 1918, *Journal of the House of Delegates,* House Document No. 5, "Inaugural Address of Governor Westmoreland Davis," pp. 9–10.

ture. All of the nominees of the Readjuster caucus, including one Republican, Lunsford L. Lewis, were elected. The voting in the General Assembly took place strictly along party lines. Benjamin W. Lacy and Robert A. Richardson decisively defeated Joseph Christian and Waller R. Staples, incumbent members of the court. Lunsford Lewis and Thomas R. Fauntleroy defeated James Keith and John W. Riely, respectively, by identical seventeen-vote margins.[56] Drury A. Hinton was unopposed.

On December 31, 1894, with the expiration of the terms being served by the Readjuster justices, five new persons were seated on the court. The Readjuster party had lost control of the legislature in the elections of 1883, and consequently all of the nominees of the Democratic caucus were elected. Votes were cast for ten persons in the caucus, with the five individuals having the largest number of votes qualifying as the Democratic candidates in the General Assembly election. Of the five Readjuster justices, the only one to receive votes in the Democratic caucus was Judge Lacy, who received two;[57] none of the incumbents was nominated for reelection in the legislature. The 1882 precedent of electing all new justices was therefore repeated in 1894.

With these experiences fresh in mind, the delegates to the Constitutional Convention of 1901–2 took steps to minimize complete turnovers in the personnel of the Supreme Court. The simultaneous expiration of the justices' terms was avoided by a stipulation in section 91 that at the first election of justices under the new constitution, the General Assembly should elect members for terms of four, six, eight, ten, and twelve years, respectively, and thereafter for full twelve-year terms.

In 1883 the first case decided by the Readjuster court, *Burks* v. *Hinton*, clarified state policy with respect to the length of terms for justices filling vacancies on the Supreme Court. The constitutions of 1851 and 1864 had left the matter of filling vacancies to the legislature except where there was a vacancy in the office of justice or judge, in which case it was specified that the election to fill that vacancy was to be for a full term. The Constitution of 1870,

[56] Va., General Assembly, 1881–82, *Journal of the House of Delegates,* pp. 392–96. Interestingly enough, both Keith and Riely were elected to the court when the terms of the Readjuster justices expired, twelve years later.

[57] *State* (Richmond), Jan. 6, 1894.

under which the court was functioning in the 1880s, had eliminated the special provision with respect to filling vacancies on the courts. In 1880 the Supreme Court had invalidated an 1872 joint resolution stipulating that "all elections by the general assembly to fill vacancies in the office of judge shall be only for the unexpired term of his predecessor."[58]

In the case of *Burks* v. *Hinton,* decided three years later by a four-man bench (Judge Hinton for obvious reasons did not participate in the decision), the new court ruled otherwise. With only the president of the court, Lunsford Lewis, dissenting, the justices elected by the Readjuster-controlled legislature upheld the right of the General Assembly to specify that elections to fill vacancies would be for the unexpired term only.[59] This decision, reinforced by the Constitution of 1902, was controlling until the Constitution of 1971 stipulated that upon election by the General Assembly, a new member of the court begins service for a full term.[60] Consequently, the system of staggered terms for justices established at the beginning of this century has been superseded by a policy of permitting the timing of the resignation, retirement, or death of a justice to determine the commencement of a new twelve-year term. It is highly unlikely that this new policy will result in the simultaneous election of all new justices.

[58] *Meredith, ex parte,* 33 Grattan (74 Va.) 119 (1880).
[59] 77 Va. 1 (1883).
[60] Con., 1902, art. VI, sec. 102; Con., 1971, art. VI, sec. 7.

# II *The Justices*

BEGINNING with the five men elected in 1788 to the newly established Supreme Court, seventy-six persons have been selected to sit on the Virginia high bench.[1] An effort to understand why those few men were chosen from among the many Virginia citizens requires an examination of both the formal and the informal framework of recruitment. The quasi-insulated character of the high court magnifies the importance of measuring one of the primary influences on the court, the recruitment process.

Throughout most of the state's history the official membership of the Supreme Court has been set at five, although it has been as low as three (1809–11, 1866–69) and as high as seven (1930 to the present). From 1779 to 1788 the court comprised five judges of the Chancery, General, and Admiralty courts. The new Supreme Court, which first convened on June 20, 1789, was also composed of five members. The membership remained at five until the resignation of Judge Paul Carrington, effective January 1, 1807. The General Assembly acted on the fourteenth of that month to limit the number of justices to three by resolving not to fill the current vacancy or that occasioned by the death or resignation of one of the four remaining justices. Judge Peter Lyons died on July 30, 1809, thereby reducing the number of seats on the bench to three. An 1811 statute increased the size of the court to the initial figure of five. The court's size was again reduced to three by the Constitution of 1864, then restored to five with the implementation of the Underwood Constitution, six years later. The membership was increased to seven as a result of the constitutional revisions of 1928 and has remained unchanged since the two new seats were filled in 1930.[2]

[1] Appendix A lists the members of the court and their terms of office.

[2] William W. Hening, ed., *The Statutes at Large . . . of Virginia,* 13 vols. (reprint; Charlottesville: Published for the Jamestown Foundation by the University Press of Virginia, 1969), 10:90; *A Collection of All such Acts of the General*

The report of the Commission on Constitutional Revision recommended that the size of the state's highest court remain at seven in the present constitution. The final text of the constitution did not alter the size, but it did authorize the General Assembly to change the number of members without resorting to a constitutional amendment. In the period before the Constitution of 1851 first specified the size of the court, the General Assembly had exercised its discretion to legislate the number of justices: in 1779, when the Supreme Court was first established; in 1788, when it was reconstituted; and between 1807 and 1811, when the size was changed. The United States Congress has similarly exercised its statutory discretion to alter the size of the nation's highest court provided no justice is removed from office as a result of a reduction in membership.[3] Under the present Virginia Constitution, the General Assembly can act to increase or decrease the court's membership only according to specified limitations. The number of justices cannot be set at less than seven or more than twelve, and three-fifths of the elected membership of each house of the legislature must vote in favor of the change at two successive regular sessions.[4] If the size is increased to greater than seven, the state legislature cannot then effectuate a decrease in membership until one or more vacancies occurs on the court.[5]

## Formal Qualifications

For the first seventy years of the Virginia Supreme Court's history, there were no official qualifications for its justices. Such qualifications were first established in the Constitution of 1851, which stipu-

*Assembly . . . Passed since the Session of 1801* (Richmond: Samuel Pleasants, Jr., 1808), p. 127; 2 Munford (16 Va.) xvii; Con., 1864, art. VI, sec. 11; Con., 1870, art. VI, sec. 2; Con., 1902, art. VI, sec. 88; *Constitution of Virginia as Amended June 19, 1928* (Richmond: Division of Purchase and Printing, 1929), pp. 33–35.

3 The membership of the United States Supreme Court, which has been set at nine since 1869, has been as few as five (1789) and as high as ten (1863). Henry J. Abraham, *The Judicial Process*, 3d rev. ed. (New York: Oxford University Press, 1975), p. 169.

4 Con., 1971, art. VI, sec. 2.

5 The tenure of the justices is constitutionally protected by the provisions stipulating their election to serve a full term (art. VI, sec. 7) and that their salaries "shall not be diminished" during a term of service (art. VI, sec. 9).

lated that a Supreme Court justice was to have reached the age of thirty-five at the time of his election and was to reside during his term of office in the judicial section for which he was elected. The Constitution of 1864 lowered the age requirement to thirty and required residency of at least one year in the state. The constitutions of 1870 and 1902 eliminated all age and residency requirements in favor of the stipulation that, when chosen, the justice was to have held a judicial station in the United States, or was to have practiced law in Virginia or some other state for five years. The present constitution simply requires a justice to be a resident of the commonwealth and to have been a member of the state bar for five years prior to his appointment or election.[6] In recommending the change in qualifications for the present constitution, the Commission on Constitutional Revision pointed out that the change was "more theoretical than practical," since it was highly unlikely that a nonresident or nonmember of the Virginia bar would be selected.[7] In fact, all justices have been residents and have belonged to the bar in Virginia. But, while it is true that the formal qualifications limit the number of persons who might sit on the Supreme Court, the informal qualifications are much more significant in determining the composition of the court.

## Social Factors

The first years of Virginia's history as a state were marked by an abundance of experienced legal talents. Writing in 1813 about the members of the Virginia bar at the time of the Revolution, St. George Tucker observed that "Socrates himself would pass unnoticed and forgotten in Virginia, if he were not a public character, and some of his speeches preserved in a newspaper: the latter might keep his memory alive for a year or two but not much longer."[8] Given such a pool of legal talent, it is not surprising that the national judiciary was headed by a Virginian, namely, John

[6] Con., 1971, art. VI, sec. 7.

[7] Va., Commission on Constitutional Revision, *The Constitution of Virginia: Report of the Commission on Constitutional Revision* (Charlottesville, Va.: Michie, 1969), pp. 198–99.

[8] Charles Warren, *A History of the American Bar* (New York: Howard Fertig, 1966), p. 49.

Marshall, or that the roster of early members of the state Supreme Court reads like a roll call of prominent Americans: Edmund Pendleton, John Blair, George Wythe, Robert Carter Nicholas, Dabney Carr, Peter Lyons, Paul Carrington, Spencer Roane, and St. George Tucker.

Carl Brent Swisher, a constitutional historian, referred to Virginia's highest court as "one of the most eminent state courts of the early decades of the nineteenth century."[9] During its early history as a state, Virginia was ruled for the most part by the gentry class, just as it had been as a colony. Of the ninety-one men appointed to the colonial Council, nine families had accounted for one-third of the names and fourteen families for the next third.[10] The high incidence of family relationships among justices and between justices and other political figures during the state's early history is indicative of rule by politically prominent families. The extent of such judicial elitism as manifested through family ties during the period from 1789 to 1851 is demonstrated in the chart on p. 30. The tangible and intangible advantages to members of these families certainly enhanced their opportunity for political education and ambition, and consequently contributed to the reputation of preeminence enjoyed by the state Supreme Court.[11]

The nineteenth century was marked by a steady decline in family elitism on the appellate benches of America's oldest states.[12] Resistance to the decline by southern states, as evidenced by the Virginia example, was strongest during the antebellum period. Whereas a less developed economy and more homogeneous society, coupled with a politically oriented patrician class, had contributed to the persistence of judicial elitism in Virginia and its neighboring states to the south, the disintegration of Virginia's

[9] Swisher, *American Constitutional Development* (Cambridge, Mass.: Riverside Press, 1943), p. 108.

[10] Constance R. Crito, "American State Supreme Courts and Judges: A Study in Political Development" (Ph.D. diss., Yale University, 1969), p. 238.

[11] Three father-son combinations can be found among the roster of justices: St. George Tucker (justice from 1804 to 1811) and Henry St. George Tucker (1831–41), Edmund C. Burks (1876–82) and Martin P. Burks (1917–28), Stafford G. Whittle (1901–19) and Kennon C. Whittle (1951–65). There have been two examples of a grandfather being followed by his grandson: Richard Parker (1788) and Richard L. Parker (1837–40), Richard C. L. Moncure (1851–65, 1866–82) and Richard H. L. Chichester (1925–30). In addition, Waller R. Staples (1870–82) was followed by his great-nephew, Abram P. Staples (1947–51).

[12] Crito, pp. 244–71.

planter class and economy following the Civil War was paralleled by a decline in the state's judicial elitism. Nevertheless, although the visibility of political families on the Supreme Court was less pronounced following the Civil War, it was substantial throughout the remainder of the nineteenth century and the early decades of the twentieth century. Although no individuals from political families were elevated to the court during the brief period of popular election (1852–65), seven out of thirteen justices selected between 1866 and 1894 had at least one member of their immediate family who had served in the state legislature or judiciary. From 1895 to 1930, nine out of twenty justices came from such politically oriented families. The first three decades of the twentieth century witnessed an accelerated decline in judicial elitism, culminating in virtually negligible levels of this phenomenon. Since 1930 every justice has been initially elevated to the court by an interim appointment by the governor; only three of these seventeen justices have had immediate family members who held political office. Thus, to the extent that a judicial aristocracy existed in Virginia, it has clearly disappeared at the Supreme Court level.

Educational attainment is highly visible among the ingredients necessary for election to the court. Members of the state Supreme Court have been among the best-educated citizens of the commonwealth. All of the justices received legal training.[13] During most of the nineteenth century the general practice was to study law under a family member with legal training or under a prominent judge or law teacher. The first law lectures in America were offered by George Wythe in 1779 at William and Mary. Through students such as John Marshall and Spencer Roane, Chancellor Wythe's influence on legal developments in Virginia and throughout the nation was magnified many times over. Practically all of the formal legal training received by the early justices was at William and Mary. St. George Tucker, a member of the Virginia Supreme Court from 1804 to 1811, was influential beyond his active years on the bench as a result of three students who followed him on the state's high bench: William Cabell (1811–52), John Coalter (1811–38), and his own son, Henry St. George Tucker (1831–41). The younger Tucker, who retired from the bench to teach law at the University of Virginia, was followed by two of his students, George

[13] The source of each justice's legal education can be found in Appendix E.

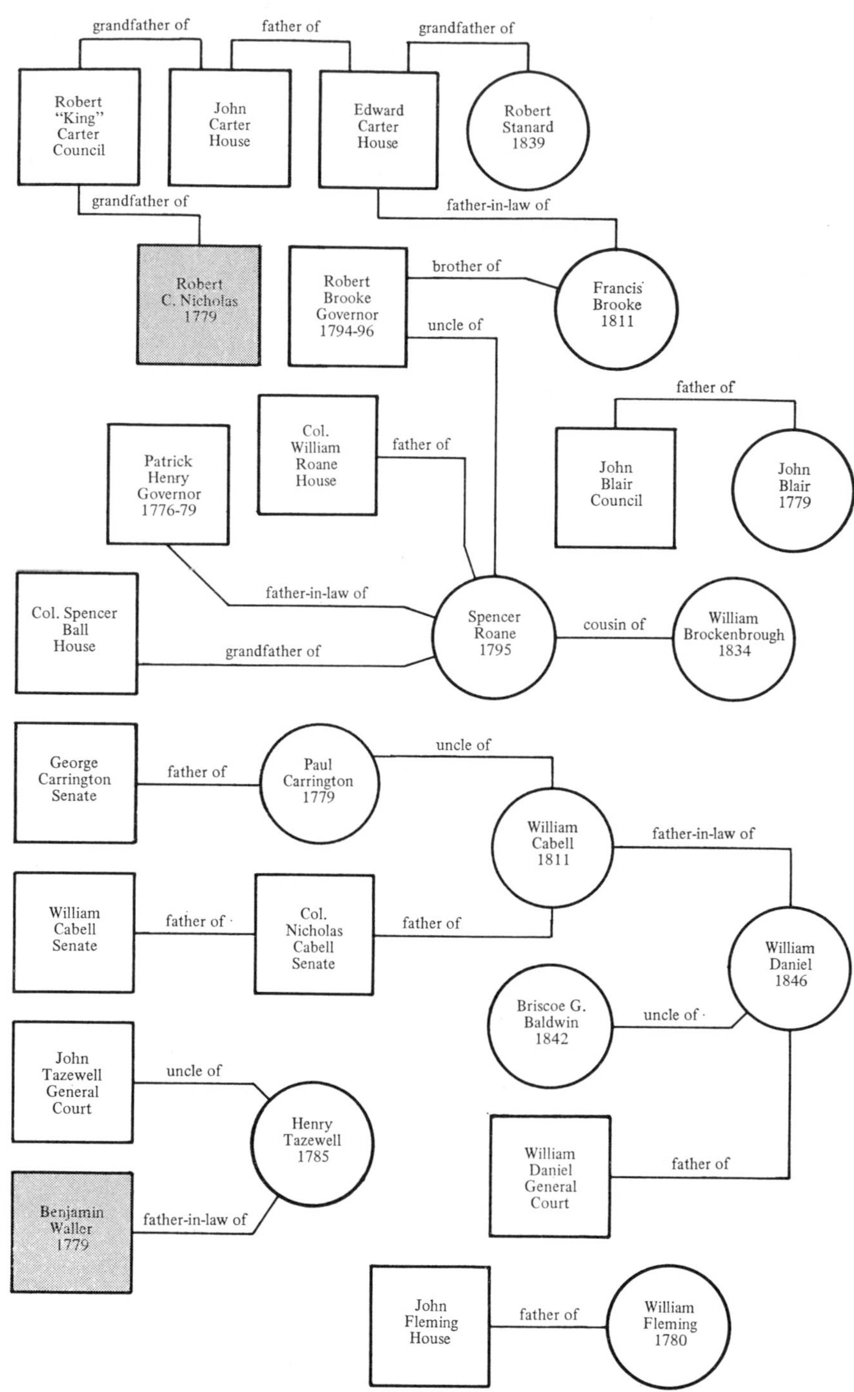
grandfather of
father of
grandfather of
Robert "King" Carter Council
John Carter House
Edward Carter House
Robert Stanard 1839
grandfather of
father-in-law of
Robert C. Nicholas 1779
Robert Brooke Governor 1794-96
brother of
Francis Brooke 1811
uncle of
father of
Col. William Roane House
Patrick Henry Governor 1776-79
father of
John Blair Council
John Blair 1779
father-in-law of
Col. Spencer Ball House
grandfather of
Spencer Roane 1795
cousin of
William Brockenbrough 1834
uncle of
George Carrington Senate
father of
Paul Carrington 1779
William Cabell 1811
father-in-law of
William Cabell Senate
father of
Col. Nicholas Cabell Senate
father of
William Daniel 1846
Briscoe G. Baldwin 1842
uncle of
John Tazewell General Court
uncle of
Henry Tazewell 1785
William Daniel General Court
father of
Benjamin Waller 1779
father-in-law of
John Fleming House
father of
William Fleming 1780

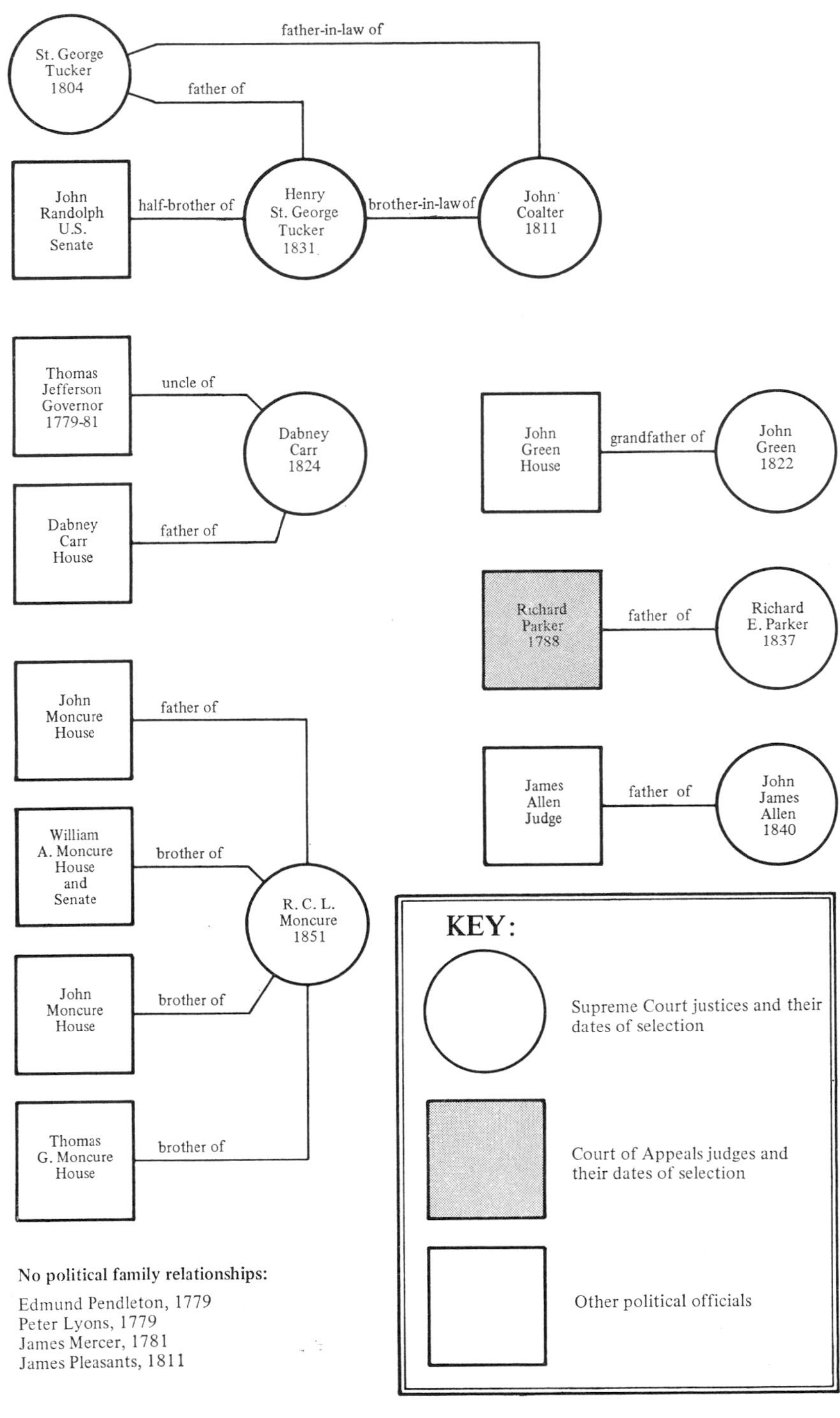


**No political family relationships:**

Edmund Pendleton, 1779
Peter Lyons, 1779
James Mercer, 1781
James Pleasants, 1811

H. Lee (1852–61) and Green B. Samuels (1852–59). Many of the justices studied law under Prof. John B. Minor at the University of Virginia during the second half of the nineteenth century.

By the turn of the century increasing numbers of the persons elevated to the high bench had received LL.B. degrees, although many of those persons did not hold undergraduate degrees. In the early years of this century it was possible to attend law school without having completed study at an undergraduate institution. That this practice was widespread is evidenced by a study of supreme court justices sitting throughout the United States during the period 1961–68: only 57.8 percent of them held any baccalaureate degrees other than in law.[14] Two Virginia justices sitting during that period had not received undergraduate degrees, and one justice since elevated to the Supreme Court had attended but had not graduated from an undergraduate institution.

Not surprisingly, Virginia justices have received their legal training almost exclusively in Virginia. Of the thirty-seven justices serving in this century, thirty-five studied law in the commonwealth and the other two were educated at law schools in Washington, D.C. At least four justices studied law in Virginia on their own or under a judge: Archer A. Phlegar, for example, "read" law under the Supreme Court justice from his area, Waller R. Staples. Several of the justices studied law at the University of Virginia around the turn of the century but were not awarded formal degrees. In 1946, for the first time in the court's history, all sitting members held law degrees,[15] and all justices appointed since that time have had such degrees. In total, twenty-three of the justices sitting on the court in this century possessed earned law degrees: eleven were granted by the University of Virginia, nine by Washington and Lee, and three by the University of Richmond.

Educational attainment and connections to politically active families have typified Virginia justices throughout much of the state court's history. As a result, the justices have been selected

[14] Bradley C. Canon, "Characteristics and Career Patterns of State Supreme Court Justices," *State Government* 45 (Winter 1972):34.

[15] By comparison, not until Charles Whittaker was appointed to the United States Supreme Court in 1957 were the seats on that Court simultaneously filled by recipients of law degrees. See Leon Friedman and Fred L. Israel, eds., *The Justices of the United States Supreme Court, 1789–1969: Their Lives and Major Opinions*, 4 vols. (New York: R. R. Bowker Company, 1969), 4:3197.

largely from the socially advantaged families of the commonwealth. In a profile of the members of the nation's highest court, John R. Schmidhauser observed: "The typical Supreme Court justice has invariably been white, generally Protestant with a penchant for a high social status denomination, usually of ethnic stock originating in the British Isles, and born in comfortable circumstances in an urban or small town environment. In the earlier history of the Court, he very likely was born in the aristocratic gentry class, while later he tended to come from the professionalized upper middle-class."[16] For Virginia justices, coming from the more homogeneous Virginia society, these characteristics have been even more pronounced. Members of the Virginia high court have invariably been white, male, Protestant, Virginia-educated, and native-born. Individuals outside the upper middle class without these characteristics have by and large been disqualified from consideration.

The distintegration of family elitism and the greater opportunity for legal education have broadened the scope of persons informally qualified to sit on the Virginia Supreme Court. No longer is it possible to win a place on the bench simply through family connections, nor does the attainment of legal education stand as a unique accomplishment. Political and professional contacts are now emphasized as the unwritten prerequisites for appointment to the state's highest tribunal.

## Career Patterns

Four of the early justices had sat on the powerful Committee of Safety that presided over the revolutionary government of Virginia at the close of British rule in the colony. The members of the original Supreme Court (1779–88) had all been involved to varying degrees in the establishment of the state of Virginia. Prior public experience has since been a common characteristic of men selected for the Virginia Supreme Court. A profile of the justices suggests that the selection of a person who has held no public office is highly unlikely. Of the seventy-six men chosen to sit on the court since 1788, only three had never held public office: George M.

16 Schmidhauser, "The Justices of the Supreme Court: A Collective Portrait," *Midwest Journal of Political Science* 3 (Feb. 1959):45.

Harrison (1895–1917), Thomas C. Gordon, Jr. (1965–72), and Martin P. Burks (1917–28). The first two were distinguished members of the bar at the time of their selection, and Judge Burks, dean of the Law School at Washington and Lee University, had served as the reporter of the court for twenty years prior to his appointment.

Table 1 presents a summary of the prior public experience of the justices. The office of legislator, and that of prosecutor, may be

*Table 1.* Summary of prior public experience of Virginia Supreme Court justices, 1789–1974

| Office | No. having held this office | No. with this office when selected | No. with this as first public office |
|---|---|---|---|
| *Legal-judicial* | | | |
| Judge on General Court | 15 | 13 | 4 |
| Judge on Chancery Court[a] | 5 | 5 | — |
| Judge on circuit and city courts of record | 27 | 20 | 8 |
| Judge on courts not of record | 6 | — | 5 |
| Judge on Special Court of Appeals | 3 | 2 | — |
| Prosecutor | 20 | 4 | 17 |
| *Legislative-administrative* | | | |
| Member of House of Burgesses | 6 | — | 5 |
| State delegate | 31 | 4 | 25 |
| State senator | 15 | 1 | 6 |
| Member of state executive[b] | 10 | 4 | — |
| Member of state regulatory body | 2 | 2 | — |
| U.S. congressman | 10 | 4 | 2 |

[a] Includes the superior courts of chancery in existence from 1802 to 1831.

[b] The office of attorney general is classified as executive in conformity with the Virginia Constitution, 1971, art. V, sec. 15.

classified as a "base office," that is, one of the first offices held in a person's career but one from which he is seldom elevated to the Supreme Court. Although over two-thirds of the justices served in Virginia's legislature at some time during their public career, a much smaller fraction were elected to the court while serving in that capacity. On the other hand, justices with experience on a court of record were much more likely to be serving in that office when chosen to sit on Virginia's highest court.

The fact that so many of those chosen to sit on the court were at one time state legislators is not surprising in view of the fact that the General Assembly has been responsible for election of the justices for all but a brief period in the court's history. Four speakers of the House of Delegates have been elected to the high court, but only one was holding that position at the time of his election to the court. In fact, the average period of state legislative service for Virginia justices has been relatively short: just a little over two terms for delegates (4.5 years) and less than one term for senators (3.6 years). No justice has served as many as two terms in the Senate, and only five justices have served as many as five terms in the lower house. One United States senator and nine congressmen (including two members of the Continental Congress and one member of the Confederate Congress) have been selected as Supreme Court justices. Seven of the nine congressmen, nevertheless, were not in office when chosen. The two congressmen elevated while in office served on the twentieth-century court, as did John A. Buchanan, who was elected to the court within a year of his voluntary retirement from Congress. Two members of the State Corporation Commission, a regulatory body organized in 1903, have been promoted to the court. The two governors who sat on the court (and their gubernatorial terms) are William Cabell (1805–8) and Albertis S. Harrison, Jr. (1962–66). Justice Harrison (1958–62) was one of two attorneys general of the state to be appointed to the court; the other, Abram P. Staples (1934–47), was elevated while in office.

The public experience of the justices can also be examined according to relatively distinct time periods. The first major period in the history of the court was 1789 to 1852. Throughout this time justices were elected to serve during good behavior. From 1852 to 1865 justices were elected by popular vote. Unfortunately, this period has limited analytical value because of the small number of justices elected by this procedure. Six were elected by the qualified voters, but three of those men had originally been elected by the General Assembly before 1852. A third period can be identified, from 1866 to 1894, during which the justices were elected by the legislature for twelve-year terms. This period is marked by shifting party control in Virginia government. The twentieth-century court, which is dated from 1895, continued the formal method of legislative election. However, the period can be divided so as to reflect the uninterrupted practice beginning in 1931 of initial selection for the court by interim appointment of the governor. The twentieth-century time span is distinguished by Democratic dominance of both the governorship and the General Assembly. The only Republican member of the court during this period, Richard H. Poff, was appointed in 1972 by the state's first Republican governor of the twentieth century.

Table 2 demonstrates the extent to which judges serving on the court directly below the Supreme Court have been elevated to Virginia's highest court. During the first period of the court's history the General Court and the Chancery Court fell into this category. Beginning in 1852 the circuit and city courts of record were the next highest courts.[17] The Special Court of Appeals can also be so designated during the brief periods it was in existence.

As evidenced in Table 2, prior legal-judicial experience has been important in all periods of the court's history with the exception of the 1866–94 period. This deviation can be explained in part by the disruption in career patterns caused by the Civil War and its aftermath. After 1870, the low rate of judicial experience is traceable to the turnover in judicial personnel as a result of alternate control of the legislature by the Conservative Democrats and the Readjusters. Of the five Readjuster justices elected in 1882, only one had prior experience as a judge: Benjamin Lacy had served for three years as a county judge and two years as a circuit judge when he was elected. Three of the other four justices had served as prosecutors, but that experience was largely independent of state politics at the time. One justice had served as an appointed federal district attorney, and another had served as commonwealth's attorney prior to the Civil War. The partisan struggles in Virginia during the late 1870s and early 1880s were also reflected in the career patterns of the five persons elected to sit on the high bench beginning in 1895. While in control of the legislature, the Read-

[17] As of July 1, 1973, the various city courts of record have been known uniformly as circuit courts. Va. Acts, 1973, ch. 544.

*Table 2.* Summary of highest legal-judicial and legislative-administrative offices previously held by Virginia Supreme Court justices, 1789–1974

| Highest office previously held | No. (and %) of justices, according to years in office, having held this as highest office 1789–1851[a] | 1852–1865 | 1866–1894 | 1895–1930 | 1931–1974 | Total |
|---|---|---|---|---|---|---|
| *Legal-judicial* | | | | | | |
| Judge on General Court[b] | 12 (52) | 1 (33⅓) | 1 (8) | — | — | 14 (19) |
| Judge on Chancery Court[c] | 5 (22) | — | — | — | — | 5 (6) |
| Judge on circuit and city courts of record | 1 (4) | 1 (33⅓) | 3 (23) | 10 (50) | 10 (59) | 25 (33) |
| Judge on courts not of record | — | — | — | 1 (5) | — | 1 (1) |
| Judge on Special Court of Appeals[d] | — | — | — | 2 (10) | 1 (6) | 3 (4) |
| Prosecutor | 1 (4) | 1 (33⅓) | 3 (23) | 2 (10) | 1 (6) | 8 (11) |
| None | 4 (18) | — | 6 (46) | 5 (25) | 5 (29) | 20 (26) |
| Total | 23 (100) | 3 (100) | 13 (100) | 20 (100) | 17 (100) | 76 (100) |
| *Legislative-administrative* | | | | | | |
| Member of House of Burgesses[e] | 2 (8) | — | — | — | — | 2 (3) |
| State delegate | 5 (21) | 1 (33⅓) | 6 (46) | 4 (20) | 1 (6) | 19 (25) |
| State senator | 4 (18) | — | 2 (15) | 2 (10) | 2 (12) | 10 (13) |
| Member of state executive | 3 (13) | — | 1 (8) | — | 3 (17) | 5 (6) |
| Member of state regulatory body | — | — | — | 2 (10) | — | 2 (3) |
| U.S. congressman | 5 (22) | 1 (33⅓) | 1 (8) | 2 (10) | 1 (6) | 10 (13) |
| None | 4 (18) | 1 (33⅓) | 3 (23) | 10 (50) | 10 (59) | 28 (37) |
| Total | 23 (100) | 3 (100) | 13 (100) | 20 (100) | 17 (100) | 76 (100) |

[a] Justices serving on the court for more than one period are counted only in the period in which they were first selected.
[b] Not in existence after 1852.
[c] Not in existence after 1831.
[d] Functioned for the following periods: 1848–51, 1872, 1924, 1924–28.
[e] Not in existence after 1776.

justers had elected ninety-five county judges, thirteen corporation court judges, and five circuit court judges in addition to the five state Supreme Court justices.[18] Consequently, the 1895 court was composed of two persons having only legislative experience, one with no prior public experience, one whose circuit court election and reelections did not coincide with Readjuster control, and one with experience as a comonwealth's attorney.

The predominant pattern of experience over the first sixty years of the court was for its members to have served in both legal-judicial and legislative offices, with elevation to the court normally occurring while the person was holding the former office. From 1866 to 1894, for reasons already discussed, the court was distinguished by the number of justices whose careers had not included legal-judicial experience. Less than one-third of the justices had served on a court of record. In the twentieth century over half of the justices never held a public office other than one of a legal-judicial nature. Prior service in the state legislature declined to a new low of less than one-fourth of the members in the most recent court period.[19] Over half of the twentieth-century justices were serving on the next highest court in the commonwealth at the time of selection for the Supreme Court. This figure, considered in conjunction with declining state legislative service, suggests an increasing level of judicial expertise and professionalization among members of the court. Although the emerging distinction in career patterns from other elected officials in the state is significant, it can be overemphasized. Six of the seventeen justices elected since 1930 entered the state political system as commonwealth's attorneys at a time when the office was acknowledged to be one of the crucial steps of political advancement in the dominant Byrd organization.[20]

18 James Tice Moore, "Two Paths to the New South: Funders, Readjusters, and the Virginia Debt Controversy, 1870–1883" (Ph.D. diss., University of Virginia, 1972), p. 231, n. 50.

19 See Appendix E. These figures contrast with the career patterns of Virginia's twentieth-century governors and United States senators. Over 50 percent of the persons holding these offices had previously served in the state legislature, whereas less than 30 percent had held a law enforcement position (public attorney, sheriff, judge). See Joseph A. Schlesinger, *Ambition and Politics: Political Careers in the United States* (Chicago: Rand McNally, 1966), pp. 72–76.

20 J. Harvie Wilkinson III, *Harry Byrd and the Changing Face of Virginia Politics, 1945–1966* (Charlottesville: University Press of Virginia, 1968), pp. 23–24.

## Age and Length of Service

The average age of justices when initially selected to sit on the Virginia Supreme Court is 51 years. Table 3 demonstrates that members elected before 1895 were more likely than twentieth-century justices to be 45 years or younger. Conversely, justices serving in the twentieth century have been more likely than earlier judges to be 56 years or older. The table also indicates a gradual increase in the average age of the justices when one discounts the brief exception of the popular election period. The 53.6 average age for the latest court period is in line with the figure of almost 56 years as an average selection age for supreme court justices sitting in all states during the period 1961–68.[21] Given the age distribution for the Virginia Supreme Court, it is not surprising that the youngest man ever elected was Spencer Roane, at age 32 in 1794, whereas the oldest man elected was Martin P. Burks, at age 66 in 1918. Judge Burks had just completed over twenty years as reporter for the court when he was appointed. Two twentieth-century justices, Harry L. Carrico and A. Christian Compton, were appointed to the court at age 44.

*Table 3.* Age of justices upon selection to the Virginia Supreme Court, according to year of selection, 1789–1974

| | No. of justices | | | | | |
|---|---|---|---|---|---|---|
| Age | 1789–1851 | 1852–1865 | 1866–1894[a] | 1895–1930 | 1931–1974 | Total |
| 45 or under | 7 | 2 | 5 | 1 | 2 | 17 |
| 46–55 | 13 | 1 | 3 | 13 | 8 | 38 |
| 56–60 | 2 | — | 2 | 2 | 5 | 11 |
| 61–66 | 1 | — | 2 | 4 | 2 | 9 |
| Average age | 48.3 | 43.7 | 49.9 | 53.6 | 53.6 | 51.0 |

[a] Excludes Lucas P. Thompson and Robert A. Richardson.

Death has caused almost half of the vacancies on the court, and poor health has forced justices to retire in at least four additional cases. Defeat or expiration of term has accounted for a very small

[21] Canon, p. 36.

portion of the vacancies. Before 1852, when justices retained their office during good behavior, terms were ended by either death or resignation. The creation of a new court by the Constitution of 1830 had little effect on the rate of vacancies, since only one member retired and the other four were reelected to continue their appellate service. No justice was defeated for election under the Constitution of 1851. The adoption of a new constitution in 1864 meant the suspension of the terms of all the justices. Only four were sitting at the time, George H. Lee having resigned in 1861 when West Virginia was recognized as a separate state. Richard C. L. Moncure was reelected under the Constitution of 1864, but the service of the remaining three justices was terminated. Of the three justices serving on the court under the Constitution of 1864, two were reelected following adoption of a new constitution in 1869, and one, Alexander Rives, was defeated in the legislature in a head-on contest with a former colleague, Judge Moncure. From

*Table 4.* Cause of vacancies on the Virginia Supreme Court, 1789–1974

| | No. of vacancies | | | | | |
|---|---|---|---|---|---|---|
| Cause | 1789–1851 | 1852–1865 | 1866–1894 | 1895–1930 | 1931–1974 | Total |
| Death | 12 | 1 | 3 | 7 | 9 | 32 |
| Resignation | 7 | 1 | 1 | 5 | 8 | 22 |
| Defeat | — | 1 | 3 | 1 | — | 5 |
| Expiration of term | 1 | 2 | 7 | — | — | 10 |
| Total | 20 | 5 | 14 | 13 | 17 | 69 |

1870 to 1894, ten of the twelve justices served full terms of twelve years and then were either defeated or not considered for reelection. Since 1895 no member has been defeated for reelection, although one interim appointee by the governor was not elected by the General Assembly. Thus, only during the period from 1866 to 1894 has expiration of term and failure to be reelected been an important source of vacancies.

A potential source of vacancies in the future is provided in the form of a mandatory retirement age for Virginia justices. Any justice elected or appointed for the first time after June 30, 1954, has been subject to mandatory retirement at age seventy-five. A 1970 act of the legislature reduced the age limit to seventy for any justice selected after July 1, 1970.[22] As yet no justice covered by these provisions has approached the mandatory age of retirement. Any lingering doubts about the power of the General Assembly to interrupt a justice's term once he has reached a certain age were dispelled by article VI, section 9 of the 1971 Constitution: the General Assembly is empowered to "provide for the mandatory retirement of justices . . . after they reach a prescribed age, beyond which they shall not serve, regardless of the term to which elected or appointed."

A seat on the Virginia Supreme Court has been considered a prestigious and important position by its members, as evidenced by the small number of them who have resigned while still in their active years. The major exceptions were during the early years of the court, when John Blair resigned to become the first and only Virginia Supreme Court member to be appointed a justice of the United States Supreme Court, Henry Tazewell resigned to serve as a United States Senator, and St. George Tucker resigned to become a federal district judge. Henry St. George Tucker resigned at the age of sixty, in 1841, to become professor of law at the University of Virginia. James Pleasants resigned his commission almost immediately, in 1811, but only because he distrusted his own qualifications for judicial service.

In the twentieth century only two justices have retired before the age of sixty. Joseph L. Kelly retired to private practice in 1924, at age fifty-seven, but he consented to being reappointed to the court less than a year later. Thomas C. Gordon, Jr., retired effective May 31, 1972, at age fifty-six, citing "the stronger lure of the private practice of law" as the sole reason for his decision.[23] Nevertheless, the high number of deaths of sitting justices and retirements at an advanced age confirms the proposition that few justices have left the bench while still capable of judicial service. C. Vernon Spratley and John Eggleston sat on the bench until the age of eighty-five and eighty-three, respectively.

The success enjoyed by the justices in being reelected to the

[22] Va. Code, sec. 51–12 (1967 repl. vol.); repealed by Va. Acts, 1970, ch. 779; Va. Code, 51–167 (1972 repl. vol.).

[23] *Richmond Times-Dispatch*, Apr. 1, 1972.

court is a primary determinant of length of service. The lack of success during the period from 1866 to 1894 was a major factor in establishing the average length of service during that period at less than 10 years. With the exception of Richard C. L. Moncure and William T. Joynes, who both served on the court created by the Constitution of 1864 and on that created by the Constitution of 1870, no justice during that period was elected for a second term. Since 1894 the average period of service has been 14.1 years. This figure is not significantly different from the average of 15.3 years for the period before 1852, when the justices were elected to serve during good behavior. The obvious conclusion is that the imposition of twelve-year terms on twentieth-century justices has not been a check on lengthy judicial service.

The top three justices in longevity of service, all of whom sat during the court's earliest period, achieved that status primarily because they continued as justices beyond their healthy years. To have imposed a term of a given number of years might have reduced their service slightly, but only if the end of one term had coincided with their last years on the court. William Fleming, a member of the original Supreme Court, served for almost 35 years, although infirmities of age prevented his attendance at sessions of the court for the last seven years of his life; inclusion of Fleming's 8 years on the original court boosts his total period of service to over 42 years. William H. Cabell and Francis T. Brooke were sworn in within a month of each other in 1811 and served 41 and 40 years, respectively. Twentieth-century justices with the records of longest service on the court are John W. Eggleston (34 years, 8 months) and C. Vernon Spratley (31 years, 1 month). Richard C. L. Moncure, first elected in 1851, served for a little over 30 years. Only two other justices sat on the court for longer than 25 years, Edward W. Hudgins (1930–58) and Spencer Roane (1795–1822).[24]

## The Selection Process

There are presently five systems used by different states to select judges: (1) gubernatorial appointment, (2) legislative election, (3) nonpartisan popular election, (4) partisan popular election,

[24] See Appendix E.

and (5) the Missouri plan. A majority of the states employ partisan and nonpartisan popular election methods. Dating back to 1940, the present trend has been toward adoption of the Missouri plan, in which governors appoint judges on the recommendations of a select committee and the voters decide whether to retain or remove the appointed judges after a period in office of one year or more. The more traditional methods of gubernatorial appointment and legislative election are favored by ten of the original thirteen states. Virginia is one of only five states continuing to select judges by legislative election.[25]

For all but fourteen years of the history of the Virginia Supreme Court, the justices have been chosen by the joint vote of the two houses of the General Assembly.[26] As opponents of legislative elections pointed out in the conventions of 1850–51 and 1901–2, the election of justices actually takes place in the legislative caucus of the majority political party. In close caucus elections, therefore, it is possible for a minority of the General Assembly membership to choose members of the high court. Beginning in 1894, all men chosen for the Supreme Court have been subject to election by the legislative caucus of the Democratic party.[27] Elections by the caucus have often been spirited and highly competitive, particularly when the original incumbency of a justice is being decided by the legislature.

In filling the two new seats created for the Supreme Court, the Democratic caucus in January 1930 endured seven hours of bal-

[25] Henry Robert Glick and Kenneth N. Vines, *State Court Systems* (Englewood Cliffs, N.J.: Prentice-Hall, 1973), pp. 39–40.

[26] The constitutional language requiring election "by the joint vote of the two houses" could have been interpreted to mean a majority of the combined vote of the Houses of Delegates and the state Senate, that is, any seventy-one members of the General Assembly. The present constitution avoids such a misinterpretation by requiring "the vote of a majority of the members elected to each house of the General Assembly." Con., 1971, art. VI, sec. 7. Thus, the affirmative vote of twenty-one senators and fifty-one delegates is necessary for election to the Virginia Supreme Court. A. E. Dick Howard, *Commentaries on the Constitution of Virginia*, 2 vols. (Charlottesville: University Press of Virginia, 1974), 2:742.

[27] Before 1972, the Democratic members of both houses of the General Assembly met together in a single caucus for that purpose. At the 1972 session, the Democratic delegates and senators met in separate caucuses in conformity with the language of art. VI, sec. 7, although as extraconstitutional, extralegal bodies, the political party caucuses are under no obligation to do so. See Howard, 2:742, n. 12.

loting, concluding at 2:30 A.M.; it decided on one candidate on the eleventh ballot and a second candidate on the fourteenth ballot. Echoing the criticisms historically made by the advocates of popular election of judges, the *Richmond Times-Dispatch* commented editorially on the methods employed on behalf of the various candidates: "Combination, trades, mutual understandings—anything for an advantage—were the order of the day."[28] Less than a month later, the Democratic caucus selected a successor to Judge Richard Chichester by a vote of sixty-four to sixty-three. The Richmond newspaper decried once again the overt political bargaining that developed before the caucus election and suggested that "it is becoming increasingly apparent that we shall have to adopt in Virginia the method of gubernatorial appointment if our judiciary is to measure up to such a standard as we would like to see."[29] In point of fact, the election in February 1930, about which the newspaper was commenting, was the last such election in which the original incumbency of a Supreme Court justice was determined by the General Assembly. Although no change has been made in the constitutional provision for election by joint vote of the General Assembly, all justices taking their seats on the court since 1930 have done so initially as a result of an interim appointment by the governor.

Virginia, like most other states with elective systems, has specified that vacancies are to be filled by the governor until a formal election can be held.[30] If the legislature is not in session when a vacancy occurs on the state's high court, the governor has been authorized to make an interim appointment to be effective until thirty days after the end of the next session of the General Assembly. Over the period since 1788, vacancies have occurred on the Virginia Supreme Court on the average of one every two and one-half years. Election by the legislature rather than interim appointment by the governor was the predominant means of accession until the twentieth century (see Table 5). The first five justices serving in the twentieth century were elected simultaneously by the General Assembly in 1894. Of the remaining thirty-two justices serving in this

[28] Jan. 18, 1930.

[29] Ibid., Feb. 8, 12, 1930.

[30] Con., 1971, art. VI, sec. 7.

century, twenty-three (72 percent) were initially appointed by the governor.

*Table 5.* Mode of accession of justices to the Virginia Supreme Court, 1789–1974

| Mode of accession | No. of justices 1789–1851 | 1852–1865 | 1866–1894 | 1895–1930 | 1931–1974 | Total |
|---|---|---|---|---|---|---|
| Election | 21 | 3 | 12 | 14 | — | 50 |
| Appointment | 2 | — | 1 | 6 | 17 | 26 |
| Total | 23 | 3 | 13 | 20 | 17 | 76 |

The death of incumbent justices offers obvious opportunities for governors to make interim appointments. Moreover, in the twentieth century only two of the thirteen justices who have retired from the court did so at a time convenient for the General Assembly to elect a successor. This increase in interim appointments is not unique to the state of Virginia. An analysis of the initial selection of justices in states employing a popular election method during the period 1948–57 attempted to measure this development. It was found that 55.8 percent of the justices were initially appointed to the bench. Furthermore, the percentage of appointed justices was highest (67.5 percent) in those states undergoing the least amount of change in partisan control of the governorship.[31] Undoubtedly, stability in the political control of the state and sharp criticism of caucus elections encouraged the evolution of the widely accepted appointive system in Virginia. The 1930 experiences with initial selection by the legislature tended to verify the wisdom of interim appointment by the chief executive followed by legislative confirmation through the mechanics of election by the legislature.

## Role of the Governor

Legislative opposition to incumbent appellate justices has with one exception been inconsequential in this century. On October 1, 1900,

[31] James Herndon, "Appointment as a Means of Initial Accession to Elective State Courts of Last Resort," *North Dakota Law Review* 38 (1962):64, 69.

Gov. J. Hoge Tyler appointed Archer A. Phlegar of Montgomery County to the Virginia Supreme Court. This interim appointment is noteworthy not only because it was the first such appointment in the twentieth century but also because of the failure of the General Assembly to elect Phlegar when it convened less than four months later. The Democratic governor's lack of political strength within both his party and the legislature had been dramatically demonstrated in 1898 in his unsuccessful bid to unseat the leader of the dominant organization in the Virginia Democratic party, United States senator Thomas S. Martin. Governor Tyler was soundly defeated by Martin in the Democratic caucus of the General Assembly by a vote of 103 to 27.[32] Thus, when Tyler appointed Phlegar to the Supreme Court, his political influence with the legislature had already been seriously undermined.

Judge Phlegar was challenged primarily by two candidates in the caucus, one backed by Senator Martin and one by the antiorganization Independents. After five ballots the caucus was deadlocked. A few days later the deadlock was broken, through the efforts of Rep. Claude A. Swanson, and Stafford G. Whittle was elected to serve on the Supreme Court.[33]

It is significant that both of Phlegar's principal opponents were from Southside Virginia. Since 1870 there had been a custom dictating that there should be an appellate justice from each of the five grand divisions of the state: Tidewater, Piedmont, Valley, Southside, and Southwest. Legal precedent for the custom could be found in the constitutions of 1851 and 1864, which provided for the election of justices according to the judicial sections within the state. The practice of selecting justices from each of the divisions had been strictly adhered to before the appointment of Phlegar. The seat on the court to which Phlegar was appointed had been occupied by Judge John W. Riely of Halifax County. The appointment of Phlegar, who was from Governor Tyler's home county of Montgomery, gave Southwest Virginia two justices (the second one being incumbent Judge John A. Buchanan of Abingdon) and left Southside with no justice on the court. The defeat of Judge Phlegar

32 Thomas Edward Gay, Jr., "The Life and Political Career of J. Hoge Tyler, Governor of Virginia, 1898–1902" (Ph.D. diss., University of Virginia, 1969), p. 194.

33 Ibid., pp. 223–24.

Justices in conference, 1961. *Left to right*: Lawrence W. I'Anson, Kennon C. Whittle, C. Vernon Spratley, Chief Justice John W. Eggleston, A. C. Buchanan, Harold F. Snead, and Harry L. Carrico. (Photo, Richmond Newspapers, Inc.)

Justices on the bench, 1974. *Left to right*: Richard H. Poff, George M. Cochran, Harry L. Carrico, Chief Justice Lawrence W. I'Anson, Albertis S. Harrison, Jr., Alex M. Harman, Jr., and A. Christian Compton. *Seated in the foreground, left to right*: Hubert D. Bennett, Executive Secretary of the Court, and Howard G. Turner, Clerk of the Court. (Photo, Richmond Newspapers, Inc.)

in 1901 is instructive primarily because of the contrast it provides to subsequent appointments by Virginia governors. It is the only instance of legislative rejection of a gubernatorial Supreme Court appointee in the twentieth century. Phlegar's defeat can be attributed to Governor Tyler's rejection of a well-established custom as well as his weak position vis-à-vis the General Assembly. Subsequent governors have encountered no difficulty in securing legislative election of their interim appointees. Governor Godwin has made four appointments to the high court (including three in his first administration), thus establishing himself as the only twentieth-century governor to appoint a majority of the court's membership. Governor Tuck is the only other twentieth-century chief executive to make as many as three appointments during his administration. Governors Stuart, Byrd, Perry, Battle, and Almond each made two appointments. Six other governors made one appointment. Since 1922, only Governors Price and Darden, who served successive terms from 1938 to 1946, did not make appointments to the Supreme Court.

Geography was a factor in the first appointment made by Gov. William Tuck. Chief Justice Campbell of Abingdon notified Governor Tuck in advance of his intention to retire and expressed a preference that circuit court judge Archibald C. Buchanan of Tazewell be appointed in his place.[34] Judge Buchanan, a former law partner of Gov. George C. Perry (1934–38), had been mentioned as a possible appointee with respect to earlier vacancies. Sensing the overwhelming support for Judge Buchanan, a man with whom he was only casually acquainted, Governor Tuck acted quickly, naming him to the Supreme Court the same day that he received Chief Justice Campbell's formal letter of retirement.

The following year Governor Tuck made his second and third appointments to the Supreme Court. The first vacancy was created by the death of Justice George L. Browning of Culpeper, August 26, 1947. Two days later Governor Tuck announced the appointment of Attorney General Abram P. Staples to succeed Justice Browning. Tuck recalled that he "drafted" Staples for the position because of his distinguished twelve years of service as the state's top legal official. Along with state senator John W. Eggleston, Staples had gained widespread recognition for his active role in drafting the Alcoholic Beverage Control Act enacted in 1934. Then

[34] Interview with Tuck, Mar. 3, 1971.

he had been appointed to the office of attorney general in March 1934 by Governor Perry and had subsequently been elected by popular vote in 1937, 1941, and 1945. As attorney general, Staples had continued to draft important legislation.[35] He also had demonstrated his legal and political acumen in challenging the executive authority of the antiorganization governor, James H. Price. His two opinions ruling against the power of the governor were subsequently upheld by the state Supreme Court; one of Staples's opinions had been rendered in response to a letter from William Tuck, who was then serving in the state Senate.[36]

Staples had begun his political career in Roanoke, but he had spent the twelve years preceding his succession to the Supreme Court in Richmond as attorney general. For this reason, Governor Tuck, who had worked closely with Staples the first two years of his administration, felt justified in appointing his attorney general in spite of the presence on the court of Justice Herbert B. Gregory, also of Roanoke. Governor Tuck recalled that following the addition of two new seats to the court, it was generally understood among the politicians of the state that appointments need not adhere strictly to regions so long as geography was not totally ignored. Governor Tuck acted on this new understanding once again when he filled the Valley seat on the court vacated by the death of Justice Henry W. Holt of Staunton with an appointee from Richmond.

There was no consensus candidate for Tuck's third appointment, and, as a result, the governor found it necessary to hold hearings for delegations appearing on behalf of eleven different candidates. The two primary contenders for the appellate seat were Judge Willis D. Miller of the Richmond Law and Equity Court and Frank S. Tavenner, Jr., of Woodstock, United States attorney for the Western District of Virginia. At the time of the vacancy, Tavenner was serving as the associate prosecutor in the war crimes trials at Tokyo. The delegation on Tavenner's behalf was led by Harry F. Byrd, Jr., of Winchester, who was a Democratic nominee for the state Senate.[37] While it was understood that Tavenner could be released from

[35] *Proceedings of the Virginia State Bar Association* 62(1951):191–93.

[36] Va., Opinions of the Attorney General, 1939–40, pp. 194–99, 256–60. See Chaper VI below for a discussion of the cases upholding the opinions of Attorney General Staples: *Jackson* v. *Hodges*, 176 Va. 89, 10 S.E. 2d 566 (1940); *Commonwealth* v. *Dodson*, 176 Va. 281, 11 S.E. 2d 120 (1940).

[37] *Richmond Times-Dispatch,* Oct. 16, 1947.

his duties in Tokyo, Governor Tuck felt that his experience more properly qualified him for a federal judgeship. Although not a close acquaintance of Judge Miller, the governor was impressed by his record and was persuaded by the argument that Richmond deserved to be represented on the state Supreme Court. The decision to name Miller was described by Governor Tuck at the time of the appointment as "one of the most difficult that has confronted me since the beginning of my term as Governor."[38]

The most significant development in the judicial selection process over the past seventy years is the dominant role that has been assumed by the governor. The legislators, of course, are not totally left out of the selection process at the appointment stage. For a governor to ignore completely the feelings of the legislators would be imprudent and perhaps would endanger the subsequent election of his nominee. It is safe to assume that the reactions of key members of the General Assembly to possible appointees are either solicited or easily predicted. Nevertheless, the dispersal of legislators around the state when the legislature is not in session, coupled with their divided loyalties, has minimized the influence of the General Assembly. More often than not the legislators support the candidate from their region of the commonwealth when several strong contenders are being considered.

Virginia governors have enjoyed a considerable amount of independence and flexibility in making interim appointments. Gov. William Tuck dramatically demonstrated the strength of the governor in the selection process by announcing two of his appointments within one or two days after the creation of a vacancy. As was the case with Governor Tuck's last appointment, the governors have generally consented to hear any delegation of citizens wishing to speak on behalf of a candidate. The expressed views of members of the legislature and the bar have been cordially accepted. In the final analysis, twentieth-century governors have been confident that the legislature would elect any one of the persons they were considering for the position. Legislators, although sometimes disappointed that the governor did not appoint their preferred nominee, have been reluctant to oppose an otherwise qualified appointee. The governors for the most part have merited this deference by acting on the basis of political realities: they have not

[38] Ibid., Oct. 18, 1947.

ignored geography, party affiliation, or judicial philosophy in their appointments, nor have they named political cronies or poorly qualified friends. Nevertheless, the defeat of Governor Tyler's appointee in 1901 serves as a reminder of the limits on the gubernatorial prerogative to make interim appointments.

## Influence of the Bar

For some years the sentiment had been growing among members of the Virginia bar that practicing attorneys should be considered for appointment to the appellate bench. Writing in the December 1952 issue of the *Virginia Law Review*, Robert B. Tunstall, a former president of the Virginia Bar Association (formerly known as the Virginia State Bar Association) gave concrete expression to that sentiment.[39] He characterized the practice of appointing only judges of inferior courts and an occasional public officeholder to the Supreme Court as a "habit." Tunstall pointed out that, since 1900, only four members of the bar in active practice had been chosen for the Supreme Court: of these four, one was a United States congressman, one a state senator, and two former members of the General Assembly. He cited the historical preponderance of nonjudicial appointees serving on the United States Supreme Court. He also presented statistics showing that of all the judges then sitting on the highest state courts across the country, the number who had held no prior judicial position was comparable to the number who had had such experience. Tunstall concluded that the inertia of the Virginia bar had contributed to the "habit" of excluding practicing members from serious consideration as Supreme Court justices.

Tunstall suggested in his article that the Virginia Bar Association create a special committee to study the methods by which the collective judgment of the bar concerning the filling of vacancies on the Supreme Court could be presented to the General Assembly or the governor. The chairman of the Executive Committee of the Association complied by appointing just such a committee, with Tunstall as a member. The Special Study Committee proposed that

39 Tunstall, "Why Ignore the Bar? A Study of Accessions to the Supreme Court of Appeals of Virginia," *Virginia Law Review* 38 (1952):1091–1109.

the Virginia Bar Association set up a Committee on Nominations to the Supreme Court; when a vacancy occurs on the court, this committee is to present the governor or General Assembly a list of three candidates recommended for appointment or election (the plan does not cover reelection of justices). The association adopted this proposal at its annual meeting in 1954.

The Committee on Nominations to the Supreme Court first acted with respect to the vacancy created by the death of Justice Lemuel F. Smith, on October 15, 1956. In accordance with the procedures established by the association, the committee presented the names of three persons to Gov. Thomas B. Stanley on November 9, 1956. Less than two weeks later the governor announced the appointment of Judge Harold F. Snead of Richmond, whose name was not on the list submitted by the committee of the Virginia Bar Association. The chairman of the committee, Alex W. Parker, in a release to the press, indicated that Judge Snead had been considered by the committee but had been excluded when it was decided not to recommend any member of the Richmond bench or bar because of the presence on the court of a justice from Richmond. Mr. Parker concluded on this affirmative note: "The Bar Association recognized it to be the prerogative of the Governor of the General Assembly to make these appointments, but it feels that its Committee's considered opinion as to the eligible appointees should be of real value to either appointive power and it expects to continue to make its recommendations in all future cases."[40]

Parker's determined tone proved effective. The next six appointees to the court, named by three different governors, were all from the list submitted in each case by the Virginia Bar Association Committee on Nominations. Three of those six vacancies were filled by nonjudicial persons, thus fulfilling one of the original goals of association participation. The string of successes by the committee was broken in 1972 when it recommended two Democratic judges and a Democratic lawyer to a Republican governor. Notwithstanding this setback, the Virginia Bar Association was largely responsible for ensuring the informal participation of the bar in the selection process.

The role of the legal subculture in the selection of justices has been formalized to the point where Virginia governors routinely

[40] *Proceedings of the Virginia State Bar Association* 68 (1957):87.

wait for the recommendations of the bar before filling a vacancy on the court. Although in the past the Virginia Bar Association has been the primary spokesman for the legal profession, evidence of more diverse participation in this area has now surfaced. The Virginia State Bar, to which all lawyers in the state must belong, has a membership more than three times as large as the more elitist Virginia Bar Association. An invigorated State Bar has begun making suggestions for nominations to fill vacancies on the high bench, as well as continuing to study and make proposals regarding the pertinent issues of practice and procedure that concern the legal profession. In 1974, for example, Governor Godwin appointed Judge A. Christian Compton from among the names of three circuit judges recommended by the State Bar. The Virginia Bar Association endorsed its president-elect, who was a practicing attorney, and two of the judges recommended by the State Bar, but not the eventual choice of the chief executive. Local bar associations also often endorse candidates, especially when a judge or attorney from their area is among the leading contenders for a vacancy. Another group, the Old Dominion Bar Association, composed of black lawyers throughout the state, has sought to influence appointments by regularly endorsing a leading black attorney for each one of the vacancies occurring on the Supreme Court over the past few years.

## Criteria

Good character, acceptable judicial philosophy, and demonstrated ability are the primary qualities that Virginia governors look for in prospective justices. The chief executive must be personally satisfied as to the person's fitness for the post. Given relatively equal competency among the candidates, then geography, age, and potential compatibility with the sitting justices become important considerations.

One factor that has on occasion influenced gubernatorial appointments is the amount of support a man has previously received for an appellate seat. For example, Joseph W. Chinn lost to George L. Browning in the Democratic caucus of February 11, 1930, by one vote. (Browning had led on the first two ballots in the caucus a few weeks earlier that had chosen Edward W. Hudgins and

Herbert B. Gregory.) Chinn was appointed by Gov. John G. Pollard to fill the next vacancy occurring on the court. In 1951 Gov. John S. Battle was faced with a choice between two favorites, Judge Lemuel F. Smith of Charlottesville and Judge Kennon C. Whittle of Martinsville.[41] He appointed his former law partner, Judge Smith, to the appellate bench, but less than two months later he named Judge Whittle when another vacancy occurred on the court.

The custom of strict geographical representation on the court was continued until after the number of justices was increased to seven. Gov. William Tuck's appointment of Judge Willis D. Miller of Richmond in 1947 marked the first significant break with the custom by denying the Valley a seat on the court. Geographical considerations, although not necessarily according to rigid divisions within the state, continue to be important in the selection of justices. Geographical distribution of the justices has practical as well as political significance. For example, lawyers not living in the vicinity of Richmond can conveniently present petitions for writs of error to the justice from their region of the state.

Representation according to region is reflected in the preponderance of Supreme Court seats held by men from the rural areas of the state. This distribution of seats is consistent with the pattern of home areas for persons serving in Virginia's top three executive positions (governor, lieutenant governor, and attorney general) since 1900. The domination of state politics by the rural-based Byrd organization resulted in a paucity of statewide officials from the population centers of the commonwealth, especially from northern Virginia.[42] In recent years, however, there has been a distinct shift toward increased representation on the Supreme Court for the urban areas.[43] The shift was initiated in the mid-1930s when both Norfolk and Hampton were given representation on the court. In 1949 Judge Miller became the first Richmonder to sit on the court since 1839. Another Richmond judge, Harold F. Snead,

41 *Richmond Times-Dispatch*, Jan. 26, 1951.

42 Thomas R. Morris, *Virginia's Lieutenant Governors: The Office and the Person* (Charlottesville: Governmental and Administrative Research Division, Institute of Government, University of Virginia, 1970), pp. 40–41.

43 Robert J. Austin, "The Virginia Supreme Court of Appeals: Career Patterns and the Selection Process," *University of Virginia News Letter* 45 (Dec. 15, 1968): 15–16.

was appointed in 1956, and, following the elevation of judges from Portsmouth and northern Virginia, the peak of urban representation on the high bench was reached with the appointment in 1965 of a Richmond attorney, Thomas C. Gordon, Jr. At that time only Justice Archibald Buchanan of Tazewell was not from one of the state's major metropolitan areas. Of the nine men elevated to the court between 1956 and 1974, three have been from Richmond, one from Portsmouth, and one from northern Virginia.[44]

Harry L. Carrico, a judge from northern Virginia, was the first justice selected from that area in this century. In announcing his decision in 1961 to appoint Carrico, Gov. J. Lindsay Almond, Jr., pointed out that northern Virginia was the most rapidly growing part of the state and was supplying an increasingly large portion of the Supreme Court's work load. By 1969 Governor Godwin was faced with an entirely different situation. The retirement of Justice Buchanan left no one on the high bench from west of a line running north and south from Richmond to Lawrenceville. Governor Godwin responded by filling the two vacancies on the court in 1969 with men from Staunton and Pulaski. Nevertheless, the shift toward substantial urban representation on the court is probably irreversible because of the changes in Virginia's political climate and the heavy judicial business from the state's urban areas.

Prior judicial experience has carried different weight with different governors. As a former state judge, Gov. J. Lindsay Almond, Jr., viewed judicial training on the bench as an element deserving "weighted consideration."[45] Not surprisingly, both of his appointees were sitting judges in the state court system. On the other hand, the appointee of Gov. Albertis S. Harrison, Jr., had no prior experience in public office, and two of the three appointments made by Gov. Mills E. Godwin, Jr., during his 1966–70 term were men with no experience as a judge. When faced with filling two vacancies in 1969, however, Governor Godwin resolved that in order not to make those members without prior judicial ex-

[44] Justice Poff, a native of Radford who lived in northern Virginia while representing Virginia's Sixth Congressional District, is not counted as an urban justice. However, after becoming a member of the Supreme Court, he moved his residency to Richmond and can be considered an urban justice in future calculations of geographical representation on the court.

[45] Interview with Almond, Feb. 23, 1971.

perience a majority, one appointee must be a judge.[46] When the resignation of Chief Justice Harold Snead in the first year of Governor Godwin's second administration presented the chief executive with a court equally divided between those men with and those without judicial experience, he responded with the appointment of a circuit court judge.

Governor Almond's first appointee was Judge Lawrence W. I'Anson of Portsmouth. Judge I'Anson had been backed by Sen. Harry F. Byrd, Sr., for appointment as a United States district judge in the early 1950s, but he had been passed over in favor of Republican Walter E. Hoffman. I'Anson's judicial record (only two reversals in seventeen years as judge of the Court of Hustings in Portsmouth) and high standing among the members of the bar were noted by the chief executive. Furthermore, the Portsmouth judge "had powerful support from state political leaders as well as lawyers and legislators."[47] Governor Almond, who first got to know I'Anson in the early 1940s at judicial conferences that they both attended in their capacity as state judge, knew him to be an able and industrious judge. Geography as has already been noted, was a more important factor in Governor Almond's second appointment. Perhaps in deference to the governor's demonstrated preference for men with prior service on the bench, the Virginia Bar Association recommended three state judges. Although Governor Almond hardly knew Judge Harry L. Carrico of Fairfax on a personal basis, he was familiar with some of his judicial work. As former attorney general of the state, Almond was familiar with certain records that reflected the meticulous care exhibited by Judge Carrico in presiding over cases.

Sentiment favoring the appointment of a practicing lawyer to the high bench had continued to build in intensity during the early 1960s. Gov. Albertis S. Harrison, Jr., complied in 1965 by naming the immediate past president of the Virginia Bar Association, Thomas C. Gordon, Jr., of Richmond. Along with Gordon, a corporation lawyer, the Virginia Bar Association had nominated two sitting state judges. Governor Harrison indicated the age factor (the other two nominees were over sixty) had tipped the balance

[46] Interview with Mills E. Godwin, Jr., Feb. 17, 1971.
[47] *Richmond Times-Dispatch*, Aug. 26, 1958.

in Gordon's favor. Governor Harrison's appointment of a nonjudge to sit on the court was greeted with such a favorable response that three of the next four men appointed to the court possessed no prior experience on the bench. Two years after the appointment of Gordon, former governor Harrison was named by Governor Godwin to sit on the appellate bench. Harrison had no previous experience as a judge, but he had served one term as the attorney general of the state.

In 1969 Governor Godwin appointed George M. Cochran of Staunton to the high court. Cochran and Governor Godwin had both been sent by the voters of their respective districts to the House of Delegates in 1948. Cochran, one of the "Young Turks" who had opposed the Byrd organization in the mid-1950s, had been an announced candidate for speaker of the House of Delegates in 1957 against the incumbent, E. Blackburn Moore, but had withdrawn when it had become obvious he could not win. He had served in the lower house until 1965, at which time he had been elected to the state Senate. Having been defeated for reelection in 1967, Cochran was practicing law in Staunton at the time of his appointment.

Gov. Linwood Holton also turned to a man with a long political career when he selected retiring congressman Richard H. Poff of Radford. Poff had never been a judge and had little experience as a practicing attorney; nevertheless, in 1971 it had been widely assumed that Congressman Poff was President Nixon's first choice for appointment to the United States Supreme Court. As opposition to Poff began to develop among certain groups because of his anti–civil rights voting record, he asked that his name be withdrawn from consideration so as to avoid the possibility of a bitter, divisive battle in the United States Senate over his nomination. One of President Nixon's earlier nominees from the South, Judge G. Harrold Carswell, had been rejected after senatorial debate focusing on his record in the area of race relations.

Governor Godwin's decision to name two circuit judges to the court was governed by the composition of the high bench at the time of the vacancies. One of his two 1969 appointees was Judge Alex M. Harman, Jr., of Pulaski. Harman, who was born and raised in War, West Virginia, had served as a circuit judge beginning in 1965. He had been backed by Sen. Harry F. Byrd, Jr., for a federal district judgeship for western Virginia, but the Johnson administration had left the post unfilled because of Sen. William Spong's sponsorship of another candidate.[48] In 1974 Governor Godwin elevated circuit court judge A. Christian Compton to the Supreme Court. Compton had been appointed in 1966 to the law and equity court in Richmond during Godwin's first term as governor. Compton's excellent reputation as a judge and his relatively youthful age enhanced his standing in the eyes of the governor.

Political party considerations in the selection of justices were taken for granted throughout most of the twentieth century as a result of Democratic dominance of both the governorship and the legislature. The election year of 1969 provided the first evidence that changes in Virginia's political environment would affect the Supreme Court selection process. In the early summer of 1969, Chief Justice Eggleston and Justice Buchanan met with Governor Godwin to inform him of their decision to retire simultaneously as of October 1, 1969. Both men had served long tenures and doubtless had contemplated retirement for some time. The timing of their decision, however, was undoubtedly influenced by political realities within the state. Governor Godwin was, at the time, nearing the end of his term, and the outcome of the next election was uncertain. Organization control of the governor's office was being strongly challenged from both within and outside the Democratic party. If the justices were to be assured that their successors would be selected by a like-minded individual, their resignations could not be postponed. The instincts of the justices proved to be accurate, because the 1969 appointments to the court were the last to be made in the placid, predictable atmosphere of dominance by the conservative Democratic organization.

The early retirement of Justice Gordon afforded Republican governor Linwood Holton his only opportunity to make an appointment to the state's highest court. Speculation as to his choice centered on retiring Republican congressman Richard H. Poff of Radford as soon as the vacancy was made known. In appointing Poff to the Virginia Supreme Court, Governor Holton bypassed three Democrats who had been suggested by the Virginia Bar Association. Only one Republican—and he had been in office for only a short time—was a sitting state judge at the time of the

48 *Richmond Times-Dispatch*, Oct. 2, 1969.

vacancy. It was therefore apparent that if the governor wanted to name a person from his own party, it would have to be someone without experience on the bench. He took note of Poff's recognized legal scholarship emanating from his long service on the House Judiciary Committee, where he had become the second-ranking Republican in seniority.

## Removal

Before adoption of the 1971 Constitution, there were two constitutionally sanctioned methods by which justices could be removed from office (other than defeat of appointees in the legislature): (1) impeachment and (2) removal for cause by a concurrent vote of the General Assembly. No justice of the Virginia Supreme Court has ever been removed from office by either of these procedures. The present constitution retains the impeachment section without substantive change. A justice, like all officers elected by the General Assembly or appointed by the governor, may be impeached by the House of Delegates for "malfeasance in office, corruption, neglect of duty, or other high crime or misdemeanor" and convicted with the concurrence of two-thirds of the senators present.

Under the Constitution of 1971, the provision authorizing removal simply "for cause" was eliminated in favor of a mandate to the General Assembly to create a Judicial Inquiry and Review Commission composed of members of the judiciary, the bar, and the general public. The commission is vested with the authority to investigate charges made against any justice or judge, conduct hearings with full power to subpoena witnesses and documents, and, if satisfied the charge is well founded, either urge the justice or judge to retire voluntarily or file a formal complaint with the Supreme Court. Following a hearing in open court, the Supreme Court may take one of several actions. In cases of physical or mental disability, it may retire the justice or judge from office on the ground of unfitness for further judicial service, in which case the justice or judge remains eligible for retirement benefits. In cases of neglect of duty or misconduct in office, the court may retire the justice or judge, censure him as a deterrent to further misconduct, or remove him from office.[49] Flexibility in the alternatives available to the court is the major characteristic of this procedure.

The establishment of a Judicial Inquiry and Review Commission represents a vast improvement over the previous method of removal for cause. The commission is in a better position than any public or private body to urge the voluntary retirement of members of the judiciary subject to its review. If a case of physical or mental disability is filed with the Supreme Court, that tribunal can retire the justice or judge with full retirement benefits without resorting to the more extreme method of impeachment. Misconduct and prejudicial activity cases will be more sensitive for the commission and the court. If the charges against the justice or judge are substantiated, the Supreme Court has the option of censure or removal. An anomaly in the process will be apparent when and if one of the justices is accused of unfit conduct. If a formal charge is filed by the commission against one of the justices, close friendships and collegial harmony will be supremely tested in the deliberations of the Supreme Court.

[49] Con., 1971, art. VI, sec. 10. The first formal complaint filed by the Judicial Inquiry and Review Commission resulted in a censure of circuit judge William S. Jordan of Radford. In an unsigned order dated Oct. 8, 1973, the Supreme Court found Jordan had engaged in conduct "prejudicial to the proper administration of justice." Two additional charges by the commission were dismissed as not being sustained "by clear and convincing evidence." Va., Supreme Court Order Book, no. 63, p. 152.

# III *Organization and Internal Procedures*

An evaluation of the work of the Virginia Supreme Court must go beyond an examination of the political and social realities under which the court operates. Its institutional structure and processes are a major factor in determining how the court functions in the Virginia political system. The organization and operation of the court are based on constitutional and statutory provisions, as well as on the Rules of the Court and its internal customs.

## Authority of the Court

As the fundamental law of the state, the Virginia Constitution is limited by the provisions of the United States Constitution and the federal laws passed in pursuance thereof. Whenever there is a manifest conflict between the federal document and the state document, the former prevails. Within this federal framework, the Virginia Constitution prescribes the essential structure and limits of Virginia government. The judgment of the Virginia Supreme Court as to the meaning and effect of the Virginia Constitution is decisive and controlling. No federal courts, including the nation's highest court, can contradict the interpretation given by the Virginia Supreme Court to the state's own constitution.[1] In interpreting the state constitution, the court does not pronounce policy in the abstract, but limits itself to rendering decisions in concrete cases. The court is inherently a passive institution making largely specific and retrospective judgments.

The Virginia Supreme Court possesses both original and appellate jurisdiction. Its original jurisdiction includes cases of habeas corpus, mandamus, and prohibition, and matters of judicial cen-

[1] *Highland Farms Diary, Inc.* v. *Agnew*, 300 U.S. 608 (1937).

sure, retirement, and removal filed by the newly created Judicial Inquiry and Review Commission. All other jurisdiction of the court is appellate. The state constitution specifically vests the court with appellate jurisdiction in cases involving the constitutionality of a law under the Virginia Constitution or the United States Constitution, and those involving the life or liberty of any person. With the exception of the above-named matters of original and appellate jurisdiction, which are enumerated in the constitution, the General Assembly is empowered to expand or contract the jurisdiction of the Supreme Court.[2]

Before the adoption of the Constitution of 1851, appellate authority in Virginia was shared by the state Supreme Court and the General Court. After the abolishment of the latter, in 1852, the Supreme Court served as the Virginia court of last resort in criminal as well as civil matters. The jurisdiction of the court was first constitutionally defined in 1851, and few substantive changes have been made since that time. The most noticeable alteration made by the 1971 Constitution in this regard is the expansion of the court's original jurisdiction to encompass cases initiated under article VI, section 10, pertaining to judicial censure, retirement, and removal.

## Operation of the Court

Throughout most of its history the Supreme Court has met in Richmond. The first Supreme Court, organized in Williamsburg on August 30, 1779, was moved to Richmond when the seat of government was transferred there the following year. The court sat at various locations in Richmond before it came to occupy the present Supreme Court Building in 1941.[3] With the reorganization of the court following the adoption of Virginia's second constitution, in 1830, the justices were required by the legislature to hold a session annually at Lewisburg, in Greenbrier County, for the benefit of those citizens living west of the Blue Ridge Mountains.[4] The justices followed this schedule of meeting in Richmond and Lewis-

[2] Con., 1971, art. VI, sec. 1.

[3] *Dedication of Building of Supreme Court of Appeals of Virginia, Richmond, Virginia, January 6, 1941* (Richmond: Richmond Press, 1941), pp. 31–35.

[4] Va. Acts, 1830–31, p. 37.

burg for thirty years, until the outbreak of the Civil War, at which time the area of West Virginia was organized as a separate state. In 1870 the tradition of holding short sessions away from Richmond became a constitutional mandate. Court sessions were authorized at Wytheville, Staunton, Winchester, and Richmond. In the twentieth century, annual sessions were held in Wytheville and Staunton in addition to the regular sessions in Richmond.[5]

The practice of holding the court at different locations in the state in order to be closer to the litigants originated in the days of horse-and-buggy travel. The development of a modern transportation system throughout the state rendered the practice unnecessary. In 1944 there was support in the General Assembly, and reportedly among the justices, for discontinuing all sessions outside Richmond.[6] A compromise solution discontinued the Wytheville session but retained the one in Staunton. When the 1971 Constitution eliminated the requirement that the court meet in two or more places, the Staunton session was also discontinued.

The justices have historically followed a busy schedule.[7] In 1811 the General Assembly increased the number of judicial days from 126 to 250 each year, but the legislature eventually reduced the justices' sessions to 220 days a year unless the business of the court could be completed in a shorter time.[8] At present the controlling statute stipulates that the court shall hold one term annually, commencing at such time (usually the first Monday in October) and continuing for such period as the justices may determine.[9] As a general rule the court has met every seventh Monday from that date until the completion of the June session. A regular session of

5 "The Supreme Court of Appeals shall hold its sessions at two or more places in the State, to be fixed by law." Con., 1870, art. VI, sec. 7; Con., 1902, art. VI, sec. 93; Va., General Assembly, 1944, *Report of the VALC to the Governor and General Assembly of Virginia,* House Document No. 8, "Proposed Elimination of the Sessions of the Supreme Court of Appeals at Staunton and Wytheville," p. 5.

6 *Richmond Times-Dispatch,* Sept. 9, 1944.

7 On at least one occasion the schedule was cited as the cause of resignation from the bench. In submitting his resignation, Judge St. George Tucker pronounced the 1811 legislative action that increased the duties of the justices without a corresponding increase in salary as oppressive and unconstitutional. He argued that the increase in the number of judicial days would leave him no choice but to desert his property and family in Williamsburg or move his family to Richmond. 2 Munford (16 Va.) xvii–xix (1811).

8 Va. Acts, 1869–70, p. 219.

9 Va. Code, sec. 17–99 (1974 suppl.).

oral arguments and conferences lasts seven weekdays, with a short session of three days being held in September.

From 1870 to 1933 the statutes governing the composition of the court instructed the members to select one of their number to reside in Richmond. It was felt to be in the public interest for one member to maintain a permanent residency in the capital city.[10] Since the appointment of Willis D. Miller to the court in 1947, there has always been at least one justice from Richmond sitting on the high bench. In fact, two of the justices elevated to the court during the past fifteen years chose to move their residency from another part of the state to Richmond. Traditionally, however, those justices not living in the Richmond area return to their homes when the court is not in session. The out-of-town justices utilize their home offices for writing their opinions and carrying out the judicial duty of hearing petitions for review of lower court decisions.

The Constitution of 1851 and successive constitutions of Virginia specified that a majority of the elected justices would constitute a quorum for hearing and deciding cases. The constitutions of 1870 and 1902 also specified that a majority of the total number of justices would have to concur before a law could be declared unconstitutional.[11] Under the 1971 Constitution the quorum requirement has been replaced: the document specifies that at least three justices must concur before a decision can become the judgment of the court, and that a majority of the justices must concur before a law can be found unconstitutional.[12]

When the number of justices was increased to seven by a 1928 amendment, the court was authorized to sit in two divisions, provided each division consisted of not less than three justices, for the purpose of hearing cases. The explicit rationale for the provision was to expedite the court's handling of the large number of cases on its docket.[13] The concurrence of three justices was sufficient

[10] Va. Acts, 1869–70, p. 219; 1874–75, p. 388; Va. Code, 1887, sec. 3048; 1919, sec. 5863.

[11] Con., 1851, art. VI, sec. 11; Con., 1864, art. VI, sec. 11; Con., 1870, art. VI, sec. 2; Con., 1902, art. VI, sec. 88.

[12] Con., 1971, art. VI, sec. 2.

[13] A Special Court of Appeals, composed of selected judges of the lower courts of record, had been employed from 1924 to 1928 for the purpose of relieving the congestion of the high court docket by adjudicating those cases assigned to it by

for the decision of one division to become the court's decision except in those cases involving construction of a constitutional provision.

With the addition of two new justices in 1930, the court continued to sit with only five justices in most cases.[14] This practice of utilizing only five members on a rotating basis was employed as a means of expediting the court's handling of cases on its overloaded docket. So commonplace was the use of a five-member court that the court reporter eliminated the historical practice of listing the justices who were "absent" when a case was being argued. In order to avoid giving the false impression that the justices not in attendance were shirking their judicial duties, the reporter initiated the practice, which continues today, of listing those members "present."[15] When the immediate docket crisis subsided several years later, the system of rolling panels was abandoned. Since that time the justices have followed the pre-1930 practice of sitting as a full court to hear all cases. The current justices have rejected suggestions that the court handle the heavy workload of the 1970s by reverting to the practice of sitting in panels to hear certain cases accepted for review.

Throughout the nineteenth century and the first quarter of the twentieth century the presiding officer of the Supreme Court has been designated as its president. In the first years of the court's history the General Assembly decided who was to serve in that position, but the practice evolved of electing as president the member who had served for the longest period. The 1928 constitutional amendments, which included an increase in the size of the court, formalized the practice by providing that the justice longest in continuous service should be chief justice. Robert R. Prentis, who was at that time serving as president of the court, thus qualified as the first chief justice. Under the 1971 Constitution the chief

---

the state Supreme Court. There is no provision for the creation of such a court in the present constitution. For a thorough examination of the historical role of the Special Court, see David K. Sutelan and Wayne R. Spencer, "The Virginia Special Court of Appeals: Constitutional Relief for an Overburdened Court," *William and Mary Law Review* 8 (1967):244–76.

14 Graham C. Lilly and Antonin Scalia, "Appelate Justice: A Crisis in Virginia?" *Virginia Law Review* 57 (1971):40–41.

15 Compare 155 Va. 413, 154 S.E. 545 (1930), and 155 Va. 419, 155 S.E. 683 (1930).

justice is to be selected from among the justices in a manner provided by law (art. VI, sec. 3). The 1971 General Assembly continued the seniority method of selecting the chief justice with the provision that the senior justice may decline the office if he so desires.[16]

## The Influence of Pendleton and Roane

Edmund Pendleton was the dominant figure on the bench in the first years of the Supreme Court. His influence over his fellow justices can be attributed at least in part to his extraordinary command of English law. His commanding presence during his twenty-four years as president of the court was primarily responsible for the harmonious relations among the early justices. His leadership discouraged the practice of the justices' writing seriatim opinions, as was commonplace on most state courts of last resort and on the United States Supreme Court prior to the ascendancy of John Marshall.

Thomas Jefferson was critical of judicial leadership that encouraged the presentation of a court's opinion in such a way as to minimize dissension and to give the outward appearance of unity. Writing to United States Supreme Court justice William Johnson in 1822, the former president reviewed the historical development of seriatim opinions:

> You know that from the earliest ages of the English law, from the date of the yearbooks, at least, to the end of the IId George, the judges of England, in all but self-evident cases, delivered their opinions seriatim, with the reasons and authorities which governed their decisions. If they sometimes consulted together, and gave a general opinion, it was so rarely as not to excite either alarm or notice. . . . It sometimes happened too that when there were three opinions against one, the reasoning of the one was so much the most cogent as to become afterwards the law of the land. When Ld. Mansfield came to the bench he introduced the habit of caucusing opinions. The judges met at their chambers, or elsewhere, secluded from the presence of the public, and made up what was to be delivered as the opinion of the court. On the retirement of

16 Va. Code, sec. 7–93 (1974 suppl.). Appendix C lists the presidents and chief justices of the court.

Mansfield, Ld. Kenyon put an end to the practice, and the judges returned to that of seriatim opinions, and practice it habitually to this day. . . .[17]

Jefferson implored Justice Johnson to use his influence to persuade his colleagues on the United States Supreme Court to return to the practice of writing seriatim opinions. The former president cited with approval the development of the Virginia Supreme Court:

I know nothing of what is done in other states, but in this Virginia our great and good Mr. Pendleton was, after the revolution, placed at the head of the court of Appeals. He adored Ld. Mansfield, and considered him as the greatest luminary of law that any age had ever produced, and he introduced into the court over which he presided, Mansfield's practice of making up opinions in secret and delivering them as the Oracles of the court, in mass. Judge Roane, when he came to that bench, broke up the practice, refused to hatch judgments, in Conclave, or to let others deliver opinions for him.[18]

Although Jefferson's historical analysis of the English precedent is accurate, he errs in presenting the tenure of Spencer Roane on the bench as marking such a sharp departure from the first twenty-four years of the court.

Upon the death of Pendleton, in 1803, Roane immediately began to take control of the operations of the court. On the day of Pendleton's death the court was to have handed down its decision in the important case of *Turpin* v. *Locket*.[19] Perhaps the most exciting case since the court was reorganized in 1788, it involved the constitutionality of a Virginia act passed in 1802, expropriating the vacant glebe lands of the Episcopal church. Judge William Fleming had disqualified himself from the case because the lands in question were in his county. The remaining justices were divided three to one, with only Roane in favor of upholding the decision of Chancellor George Wythe that the act was constitutional. Pen-

[17] Paul L. Ford, comp. and ed., *Writings of Thomas Jefferson*, 10 vols. (New York: G. P. Putnam's Sons, 1892–99), 10:223–24.

[18] Ibid., p. 224.

[19] 6 Call (10 Va.) 113 (1804); see "Judge Spencer Roane of Virginia: Champion of States' Rights—Foe of John Marshall," *Harvard Law Review* 66 (1953):1246–47.

dleton's handwritten opinion reversing Wythe was found in his room, but it had not been officially delivered.[20] In view of Fleming's disqualification and Pendleton's death, and considering it unseemly for two justices on the five-man court to pronounce the act unconstitutional, Roane suggested that the case not be finally decided until the vacancy had been filled. The two surviving members of the majority agreed with Roane. Meanwhile the General Assembly was anxious to fill Pendleton's seat with someone who would uphold the constitutionality of the glebe law. When queried by his legislative supporters concerning his feelings on the glebe case, St. George Tucker refused to express an opinion on a pending case or to pledge himself to a position in order to be elected to replace Pendleton. However, he referred the inquirer to a recently published essay in which Tucker had found no conflict between a state-financed plan of religious education and the constitutional guarantees of freedom of religion and separation of church and state. His supporters were satisfied that he would also support the power of the legislature to authorize the sale of vacant glebe lands; once on the court, Tucker vindicated that view by voting with Roane, thereby upholding Wythe's decision because of an equal division of the justices.[21]

The first few years after the death of Pendleton were marked by dissension within the court. Notwithstanding the agreement of Roane and Tucker in the glebe case, feelings between the two became so bitter that they ceased speaking to one another. It has been suggested that Roane's irascibility, coupled with the heavy workload of the court, influenced Tucker to resign from the bench in 1811, at the age of fifty-nine. The election that year of three new justices who were in sympathy with the political control exercised by the Richmond oligarchy headed by Roane, and the fact that after 1817 infirmities of age prevented Judge Fleming from sitting with the court, substantially altered the complexion of the high bench. A degree of harmony had returned under the leadership of Spencer Roane. In the period from February 1813 to April 1820,

[20] David J. Mays, *Edmund Pendleton, 1721–1803, A Biography,* 2 vols. (Cambridge: Harvard University Press, 1952), 2:345.

[21] Charles T. Cullen, "St. George Tucker and Law in Virginia, 1772–1804" (Ph.D. diss., University of Virginia, 1971), pp. 249–52.

Roane wrote 157 of 223 majority opinions, while delivering only 15 seriatim opinions.[22]

In 1808, before the election of the three new members, Judge Roane proposed certain novel reforms of procedure to his colleagues on the Supreme Court. Emphasizing the importance of "unanimity of opinion among the members," especially in light of the legislature's action to reduce the number of justices to three, Roane suggested that the members meet in conference for full consultation before reaching a final decision on a case. He also suggested that when there was a division of opinion among the members, their written opinions should be interchanged before the court handed down a decision. Finally, he recommended that the members refrain from writing elaborate seriatim opinions in those cases presenting no important principles or division among the justices. Roane withdrew his proposals the following year when it became obvious that his colleagues were not in agreement with them.[23]

The pressure of business before the court, together with the election of more compatible justices, eventually resulted in the de facto adoption of Roane's proposals. The justices followed Roane's lead in writing relatively short majority opinions stating the position of the court in all but the most important cases. On occasion the justices continued to write seriatim opinions. One of those occasions was the case in which the Virginia court challenged the power of the United States Supreme Court to review judgments of state courts.[24] In fact, Roane actually sought the views of Jefferson and James Monroe before presenting his own opinion. The justices also wrote individual opinions in the 1848 decision upholding the constitutionality of the Special Court of Appeals.[25] Roane's lasting impact on the opinion-writing traditions of the Virginia Supreme Court was not lessened by the court's occasional resort to seriatim opinions in important cases during the first half of the nineteenth century.

22 "Judge Spencer Roane," p. 1245.

23 Rex Beach, "Spencer Roane and Richmond Junto," *William and Mary Quarterly*, n.s., 22 (Jan. 1942):10–15.

24 *Hunter* v. *Martin*, 4 Munford (18 Va.) 1 (1815).

25 *Sharpe* v. *Robertson*, 5 Gratt (46 Va.) 518 (1849).

## The Decision-making Process

Appeal to the Virginia Supreme Court is a matter of right only in those cases originating in the State Corporation Commission and those involving disbarment. Unlike practically all other states, Virginia does not allow a general "appeal of right." Since the exceptions just named constitute only a small category of appeals and the number of cases heard exclusively under the court's original jurisdiction is severely limited, it can be stated that the court is given broad jurisdictional discretion in determining its caseload. The absence of a general appeal as a matter of right means that the method by which the justices grant reviews of lower court decisions is an extremely important aspect of the decision-making process.

### The Sifting Process

A petition for appeal may be presented to the clerk of court or to one of the justices. Procedures and deadlines for filing petitions are governed by part 5 of the Rules of the Court and are administered by the court clerk. The attorney for the petitioner (the appellant) is allowed up to thirty minutes to present orally the reasons for granting the appeal. Although the counsel for the appellee is not allowed to present an oral argument against granting the petition, he may file a written brief opposing the granting of the petition for appeal.

Whenever possible, the justices prefer to hear the arguments for petitions while sitting in panels of three. This practice is preferable because, although one justice may grant an appeal, one justice cannot deny a petition with finality. The justices are governed in this regard by a statute stipulating that "the rejection of such petition by a judge in vacation shall not prevent the presentation of such petition to the court at its next term."[26] The Rules of the Court reflect this statute by acknowledging that if counsel has been refused an appeal by one justice, he may apply to another member of the court but will not be accorded an opportunity to

[26] Va. Code, sec. 8–476 (1957 repl. vol.).

make his argument orally: "Oral argument before a Justice shall be a waiver of the right to oral presentation to any other Justice or to the Court."[27] When a petition is presented to a single justice, the practice has developed whereby the justice causes the petition to be summarized and presented to two other justices for their concurrence. By following this practice, the court avoids the possibility of the same petition being submitted once again, since the concurrence of three justices is in effect the final judgment of the court except in cases involving the construction of a constitutional provision.

With the assistance of a statute permitting retired Supreme Court justices to sit on a panel reviewing petitions, the court has been able to handle most of its petitions while sitting in panels of two or more in Roanoke, Richmond, Norfolk, or some other area of the state. Although attempts are made to distribute this responsibility evenly among the justices, it is quite probable that the screening process gives greater influence to justices hearing petitions from the heavily populated urban corridor area of the commonwealth, which accounts for much of the court's business.[28] The court sits *en banc* to hear petitions only in exceptional circumstances.

The handling of petitions for appeal is one of the most difficult tasks facing the justices. The review of petitions probably consumes more of the justices' time than any other aspect of their duties except writing opinions. It is physically impossible for the justices to read the entire record in every case submitted for review without neglecting their other duties. The law clerks provided for the justices since 1962 are immensely valuable in lightening this burden. They draw up a memorandum on each petition summarizing the basic points of the appeal.

Even though review of petitions is largely discretionary, the court has historically reviewed petitions on their merits. In a 1905 case Judge James Keith stated the policy followed by the members of the court: "It is as much the duty of the court, or judge, to deny the petition when of opinion that the decision complained of is

[27] Rule 5:28, 212 Va. 379 (1972).

[28] John T. Wold, "Internal Procedures, Role Perceptions and Judicial Behavior: A Study of Four State Courts of Last Resort" (Ph.D. diss., Johns Hopkins University, 1972), pp. 113–14.

plainly right as it is to grant it when any doubt exists as to the propriety of the decision."[29] More recently, the rapid rise in the number of petitions filed with the court and the decrease in the percentage of petitions granted suggested an abandonment of the "merits review" standard. Based in part on a 1971 statistical study published in the *Virginia Law Review*, the standard of discretionary review practiced by the Virginia Supreme Court was challenged as being violative of the equal protection clause of the Fourteenth Amendment. In unequivocal language, Chief Justice Harold F. Snead defended the court's policy of review:

> We readily acknowledge that the increased number of petitions filed in recent years has created a greater burden for this court. We cannot agree, however, that this burden, or anything else, has caused us to depart from our traditional merits standard of discretion in favor of some other test. The societal importance of the issues presented may, and properly should, play some part in the decision to grant a petition, but that has always been true, given the role of this court in matters of general application. This is certainly not to say, however, that societal importance is a controlling consideration or that a petition would be refused simply because it lacked such importance.[30]

A recent study of the appellate process in Virginia sponsored by the National Center for State Courts confirmed the standard of review espoused by the court's members. The final report, written by Prof. Graham C. Lilly (coauthor of the 1971 statistical study questioning whether the court was continuing to apply the merits standard), made this observation: "The staff concluded that insofar as it was able to observe the process of decision making, the justices conducted a thorough merits review."[31] The report further conceded that the decline in the percentage of petitions granted could be attributed to the increase in the number of frivolous petitions filed with the court. New constitutional interpretations in the federal courts have resulted in free legal counsel and free transcripts for indigent criminal defendants, and counsel for an indigent is

[29] *McCue* v. *Commonwealth*, 103 Va. 870, 1008, 49 S.E. 623, 632 (1905).

[30] *Saunders* v. *Reynolds*, 214 Va. 697, 700, 204 S.E. 2d 421, 423–24 (1974).

[31] Lilly, *The Appellate Process and Staff Research Attorneys in the Supreme Court of Virginia: A Report of the Appellate Justice Project of the National Center for State Courts, 1972–1973* (Washington, D.C.: National Center for State Courts, May 1974), p. 56, n. 36; see also Lilly and Scalia, p. 14.

obligated to file a petition in order to avoid charges of incompetence in representing the client. Consequently, many of the petitions pertaining to criminal issues can be and have been summarily rejected.

## Assignment of Opinions

A committee of the American Bar Association has stated that there is "perhaps no more important internal procedure of an appellate court than that which is involved in designating the judge who is to draft the opinion in a particular case."[32] The chief justice of the United States assigns opinions for the Court on which he sits except when he has voted in the minority, in which case the senior justice voting in the majority makes the assignment. The Virginia Supreme Court utilizes the other major method of assigning cases, that is, the rotation system. Before the beginning of each session of the court, the assignment of cases is determined by lot. Seven slips of paper are prepared by the clerk of the court, with one bearing the number 1 and the remainder being blank. The member drawing the marked paper writes opinions in the first, eighth, and fifteenth cases, etc.; the justice immediately below him in seniority is responsible for the second, ninth, and sixteenth cases, etc.; and so on until all cases are assigned.[33] Occasionally the justices do exchange responsibility for the writing of an opinion: for example, in cases where a justice is in the minority on a case that he has drawn, has disqualified himself from participation in the case, or for some reason is overburdened at the time. The subject matter of the case is almost never the basis for an exchange.

Prior to each new session of the court, the clerk of the court forwards to each justice a copy of the printed docket showing the cases to be heard at that session together with a copy of the record

[32] American Bar Association, Special Committee of the Section of Judicial Administration, "Internal Operating Procedures of Appellate Courts" (Aug. 1961), p. 12.

[33] The division of cases by lot appears to have been the predominant practice throughout this century in view of its current usage and Judge Joseph L. Kelly's acknowledgment of the court's use of the method in 1923. Kelly, "An Inside View of the Work of the Virginia Supreme Court," *Proceedings of the Virginia State Bar Association* 35 (1923):216.

and the written briefs filed by the opposing counsel in each case. Before the commencement of the session, each justice, with the aid of memorandums drawn up by his law clerk, reviews the briefs in those cases scheduled to be heard. In this way the justices are able to familiarize themselves with the basic arguments, although they are careful not to study the briefs in such a thorough manner as to make up their minds before hearing the oral arguments. This procedure was not followed prior to the elevation of John Eggleston to the court in 1935. Chief Justice Eggleston recounted the origination of the practice: "When I joined the court, none of the judges ever looked at the record and briefs before the case was argued. That astounded me. The other judges contended: 'If you do that, you might be prejudiced before you hear the case.' But I said, 'That doesn't make sense. All I wanna do is know what the case is about.' As new judges came on the bench, they adopted my view, and now all of us read the cases in advance and prepare detailed memorandums on each of them."[34]

## Court in Session

The court convenes in a third-floor chamber of the Supreme Court Building. The walls of the courtroom are lined with portraits of former members of the court, as are the walls of the entrance hall. The current members of the court, clad in black robes, sit behind a raised bench stretching across the front of the courtroom. The chief justice is seated in the center chair and is flanked by the justice second in seniority to his immediate right and the justice third in seniority to his immediate left (see Figure 1). This alternating seating arrangement in declining order of seniority places the junior justice in the end chair to the left of the chief justice.

Oral arguments are heard by the justices sitting *en banc*. Except by special permission, the attorneys for the appellant and the appellee are allowed no more than thirty minutes each.[35] The opening

[34] *Richmond News Leader,* July 2, 1969.

[35] When the present Rules of the Court became effective, in 1950, each side was permitted one hour. The allotted time was reduced to forty minutes in 1969 and finally to the current thirty minutes in 1971. 190 Va. cxxii (1950); 210 Va. clxxiii (1969); 211 Va. 468 (1971); rule 5:52, 212 Va. 305 (1972).

*Figure 1.* Courtroom arrangement for the Virginia Supreme Court

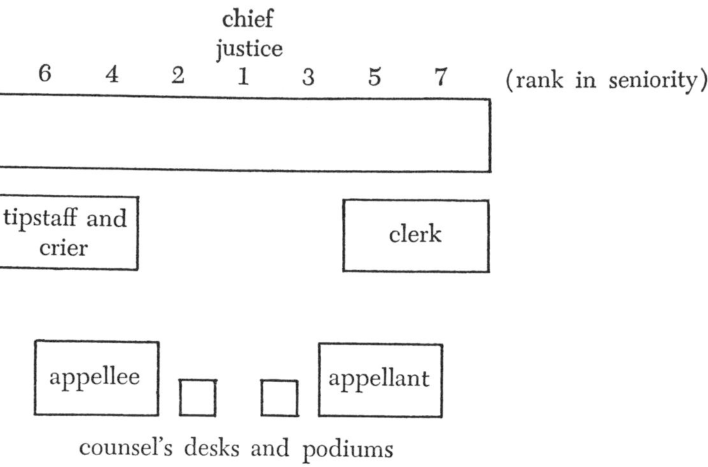


argument is presented by the appellant's attorney and followed by the presentation of the appellee's argument. The attorney for the appellant is granted the right of rebuttal provided he did not exhaust his time in the initial argument. A clear and well-presented oral argument is invaluable as a means of clarifying the fundamental issues involved in a case. In speaking to a meeting of the Virginia Bar Association, Justice Lawrence W. I'Anson stressed the importance of the oral argument and suggested that the attorneys for the appellant make their strongest argument first. He further recommended that in making "the opening argument counsel should clearly and fully state: (1) what the case is about; (2) what disposition was made of it in the lower court; (3) the points raised on the appeal; and (4) the facts pertinent to the issues on appeal, bearing in mind that usually . . . the justices do not weigh the evidence, but consider the case in the light of the verdict or finding of the trial court."[36] The justices frequently exercise their prerogative to interrupt the attorneys for the purpose of asking questions.

In terms of the internal operation of the court and the consultation about cases, the formal role of the chief justice is extremely limited. He serves as timekeeper during oral arguments and pre-

[36] I'Anson, "How the Supreme Court of Appeals of Virginia Functions," *Proceedings of the Virginia State Bar Association* 71 (1960):224–25.

sides over the private conferences of the justices. In conference, however, the chief justice does not possess any special authority. Unlike the chief justice of the United States, he is not necessarily the first member to give his opinion about a case and he does not assign justices to write the opinions of the court. He possesses only that influence which his ability and his years of appellate experience merit him in the eyes of his colleagues.

During a typical session of the court, the assembled justices hear oral arguments each morning, beginning Monday and adjourning Tuesday of the following week. After a short recess for lunch, the justices reconvene each day in the conference room for a private discussion of the cases heard in the morning. The justices gather around a large, rectangular conference table, with the chief justice seated in the head chair. To the right of the chief justice are seated the members second, fourth, and sixth in seniority; to his left, the justices third, fifth, and seventh in seniority (see Figure 2). The

*Figure 2.* Seating of Virginia Supreme Court justices during conference

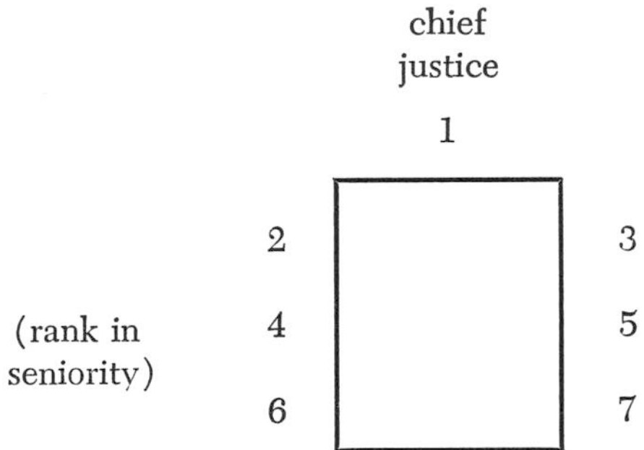


member responsible for writing the opinion initiates the discussion of the case by asking the justice on his right for his opinion on how the case should be decided. The justices then proceed to comment in turn with the member designated to write the opinion expressing his views last.[37] In addition to identifying potential dissenters, this

[37] According to former Chief Justice John W. Eggleston, Henry W. Holt initiated this practice while substituting for Chief Justice Preston W. Campbell as the presiding officer of the court. Since Holt's succession to the position of chief justice in 1946, it has been the standard procedure. Before this time it had been customary for the senior member to speak first. Interview with Eggleston, Aug. 20, 1971.

period of discussion and debate provides the opinion-writer with an indication of the legal grounds on which the opinion should be based and how it should be cast in order to receive the greatest possible support from his colleagues.

Only the justices are present during the conference deliberations, thus preserving the secrecy of this aspect of the court's work. The Virginia justices, however, have not absolutely excluded the personal delivery of messages by clerks or other court personnel during the conference sessions, as have the members of the nation's highest court.[38] Nevertheless, the precise nature of conference debates on specific cases is not revealed by the justices. A relatively recent innovation is to record on tape the deliberations of the justices in conference. Although some of the justices initially expressed concern that the presence of microphones might inhibit conference discussion, the continued use of the tape recorders suggests that the justices have found the tapes most helpful. The justice responsible for writing the opinion in a particular case is given a tape of the conference discussion of that case along with a tape of the oral arguments before the bench for use in writing the opinion of the court. Needless to say, the conference tapes are available only to members of the court and their law clerks.

## Writing Opinions

Beginning with the Constitution of 1851, the Supreme Court has been required to state in writing its reasons for reversing or affirming a judgment or decree. The present constitution also requires a written statement when the court modifies a judgment or decree, or when it resolves original cases on their merits. Thus, if the court decides the merits of a case, as opposed to dismissing or denying review of a case, a written opinion is required, and that opinion is to be preserved with the record of the case.[39]

[38] Since 1910 when the justices suspected a "leak" by one of the pages present in the conference room, messages to members of the United States Supreme Court are taken at the door by the justice who is junior in seniority. See Henry J. Abraham, *The Judicial Process*, 3d rev. ed. (New York: Oxford University Press, 1975), p. 216.

[39] Con., 1851, art. VI, sec. 13; Con., 1864, art. VI, sec. 13; Con., 1870, art. VI, sec. 4; Con., 1902, art. VI, sec. 90; Con., 1971, art. VI, sec. 6. See discussion of

Throughout the twentieth century, one justice in each case has assumed the responsibility for writing the opinion of the court. This procedure does not relieve the other justices from reaching an independent decision in each instance, but it does free them from the burden of writing an opinion in all, or most, cases. In this manner the workload of each justice is greatly reduced, and the court can handle more quickly the tremendous volume of work that is constantly before it. The average length of opinion has varied from five to eight printed pages, with a small number running fifteen pages or more. On a comparative basis, the opinions of the Virginia Supreme Court are much shorter than those of the United States Supreme Court.

One explanation for the shorter opinions is the almost mechanical and uniform style in which they are written. The nature of the case, as well as the research and writing habits of the individual justices, is, of course, significant in determining the length of opinions. On the whole, however, the opinions briefly restate the facts and the lower court disposition of the case, and then deal point by point with the issues raised in the briefs and oral arguments. The "judicial restraint" orientation of the justices with respect to their decisions carries over into their writing of opinions. The justices normally limit their comments to those necessary to the disposition of the case. Dicta or discursive commentary is largely absent from the opinions. One of the justices has also cautioned against a different type of temptation for the opinion-writer: "The decision will go into the permanent record, so you shouldn't try, for example, to be funny. If you do, twenty years from now they'll write about what a colorful fellow you were, but that's about all. Our court tries to stay away from 'purple prose.' Witticisms may be amusing, but they should be omitted from opinions."[40]

Virginia justices have generally adhered to the rule of precedent in deciding cases. They ascribe great weight to the doctrine of stare decisis, meaning to stand by decided cases, to uphold precedents. One of the justices has referred to this doctrine as the "golden rule of judicial restraint."[41] Sociological, economic, and other nonlegal

current article and section in A. E. Dick Howard, *Commentaries on the Constitution of Virginia,* 2 vols. (Charlottesville: University Press of Virginia, 1974), 2:736–39.

40 Wold, p. 129.

41 Harry L. Carrico, Speech delivered at dedication of Halifax County Courthouse, May 1, 1964.

reasoning is therefore rarely if ever cited by the justices in their opinions.

Throughout the 1960s each justice was responsible for writing three opinions following each session of the court. This traditional caseload was increased to five for a time during 1972, before being reduced to the current number of four in an attempt to cope with the congestion of cases on the court's docket. The current caseload of four opinions per justice each session of the court was made possible by the increased use of per curiam opinions. These short, unsigned opinions are used in certain cases involving no new points of law. During the 1960s, for example, the court averaged about two such opinions each year. With the 1970–71 term, the court began to dispose of from ten to twelve cases each session with per curiam opinions. This practice has been well received by the bar and has been continued by the justices. One of the justices residing in Richmond tentatively identifies for the court those cases in which per curiam opinions would be most likely. On occasion, however, conference deliberations or legal research by a justice will dictate a change in the manner of handling the case.

An unusually long or complex record in a case assigned to one justice might justify a reduction in the number of cases for which he is responsible. Given the work schedule of the court, approximately three weeks are reserved for writing opinions. The amount of time devoted to this task has been defended by one of the justices in terms of the need to "exercise care and precision in stating even the most familiar legal principles."[42] For the most part, opinion-writing is a solitary and lonesome task, one of the most individualized phases of a justice's work. Consultation as a group is impractical at this stage for a variety of reasons including the dispersal of the justices to the various parts of the state. Moreover, if the justice is not satisfied with the authorities cited in the attorneys' briefs, he must research the question himself. Of course, since 1962 the members have had the assistance of law clerks in such matters.

Once the justice has completed his opinions, copies are circulated among his colleagues on the high bench. Opinion conferences, another recent innovation, are held for one day approximately ten days before the beginning of a new session. At this time the justices

[42] I'Anson, p. 227.

endeavor to iron out any continuing differences that might exist among the members as to phraseology or substantive holdings. The initial conference of the new session is also utilized for this purpose if necessary. The period between the opinion conference and the initial conference of a new session is used to make final revisions in the opinions before they are announced, usually on the second Monday of the session. In those instances in which the members are unable to reach a final decision on an opinion or in which there is insufficient time for revisions, the case is held over to the next session.

The use of conferences both before and after the opinions are written is conducive to achieving that unanimity of opinion for which the justices strive. It also serves as a guard against "one-man" opinions. Nevertheless, as Judge Kelly acknowledged in his 1923 speech, there are limits to the efficacy of this process in avoiding that possibility:

> Now, of course, if I were to assert that, when an opinion has been written by the judge to whom the case has been assigned, we do not review it with due regard to the fact that the author has made a closer study of the record than is to be expected of his associates, you would not, and ought not to believe it. . . . No one of us can undertake to edit and control to any great extent the structure and phraseology of the opinions written by others. And if each of us should endeavor to give as much attention to all the other cases as to those in which we respectively write the opinions, we would go wrong oftener than we do, and besides, we would never get the work done. We are obliged to divide the responsibility to some extent, and we are obliged to divide the labor to a large extent.[43]

The scheduling of conference discussion of a case on the same day it is argued and the polling of all justices on each case during the conferences militate against "one-man" opinions. The effort of the justices to familiarize themselves before the court convenes with all the cases scheduled to be heard is also helpful in avoiding such results. Nevertheless, the justices do know before the commencement of oral arguments the cases for which they will be writing opinions barring an infrequent exchange of responsibility during

[43] Kelly, p. 219.

the conference deliberations. As a result of this prior knowledge, the justices must constantly be on guard not to relax their interest when a case is being argued or discussed for which they do not have a responsibility.

The assignment of opinions by one person can result in the emergence of specialists in certain legal areas. The practice on the Virginia court of assigning cases by an order of rotation established by lot requires the justices to be legal generalists. Each member of the court eventually handles every type of case. This absence of specialists minimizes the possibility of deference to one member's expertise in some area of the law. The occasional exchange of cases among the justices will not subvert the generalist orientation so long as the subject matter of a case is not an important basis for such exchanges.

## The Tradition of Consensus

Among the reasons for the relatively short opinions of the Virginia Supreme Court is the low percentage of nonunanimous decisions. The writer of the opinion for the court is rarely faced with the necessity of reacting to or taking into account the arguments of a dissenting opinion. Based on a 1964 sampling of cases in America's fifty-one courts of last resort, the Virginia court was among three-fifths of the courts in which dissent was noted no oftener than an average of two cases in twenty-five. (Predictably, the United States Supreme Court had the highest dissent rate.)[44] More precisely, a review of cases from 1961 to 1971 reveals that nonunanimous decisions, including those in which one or more justices dissent from the opinion of the court as well as those in which the lower court decision is affirmed because of an equal division among the justices, constitute less than 5 percent of the cases decided by the Virginia court.[45] Table 6 indicates dissents and concurrences attributed to individual justices from 1961 to 1971.

[44] Robert J. Sickels, "The Illusion of Judicial Consensus: Zoning Decisions in the Maryland Court of Appeals," *American Political Science Review* 59 (Mar. 1965):100.

[45] The Virginia justice in this century most deserving of the title "dissenter" was probably Louis S. Epes (1929–35). In less than six years on the high court he

*Table 6.* Number of dissenting and concurring decisions by Virginia Supreme Court justices, 1961–71

| Justice | 1961 D[a] | C[b] | 1962 D | C | 1963 D | C | 1964 D | C | 1965 D | C | 1966 D | C | 1967 D | C | 1968 D | C | 1969 D | C | 1970 D | C | 1971 D | C | Totals D | C |
|---|---|---|---|---|---|---|---|---|---|---|---|---|---|---|---|---|---|---|---|---|---|---|---|---|
| Eggleston | 3 | — | 2 | 1 | 1 | 1 | 1 | — | — | — | — | — | 1 | 1 | 2 | — | 2 | — | ——[d] | | —— | | 12 | 3 |
| Spratley | 4 | — | 2 | 1 | 2 | — | — | — | 1 | 1 | — | 1[c] | 2 | 1 | —— | | —— | | —— | | —— | | 11 | 4 |
| Buchanan | 2 | — | — | 1 | 1 | — | — | — | 1 | 1 | 1 | 1[c] | 1 | 1 | 1 | — | 1 | — | —— | | —— | | 8 | 4 |
| Whittle | — | — | 3 | 1 | — | — | 1 | — | — | — | —— | | —— | | —— | | —— | | —— | | —— | | 4 | 1 |
| Snead | — | — | 1 | — | — | — | — | — | — | — | — | — | 2 | — | 1 | — | 1 | — | — | — | 1 | — | 6 | — |
| I'Anson | 1 | — | — | — | 2 | — | — | — | 1 | — | — | 1[c] | 1 | — | 1 | — | — | — | — | 1 | 2 | — | 9 | 2 |
| Carrico | — | — | 1 | — | — | — | — | — | — | — | 5[c] | — | 1 | — | 3 | — | 4 | 1 | — | — | 1 | 1 | 15 | 2 |
| Gordon | —— | | —— | | —— | | —— | | 2 | 1 | 4 | 1 | 2 | — | 3 | — | 3 | 3 | 3 | 1 | 2 | 1 | 19 | 7 |
| Harrison | —— | | —— | | —— | | —— | | —— | | —— | | — | — | 3 | — | 3 | — | — | — | 1 | — | 7 | — |
| Harman | —— | | —— | | —— | | —— | | —— | | —— | | —— | | —— | | 1 | — | — | — | 2 | — | 3 | — |
| Cochran | —— | | —— | | —— | | —— | | —— | | —— | | —— | | —— | | — | — | 2 | 1 | 3 | — | 5 | 1 |
| Totals | 10 | — | 9 | 4 | 6 | 1 | 2 | — | 5 | 3 | 10 | 4 | 10 | 3 | 14 | — | 15 | 4 | 6 | 3 | 12 | 2 | 99 | 24 |

[a] D = dissenting opinions including dissents in part.

[b] C = concurring opinions.

[c] Four companion cases involving a criminal prosecution (207 Va. 135, 159, 165, 170 [1966]) are counted as one case. The same justices concurred and dissented in each case on the basis of opinions in the first case.

[d] —— = justice not a member of the court.

This infrequency of dissent is generally characteristic of the twentieth-century court. The behavior of Virginia justices in this regard was well summarized by Judge Joseph L. Kelly in addressing the 1923 Annual Conference of the Virginia Bar Association: "I believe I am justified in saying that we the members of the Virginia Supreme Court are not addicted to the habit of dissenting. We realize that we are expected to agree and not to disagree. It is our duty, as far as may be, to add the strength of unanimity to our decisions."[46] Continuous *dissensus* on the court of last resort has been interpreted by many in the legal profession as undermining the prestige of the court and reducing its effectiveness in providing guidelines for the lower courts. Virginia justices have for the most part taken the position that their opinions are written for the bench and the bar. It is the justices' view, therefore, that a frequently divided court tends to create doubt in the minds of the legal profession as to the status of certain legal principles.

High dissent rates on courts of last resort are ordinarily explained in terms of the political and social backgrounds of the appellate justices. In Virginia, not only have the justices come from homogeneous backgrounds, but they have also shared a common political and judicial philosophy. These factors have unquestionably played a large role in assuring consensus among Virginia justices. Another possible explanation for the low dissent rate is the absence of an intermediate appellate court in Virginia. Recent research by two political scientists has focused on structural variations in state judicial systems. The presence or absence of an intermediate appellate court was found to have a dramatic effect on dissent rates. The assumption was that an intermediate appellate court served to shield a state's highest court from those routine cases that tend to produce unanimous decisions; consequently, one would expect a higher proportion of potentially divisive cases in those courts insulated by an intermediate appellate court. The results demonstrated that state supreme courts operating in judicial systems containing such an intermediate court dissented at about twice the rate of similar courts hearing appeals directly from trial courts. Since

---

dissented eighty-three times, although he filed opinions in only forty cases. W. Moncure Gravett, "Louis Spence Epes," *Proceedings of the Virginia State Bar Association* 68 (1936):173.

46 Kelly, p. 219.

Virginia falls in the latter category, the structural arrangements of the state's judicial system may serve as a partial explanation of the low dissent rate for the state Supreme Court.[47]

The tradition of consensus on the Virginia court can be deceiving if one infers the absence of conflict among the justices. By the justices' own admission, proposed dissenting opinions have on occasion become the opinion of the court or have prompted a revision of the majority opinion.[48] Not infrequently, it is the tone of the majority opinion that disturbs the wavering justice or justices. Minor revisions can often transform a potentially split decision into a unanimous one.

A formal dissent has been variously described by Virginia justices as a "loser," an "admission of defeat," and an "exercise in futility." It is looked upon as a viewpoint that did not prevail in the private debate among the justices. A "disagreer" in conference is considered by many of the court's members to be actually more effective than an official "dissenter." The views of a justice who prompts a change in the opinion of the court have an immediate impact on the legal situation, whereas the views of a dissenter may never be decisive.

The utility of a dissent must also be weighed against the value of presenting a solid front. Thus dissents have normally been avoided by Virginia justices except when, in the words of Judge Kelly, "the differences are so serious as that unanimity of decision would require a sacrifice of a fixed and conscientious conviction."[49] Furthermore, once a justice has publicly recorded his dissent, he normally refrains from doing so again in future cases involving the same legal principle. The continuing, and often acrimonious, dialogue among justices, which is so characteristic of the United States Supreme Court,[50] is largely absent from the Virginia court. Finally, the tendency to sublimate dissent within the Virginia court has resulted in the justices' filing lone dissents, often without comment, much more frequently than is the case among their counterparts on the United States Supreme Court. Of the sixty cases from 1961

[47] Bradley C. Canon and Dean Jaros, "External Variables, Institutional Structure and Dissent on State Supreme Courts," *Polity* 3 (Winter 1970):191–93.

[48] Kelly, pp. 219–30.

[49] Ibid., p. 220.

[50] Abraham, pp. 219–21.

to 1971 in which dissents were registered, twenty-five (42 percent) involved a single dissenter.

Concurring opinions are even more infrequent than dissenting opinions. As evidenced by usage, Virginia justices have assigned a relatively unimportant value to concurring opinions. A separate concurrence was filed in only about 1 percent of the cases decided from 1961 to 1971. The behavior norm appears to operate, even more strongly than in the case of potential dissents, in favor of compromise or alteration of the majority opinion in conference.

## Staffing

Historically, the key elements in the operation of the Virginia Supreme Court have been the anti-Jeffersonian quest for unanimity and the absence of appeal as a matter of right. Beginning in the 1960s the internal operation of the court has also been characterized by the addition of auxiliary personnel to assist the justices in their work. Prior to that time the nonjudicial staff of the court was limited principally to the clerk of the court and his staff, who processed the written briefs and petitions filed with the court and compiled statistical information about the court's caseload. In 1952 the office of executive secretary was created to assist the chief justice in administering the lower court system.

An ever bulging caseload prompted the move toward supplementing the administrative staff of the court. Since 1962 each of the justices on the court has been assisted by one law clerk. The clerks are usually recent graduates of one of Virginia's law schools and normally serve for one year. Although each justice employs his clerk in the manner most suitable to his work habits, the clerks are generally concerned with summarizing petitions for review and assisting with the researching and writing of opinions. At the close of the 1960s the court took the additional step of employing a special assistant to review, summarize, and make recommendations on original writs (habeas corpus, mandamus, and prohibition) and criminal appeals. In 1972, for example, the special assistant, assisted by a "writ clerk," processed 92 percent of all the cases of original jurisdiction and 40 percent of all the criminal petitions disposed of by the court in that year.[51]

As part of the project undertaken in 1972 to study the Virginia appeals system, a two-man central staff was employed to assist Virginia justices in screening appeals. The staff prepared summary or prehearing reports on selected petitions presented to the Virginia Supreme Court. While acknowledging that the answer to alleviating congestion in the appellate system is a complex one, the project report concluded that the creation of a central staff for the court would lead to increased productivity and improved expedition for the Virginia appellate process.[52] The central staff, much like the special assistant, would operate at the petition stage of decision-making. It was noted that such a staff would be ideally suited to address the central inquiry in the sifting process: Does the record present a reasonable possibility that there was substantial error in the trial court? The function of law clerks would remain unaltered, since the central staff would serve the court as a whole rather than individual justices. The initial response of the justices and the endorsement of the central staff concept by the governing body of the Virginia State Bar suggests that additional staff is perceived as an important ingredient in maintaining the soundness of the decision-making process in the face of appellate congestion.

[51] Lilly, p. 13.
[52] Ibid., pp. 160–65.

# IV *Litigation, Litigants, and Intercourt Relations*

THE business of the Virginia Supreme Court can best be measured by examining what kinds of cases are brought to the high bench and by whom. An identification of the types of litigation and litigants dealt with by the court is helpful in defining its place in the political system. The activity of the court may also be viewed as a system of interactions with lower state courts and with the United States Supreme Court.

## Workload of the Court

The dramatic increase in the volume of petitions submitted to the Virginia Supreme Court over the past fifteen years is a result of several factors. The simple increase in the number of Virginia citizens—8 percent higher than the national growth rate—is a partial explanation for the rapid rise in the total number of petitions. On the other hand, much of the increase can be attributed to the rise in criminal appeals. From 1959 to 1969 criminal appeals increased from 21 to 65 percent of total appeals.[1] The impact of increased criminal appeals on the court's workload has caused a dramatic shift in the balance between civil and criminal cases. Before 1967 only a small portion of cases heard by the Virginia court were criminal in nature: of the total appeals accepted by the court in 1959, only 11 percent were criminal cases. Ten years later 45 percent of the appeals decided by the court were criminal cases. Because there is little to suggest that the volume of such appeals will decrease, it is highly probable that criminal cases will continue to constitute a major portion of the court's workload.

Criminal cases have been within the court's jurisdiction for only

[1] Graham C. Lilly and Antonin Scalia, "Appellate Justice: A Crisis in Virginia?" *Virginia Law Review* 57 (1971):8–11.

a little over half its existence. Until 1852 the General Court was vested with supreme appellate jurisdiction in criminal cases. In fact, even after 1852 the court reporter continued to place criminal cases in the back of *Virginia Reports*, as had been the practice with the cases decided by the General Court. This practice was discontinued by a new reporter who served from 1883 to 1894. However, commencing with volume 91, the practice was reinstated and followed until 1940.[2]

The lower state courts of record are the primary source of cases before the Virginia Supreme Court. Appellate cases from lower courts constituted more than 90 percent of the court's total workload during the five terms beginning in October 1961 and ending September 1966 (see Table 7). Appeals from the state commissions and original petitions accounted for the remainder of the court's business. Significantly, the court affirmed 66.7 percent of the orders of the state commissions as compared with an affirmative rate of 51.2 percent for lower court decisions.

*Table 7.* Sources of litigation before the Virginia Supreme Court, Oct. 1961–Sept. 1966

| Source of litigation | Cases No. | Cases % of total |
|---|---|---|
| Original petitions | 20 | 3.3 |
| Appeals from state commissions[a] | | |
| Affirmed | 22 | |
| Reversed | 10 | |
| Mixed | 1 | |
| Subtotal | 33 | 5.4 |
| Appeals from lower state courts | | |
| Affirmed | 284 | |
| Reversed | 249 | |
| Mixed | 21 | |
| Subtotal | 554 | 91.3 |
| Total | 607 | 100.0 |

[a] State Corporation Commission, Industrial Commission of Virginia, State Milk Commission.

A general indication of the types of litigation heard by the Vir-

[2] 91 Va. xxi (1895); 177 Va. 806 (1940).

ginia Supreme Court during the period from October 1961 to September 1966 is provided in Table 8. This period was chosen to

*Table 8.* Types of litigation before the Virginia Supreme Court, Oct. 1961–Sept. 1966

| | | | Decisions | | | |
|---|---|---|---|---|---|---|
| | | | For plaintiff, or state | | For defendant, or antistate | |
| Type of case | No. | % of total cases | No. | % | No. | % |
| Automobile injury | 102 | 16.8 | 49 | 48.0 | 53 | 52.0 |
| Criminal offenses | 89 | 14.7 | 49 | 55.0 | 40 | 45.0 |
| Nonautomobile negligence | 44 | 7.2 | 17 | 38.6 | 27 | 61.4 |
| Insurance | 42 | 6.9 | | | | |
| Pleading and practice | 39 | 6.4 | | | | |
| Contracts | 36 | 5.9 | | | | |
| Constitutional law | 35 | 5.8 | 29 | 82.9 | 6 | 17.1 |
| Domestic relations | 29 | 4.8 | | | | |
| Real property | 27 | 4.5 | | | | |
| Taxation | 23 | 3.8 | 6 | 26.0 | 17 | 74.0 |
| Eminent domain | 22 | 3.6 | | | | |
| Administrative law | 18 | 2.9 | | | | |
| Workmen's compensation | 12 | 2.0 | | | | |
| Wills, trusts, estates | 12 | 2.0 | | | | |
| Real estate | 12 | 2.0 | | | | |
| Municipal corporations | 9 | 1.5 | | | | |
| Business associations | 8 | 1.3 | | | | |
| Sales | 7 | 1.2 | | | | |
| Landlord-tenant | 6 | 1.0 | | | | |
| Annexation | 4 | .7 | | | | |
| Labor-related matters | 3 | .5 | | | | |
| Miscellaneous | 28 | 4.5 | | | | |
| Total | 607 | 100.0 | | | | |

reflect the court load before the sharp increase in criminal cases beginning in 1967. The ratio between the court's civil and criminal caseloads during the 1961–66 period is historically more typical than the ratio for the period since 1966. The cases were classified according to the dominant issue or subject matter before the court. The procedure was complicated by the numerous cases involving more than one subject matter or issue. Constitutional law cases, for example, could have been listed under other categories, such as criminal offenses, taxation, or municipal corporations. Cases might also involve several points of law, such as pleading and practice, wills, or contracts. It was decided to classify cases according to their dominant theme based on the headnotes of *Virginia Reports* and *Southeastern Reporter* and, in some instances, a close reading of the opinions.[3]

The bulk of the business before the Virginia Supreme Court was clearly in the area of private rather than public law. It is not surprising, therefore, to find cases pertaining to automobile injuries as the most common type of litigation decided by the justices. Criminal cases, although a relatively small number in terms of total cases, constituted the second largest single category. Nonautomobile negligence cases were the third most common type of litigation. When this category is combined with automobile injury cases, it demonstrates that almost one-fourth of the court's work was in the area of torts. Insurance cases, normally between the insurer and the insured, and involving provisions and coverage of insurance policies, constituted the next largest category. In a typical case in 1965 the court was faced with a suit against the National Fire Insurance Company of Hartford to recover for loss or damage to trees and shrubs under a "comprehensive dwelling" insurance policy. The court decided in favor of the policyholder by applying the "rule that where the language of an insurance contract is susceptible of two constructions, as manifested in the argument, it is universally held that it is to be construed strictly against the insurer and liberally in favor of the insured."[4] Six years later a life insurance beneficiary whose grandson was killed in Vietnam while on active duty as a member of the United States Army presented the court with the question of whether, in the context of the exclusionary clause of the insurance policy, the United States was engaged in war in Vietnam. The court held that the use of United States armed forces did not constitute war in the legal sense be-

[3] A 1966 article in the *William and Mary Law Review* lists the principal issues adjudicated by the court for a five-year period. The classifications have no correlation with the total number of cases heard by the court, but they do provide another measure of the court's workload. William F. Swindler, "The Business of the Supreme Court of Appeals: Statistical Summary 1960–65," *William and Mary Law Review* 7 (1966):272–73.

[4] *National Fire Insurance Co. of Hartford* v. *Dervishian*, 206 Va. 563, 567, 145 S.E. 2d 184, 187 (1965).

cause of the absence of a congressional declaration of war although it was assumed that the conflict did constitute war in the material sense. Acknowledging that authorities are sharply divided as to which meaning should be given to the exclusionary clauses of insurance policies, a unanimous court applied the rule used in the 1965 case to decide the case in favor of the insured's beneficiary.[5]

Other common types of litigation were pleading and practice, contracts, and constitutional law. No other category accounted for as much as 5 percent of the court's business. However, it is clear that a general category of property, comprising the categories of real property, eminent domain, and real estate, made up a significant share of the workload. Of the other types of litigation, taxation cases deserve special mention. The success rate of those parties challenging taxation policy is indicative of the success historically enjoyed by taxpayers in property tax exemption cases. By the end of 1964, sixteen of nineteen exemption cases had been decided in favor of the taxpayer under section 183 of the 1902 Constitution, which enumerated property exempt from taxation. One observer was prompted to point out that "the Court, under the banner of Virginia's unique rule of liberal construction for such tax exemptions, has stretched section 183 of the state constitution to limits never dreamed of by the drafters in 1902."[6] Begining with the first case dealing with section 183,[7] the Virginia court had applied the liberal construction doctrine to the exemption provisions notwithstanding the strict interpretation implied by the language of the constitution: "Unless otherwise provided in this Constitution, *the following property and no other* shall be exempt from taxation."[8]

This liberal exemption policy had a significant impact on local governments as the number of property tax cases increased in the 1960s. The local fiscal structure was severely challenged by the ever increasing percentage of property qualifying for tax exemption. The *Report of the Commission on Constitutional Revision*, reflecting the concern of local governments, suggested a strict con-

[5] *Jackson* v. *North America Assurance Society of Va.*, 212 Va. 177, 183 S.E. 2d 160 (1971).

[6] Waller H. Horsley, "Taxation, 1963–1964, Annual Survey of Virginia Law," *Virginia Law Review* 50 (1964):1507–8.

[7] *Commonwealth* v. *Lynchburg YMCA*, 115 Va. 745, 80 S.E. 589 (1914).

[8] Con., 1902, art. XIII, sec. 183 (italics added).

struction of exempt property. Accordingly, the 1971 Constitution contains express language to that effect.[9] However, the court continued its liberal interpretation in cases decided in the months before the new constitution became effective.[10] One case stands out as a result of a strongly stated dissenting opinion by Justice Thomas Gordon. The exemption from real estate taxes of a summer camp owned by Sullins College was upheld by six of the justices. Justice Gordon dissented on the grounds that the camp was used only incidentally for educational purposes and instead was a substantial source of revenue for the college. He implored his colleagues to "heed the will of the people," as indicated by the adoption of a new constitution, rather than liberalize the construction of section 183.[11] Justice Gordon's dissent accentuated the necessity of the "strict construction" provision in the 1971 Constitution to alter the application of the liberal construction doctrine.

## Litigants

The question of who participates has always been an important one for students of American governmental institutions and politics. Table 9 demonstrates who is responsible for bringing cases to the Virginia Supreme Court. Private individuals initiate by far the largest number of petitions accepted by the court for review. It must be remembered, however, that many of those individuals undoubtedly acted on behalf of not only themselves but also others similarly situated. Businesses, including insurance and railroad companies, account for 23.1 percent of the cases. Governmental units are responsible for bringing 8.5 percent of the disputes to the court.

Table 8 reveals the success rate of litigants in those cases dealing with torts, criminal offenses, constitutional law, and taxation. A recent sample of the appellant success rate of certain types of liti-

[9] Va., Commission on Constitutional Revision, *The Constitution of Virginia: Report of the Commission on Constitutional Revision* (Charlottesville, Va.: Michie, 1969), pp. 304–7; Con., 1971, art. X, sec. 6(f).

[10] "Taxation, 1970–1971, Annual Survey of Virginia Law," *Virginia Law Review* 57 (1971):1631–35.

[11] *Washington County, Virginia* v. *Sullins College Corporation*, 211 Va. 591, 599, 179 S.E. 2d 630, 635 (1971).

*Table* 9. Appellants or plaintiffs before the Virginia Supreme Court, Oct. 1961–Sept. 1966

| Appellant or plaintiff | Cases No. | Cases % of total |
|---|---|---|
| Private individuals | 400 | 65.9 |
| Businesses | 93 | 15.3 |
| Insurance companies | 36 | 6.0 |
| State | 22 | 3.6 |
| Cities | 16 | 2.6 |
| Counties | 13 | 2.1 |
| Railroads | 11 | 1.8 |
| Nonprofit associations | 8 | 1.3 |
| Labor unions | 3 | .5 |
| U.S.A. | 1 | .2 |
| NAACP | 1 | .2 |
| Crossfiling | 3 | .5 |
| Total | 607 | 100.0 |

gants has been taken for all state supreme courts.[12] Only Louisiana had a higher success rate (100 percent) for superior economic interests (creditors, landlords, employers, and sellers) than did Virginia (88.9 percent). The appellant success rate in Virginia for inferior economic interests (debtors, tenants, employees, and buyers) was 50 percent, and the rate for corporations was 52.9 percent.

## Interest Groups and the Court

David Truman devoted a chapter of his 1951 work, *The Governmental Process*, to "Interest Groups and the Judiciary." Since that time the extent of interest group participation in litigation has been explored in numerous works: Kenneth M. Dolbeare found little evidence of such involvement at the local trial court level; interest group support in cases before the United States Supreme Court, however, has been well documented.[13] Interviews with members of

[12] Burton M. Atkins and Henry R. Glick, "Formal Judicial Recruitment and State Supreme Court Decisions," *American Politics Quarterly* 2 (Oct. 1974):438–39.

[13] Truman, *The Governmental Process* (New York: Knopf, 1951); Dolbeare, *Trial Courts in Urban Politics: State Court Policy Impact and Functions in a Local Political System* (New York: John Wiley and Sons, 1967), pp. 40–45; Clement

four state supreme courts revealed that they had a low perception of interest group activity in judicial matters and little enthusiasm for it beyond what is provided for by formal legal procedures.[14]

The relationship between interest groups and litigation is clearly established where such groups intervene as "friends of the court." Courts may permit an interested group or individual to file an amicus curiae brief in a case to which it is not a party. This procedure is used to express points of view that may not otherwise be considered or, more frequently, to reinforce arguments of one of the litigants. If the incidence of amicus curiae briefs is used to measure the extent of interest group activity, that extent is negligible. Only 11 amicus curiae briefs were filed in the 607 cases considered for this study. Groups not a party to a case were permitted as intervenors in two additional suits. Five of the amicus briefs were filed by either state or local governments; the others were filed by the Virginia Hospital Association, Virginia Passenger Bus Association, Norfolk Cooperative Milk Producers Association, Lynchburg-Westover Dairies, Tidewater Virginia Development Council, and Portsmouth Port and Industrial Commission, the latter two being filed separately in the same case. This record indicates that the amicus brief has not been a major medium of access to the Virginia Supreme Court.

Sponsorship of litigation is yet another means for an interest group to gain access to the courts. Glick found most of the judges from four state supreme courts willing to accept sponsorship by groups such as the NAACP, labor unions, or business organizations. Five of the seven judges from Louisiana reacted negatively to the idea; Glick speculated that the inclusion of the NAACP as a sample group might have influenced their opinions.[15] When six Virginia justices were questioned about the permissibility of litigation sponsorship by an interest group, three of them were less than enthusi-

---

Vose, *Caucasians Only: The Supreme Court, the NAACP, and the Restrictive Covenant Cases* (Berkeley: University of California Press, 1959); Nathan Hakman, "Lobbying the Supreme Court—An Appraisal of 'Political Science Folklore,'" *Fordham Law Review* 35 (1966):15–50; Samuel Krislov, "The Amicus Curiae Brief," *Yale Law Journal* 72 (1963):694–721.

14 Henry Robert Glick, *Supreme Courts in State Politics: An Investigation of the Judicial Role* (New York: Basic Books, 1971), pp. 139–46.

15 Ibid., pp. 144–46.

astic about the idea. Although they conceded that such sponsorship was permissible, they indicated that groups should not "stir up" litigation.[16] As was suggested in the case of Louisiana, the "activism" of the NAACP in the state during the controversial period of race relations litigation beginning with *Brown* v. *Board of Education* in 1954 apparently influenced their perception of interest group activity. The NAACP has been particularly effective in sponsoring litigation to achieve political and social ends. A measure of its success was the legislation passed by seven southern states in the mid-1950s in an effort to frustrate the civil rights organization from pursuing its goal of eliminating school segregation and racial discrimination through the courts. Virginia legislation and a decision by the Virginia Supreme Court prompted a 1963 decision by the United States Supreme Court legitimizing NAACP sponsorship of litigation.

The Virginia State Conference of NAACP Branches, an unincorporated association, had a membership of 13,500 in 1957. A legal staff of fifteen attorneys was maintained for the purpose of sponsoring litigation, although most of the staff maintained a private practice as well. The staff made decisions as to which litigants were entitled to NAACP assistance. The staff members were paid fees of sixty dollars per day for their services in connection with litigation supported by the organization. Between 1956 and 1958, $25,000 was spent by the Virginia branch in pursuance of its legal goals.[17]

In a 1956 extra session, the Virginia General Assembly broadened the definition of legal malpractice and solicitation in such a manner as to include the activities of the NAACP. On appeal to the state Supreme Court, this legislation was declared unconstitutional on the ground that it interfered with freedom of speech and denied the due process right of access to the courts. The court agreed that the NAACP could not be prohibited from advising any person or group to institute legal proceedings. It further maintained that

[16] John T. Wold, "Internal Procedures, Role Perceptions and Judicial Behavior: A Study of Four State Courts of Last Resort" (Ph.D. diss., Johns Hopkins University, 1972), pp. 277–79.

[17] "The South's Amended Barratry Laws: An Attempt to End Group Pressure through the Courts," *Yale Law Journal* 72 (1963):1621, n. 39; *NAACP* v. *Harrison*, 202 Va. 142, 146–152, 116 S.E. 2d 55 (1960); *NAACP* v. *Button*, 371 U.S. 415, 419–422 (1963).

this legislation unconstitutionally denied indigent persons financial assistance in pursuing legal action.[18]

However, the Virginia court held that the NAACP was violating chapter 33 of the Virginia Acts of Assembly, passed during the 1956 extra session, when the organization solicited legal business for its attorneys in cases in which they were not parties and in which they had no pecuniary right or liability. The effect of the Virginia decision, therefore, was to permit the NAACP to advocate and finance litigation, but not to solicit litigation for its attorneys. This decision, although more permissive of legal sponsorship than was intended by the General Assembly, remained a barrier to the activities of the NAACP. It was the practice of the organization to hold public meetings to encourage blacks to assert their rights. Frequently, prepared forms were circulated at these meetings authorizing staff members to initiate legal proceedings on behalf of those persons signing the forms. On other occasions prospective litigants would be referred to the legal staff by an NAACP member. Both of these practices were prohibited under the Virginia court ruling.

On appeal, the United States Supreme Court found the statute to be overly broad and vague. The Court interpreted the decree of the Virginia court "as proscribing any arrangement by which prospective litigants are advised to seek the assistance of particular attorneys."[19] This proscription was held to be a violation of First Amendment speech and associational rights. Speaking for the majority, Justice Brennan went beyond the issue of the constitutionality of the statute by commenting on the nature of the organization: "The NAACP is not a conventional political party; but the litigation it assists, while serving to vindicate the legal rights of members of the American Negro community, at the same time and perhaps more importantly, makes possible the distinctive contribution of a minority group to the ideas and beliefs of our society. For such a group, association for litigation may be the most effective form of political association."[20] The restrictive Virginia legislation was thus limited by the state Supreme Court and then nullified by the nation's highest court.

[18] 202 Va. 142.
[19] 371 U.S. 415, 433.
[20] 371 U.S. 431.

The solicitation of legal business was also at issue in cases involving the Brotherhood of Railroad Trainmen. The labor union had established a Department of Legal Counsel to make available to Brotherhood members and the families of deceased members the names of lawyers recommended and approved by the Brotherhood to represent them in claims for personal injury or death arising out of railroad service. A petition filed by the Virginia State Bar for a decree to permanently enjoin the Brotherhood from carrying out its plan in Virginia was entered by the Chancery Court of the city of Richmond and affirmed by the state Supreme Court on the ground it was plainly right. On appeal to the United States Supreme Court, however, the decree was reversed to the extent that it prevented the Brotherhood from implementing its plan to advise workers or their families to seek legal advice from a list of recommended lawyers.[21] The case was remanded to the Virginia court, which modified the decree in accordance with the majority opinion of the higher court.[22]

Personal sponsorship of litigation on behalf of the consumer is yet another means of access to the court. In recent years, Henry E. Howell, Jr., first as a state senator from Norfolk and then as the state's lieutenant governor, enjoyed some success in this regard. Direct action in the courts was always one of Howell's political trademarks. He was active, for example, in challenging rate increases approved by the State Corporation Commission. During his 1969 campaign for the Democratic nomination for governor, Howell cited his recent victory before the state Supreme Court. On petition of the Virginia state AFL-CIO and Henry E. Howell, Jr., the state Supreme Court had reviewed and reversed an order by the State Corporation Commission approving an 8.2 percent increase in automobile insurance rates. The court had remanded the case to the commission with instructions that additional evidence be considered and a different computation method utilized for fixing a reasonable profit margin.[23]

[21] *Brotherhood of Railroad Trainmen* v. *Virginia ex rel. Virginia State Bar*, 377 U.S. 1 (1964).

[22] *Brotherhood of Railroad Trainmen* v. *Commonwealth of Virginia ex rel. Virginia State Bar*, 207 Va. 182, 149 S.E. 2d 265 (1966).

[23] *Howell* v. *Commonwealth of Virginia*, 209 Va. 776, 167 S.E. 2d 322 (1969).

## Blacks as Litigants

In her study of judicial review in Virginia from 1789 to 1928, Margaret V. Nelson concluded that blacks had fared poorly: "The Negro asked little and received less in the way of protection of his rights from the courts. Truly for him the harvest of judicial review was a meager one."[24] The year 1931 marked the first major decision favorable to blacks to be handed down by the twentieth-century Virginia Supreme Court. The case of *Davis* v. *Allen*[25] was later described by the executive secretary of the Virginia NAACP as marking "a turning point in the Negro's attempts to register in both primary and general elections."[26]

After January 1, 1904, the temporary provision for the registration of voters that included an "understanding clause" was superseded by a permanent provision. No general knowledge or educational test was made a part of the permanent provision, although a person wishing to register had to satisfy three prescribed requirements. He had to pay poll taxes in person for the three years preceding the time he sought to register; unless physically unable, he had to apply to register in his own handwriting; and he had to answer "any and all questions affecting his qualifications as an elector." Once the poll taxes had been paid, the other two requirements could be used as further obstacles to Negro registration. A favorite device was to give the applicant a blank piece of paper, instead of a registration form, on which to list the personal information stipulated in the constitution. If the person failed to include any of the required personal data, he was denied registration.[27]

A white registrar in the city of Hampton had refused to register a black, W. E. Davis, for failure to make application in proper form and for failure to give satisfactory answers to questions relating to the state constitution. Davis had been asked three questions: (1) What is meant by legal residence in Virginia? (2) When is the

[24] Nelson, *A Study of Judicial Review in Virginia, 1789–1928* (New York: Columbia University Press, 1947), p. 201.

[25] 157 Va. 84, 160 S.E. 85 (1931).

[26] Andrew Buni, *The Negro in Virginia Politics, 1902–1965* (Charlottesville: University Press of Virginia, 1967), p. 126.

[27] V. O. Key, Jr., *Southern Politics in State and Nation* (New York: Knopf, 1949), p. 564.

payment of the poll tax not required? (3) What are the prerequisites to enable one to register in Virginia? The Virginia Supreme Court found Davis's application sufficient in law despite its lack of good form. And the court found Davis's answer to the first question, although demonstrating his lack of education, substantially correct: "All persons Who have lived in the Stat—for one year are a Legal Residenter."[28] The lower court decision, which upheld the action of the registrar, was reversed by the state's highest court on the grounds that the second and third questions were impermissible since they were not calculated to elicit information pertaining to Davis's qualifications as a voter. The opinion of the court reviewed the records of the constitutional convention debates and affirmed the position that the constitution did not prescribe any understanding or educational requirement after January 1, 1904. Registrars would be forced to limit the scope of their questions to the specific qualifications of the prospective voter. In a stinging dissent, Justice Henry W. Holt characterized Davis as a "coached applicant" with no idea of what the provisions really meant.[29]

The number of favorable appellate decisions for blacks in Virginia was small and largely insignificant in the two decades following the *Davis* case. With the increase in the number of legal suits initiated on behalf of blacks, it was evident that blacks preferred to utilize the federal courts rather than the state courts in the South.[30] Nevertheless, for various reasons the Virginia Supreme Court was presented with several important policy cases during the ten-year period following the 1954 decision of *Brown* v. *Board of Education.* Writing in 1965, Kenneth Vines reported that between 1954 and 1964 the Virginia Supreme Court decided 50 percent of its race relations cases in favor of blacks.[31] Of the eleven Southern supreme courts, only the Georgia tribunal had a higher percentage of decisions in favor of the black litigants (54.5 percent). In considering the favorable percentage for Virginia, it must be stressed that the figures were necessarily based on a small sample of cases (no more than fifteen for the Virginia percentage)

[28] 157 Va. 87, 160 S.E. 86.

[29] 157 Va. 93, 160 S.E. 88.

[30] Kenneth N. Vines, "Southern State Supreme Courts and Race Relations," *Western Political Quarterly* 18 (1965):7–8.

[31] Ibid., p. 11. Race relations cases were limited by Vines to those so defined by the *Race Relations Law Reporter.*

and included several cases that involved issues of trial procedure.

The 50-percent figure for Virginia is misleading if interpreted to mean that the court was a significant defender of the rights of blacks. The Virginia court's record must be viewed in light of its capacity to avoid or postpone decisions in crucial cases. In a 1957 case intended to test the constitutionality of the separation of races at public assemblies, a black woman was tried and convicted of failure to take the seat assigned her by an usher at a public meeting held at an Arlington County junior high school.[32] The circuit court sustained the statute under which she was convicted. On appeal to the state Supreme Court, the conviction was reversed because of an insufficient warrant of arrest. Neither the warrant nor the trial proceedings had raised the issue of the defendant's race. Although it was conceded that the defendant's conduct was for the purpose of testing the constitutionality of the law, the court refused to rule on that issue, as it was not considered necessary to a determination of the case.

The segregated seating requirements in a Richmond courtroom and restaurant were also challenged on appeal to the Virginia Supreme Court. In both instances the court refused to grant a writ of error, thus in effect sustaining the lower court convictions of the black defendants.[33] On appeal to the United States Supreme Court, the convictions were reversed.[34] In the 1963 reversal the nation's high court asserted that it was "no longer open to question that a State may not constitutionally require segregation of public facilities."[35] Less than six months later the Virginia court handed down a unanimous opinion, in *Brown* v. *City of Richmond*, which was in accordance with the pronouncements of the nation's Supreme Court. The statutes requiring segregated seating at Richmond's Parker Field and the Mosque were invalidated as being "contrary to the Equal Protection Clause of the Fourteenth Amendment of the Federal Constitution as interpreted by the [United States] Supreme Court."[36]

The major public school decision of the Virginia Supreme Court

32 *Bissell* v. *Commonwealth of Virginia*, 199 Va. 397, 100 S.E. 2d 1 (1957).

33 *Race Relations Law Reporter* 4 (1959):1012; 8 (1963):19–20.

34 *Johnson* v. *Virginia*, 373 U.S. 61 (1963); *Boynton* v. *Virginia*, 364 U.S. 454 (1960).

35 373 U.S. 62.

36 204 Va. 471, 480, 132 S.E. 2d 495, 501 (1963).

in the decade following the 1954 *Brown* case was undoubtedly *Harrison* v. *Day*.[37] This decision invalidated the effort of the Virginia General Assembly to evade the *Brown* mandate through state-imposed school closings and tuition grants. But the court was then faced with a constitutional challenge to the action of local officials in Prince Edward County, who had responded to the prospect of integrated education by closing all of the county's public schools. L. F. Griffin, a taxpayer and resident of Prince Edward County, filed an original petition for mandamus to compel the county's Board of Supervisors to make funds available for the operation of public schools. A unanimous court held that the state constitution and the relevant statutes vested the Board of Supervisors with discretionary power to determine what amount of money should be raised by local taxation to supplement state funds provided for support of the county schools.[38] The opinion, written by Chief Justice Eggleston, explicitly excluded section 129 of the Virginia Constitution as not applicable to the case because it was directed to the General Assembly and not to local governing bodies: "The General Assembly shall establish and maintain an efficient system of public free schools throughout the State."

The following year, in *County School Board* v. *Griffin*, the court ruled on whether the commonwealth of Virginia had a mandatory duty under its constitution and laws to operate public free schools in Prince Edward County. In a six-to-one decision, the justices construed section 129, in conjunction with the companion educational provisions, as permitting the General Assembly to determine for itself what is an "efficient system" of public free schools. Only an insignificantly modest sum was made obligatory in section 135 of the constitution. In a separate concurring opinion signed by all the justices except Justice Buchanan, who wrote the majority opinion of the court, and Chief Justice Eggleston, who was in dissent, the following scenario was envisioned if it were held to be the constitutional duty of the General Assembly to provide funds: "Very soon many, if not all, of the counties and cities of the State would cease making local appropriations and the schools would have to be financed entirely by State funds. Thus would come to

[37] 200 Va. 439, 106 S.E. 2d 636 (1959). For a fuller discussion of this case, see Chapter VI.

[38] *Griffin* v. *Board of Supervisors*, 203 Va. 321, 124 S.E. 2d 227 (1962).

an end the joint effort admittedly contemplated by the Constitution and in effect now for more than sixty years."[39]

In his dissenting opinion, Chief Justice Eggleston characterized the Prince Edward situation as giving Virginia "the shameful distinction of having within its borders the only school district in this Nation where public free schools are not provided for its children."[40] He viewed the legislature's constitutional mandate to "maintain an efficient system of public free schools throughout the State" as controlling in the case. This obligation was ultimately the General Assembly's, argued the chief justice, and, if a locality closed its public schools, the constitution contemplated action by the legislature to ensure an efficient public school system. Finally, Chief Justice Eggleston maintained that the situation in Prince Edward County violated the equal protection provisions of the Fourteenth Amendment. He concluded his dissent with these prophetic words: "The refusal of the highest court of this State to recognize here the rights of the citizens of Prince Edward county, guaranteed to them under the Constitution of the United States, is a clear invitation to the federal courts to step in and enforce such rights. I am sure that that invitation will be promptly accepted. We shall see!"[41] On May 25, 1964, the Supreme Court of the United States reversed the decision of the Virginia Supreme Court.[42]

Virginia's miscegenation policy was also tested during the decade following 1954. A 1955 case before the Virginia Supreme Court provided the first major test of the constitutionality of the state's miscegenation law, which had been amended in 1924. Although the specific case of *Naim* v. *Naim* pertained to the marriage of a Caucasian and a Chinese, the legislation clearly applied to blacks, since it prohibited any white person from marrying anyone with any "trace whatsoever of any blood other than Caucasian." Out of deference to the descendants of Pocahontas and John Rolfe, an exception was made in the case of persons with one-sixteenth or less of American Indian blood.[43]

The court upheld the ban against interracial marriage as a

39 204 Va. 650, 672, 133 S.E. 2d 565, 581 (1963).

40 204 Va. 674, 133 S.E. 2d 582.

41 204 Va. 677, 133 S.E. 2d 584.

42 *Griffin* v. *County School Board*, 377 U.S. 218 (1964).

43 Walter Wadlington, "The Loving Case: Virginia's Anti-Miscegenation Statute in Historical Perspective," *Virginia Law Review* 52(1966):1200–1202.

proper governmental objective, one that had traditionally been a subject for state regulation. It was noted by the court that more than half of the states had miscegenation statutes. The doctrine of white supremacy was also manifested in the opinion of the court: "We find there [in the Federal Constitution] no requirement that the State shall not legislate to prevent the obliteration of racial pride, but must permit the corruption of blood even though it weaken or destroy the quality of its citizenship. Both sacred and secular history teach that nations and races have better advanced in human progress when they cultivated their own distinctive characteristics and culture and developed their own peculiar genius."[44]

In 1966, the Virginia court was again faced with a constitutional challenge to the state's miscegenation statute. Sociological, biological, and anthropological considerations were explicitly rejected as a basis for reversing the *Naim* decision; it "would be judicial legislation in the rawest sense of the term."[45] Furthermore, no sound judicial reason was found for departing from the earlier decision. Not only had the Supreme Court of the United States failed to overturn *Naim*, but it had also refused in 1964 to rule on a miscegenation statute; and only one state court of last resort—California's—had invalidated such a law.[46] The 1966 opinion of the Virginia court was devoid of white supremacy rhetoric.

In 1963, the state Supreme Court was presented with yet another case involving the Virginia NAACP. A joint committee of the legislature, the Committee on Offenses against the Administration of Justice, had summoned the NAACP and two affiliated organizations to disclose the names and addresses of each Virginia resident making donations to one of the organizations during a specified period. In a reversal of the lower court decision, the Supreme Court held the summonses to be an unconstitutional violation of the right of association. Citing recent decisions of the United States Supreme Court, the opinion of the state court found no overriding or compelling state interest in obtaining such information that would justify the prejudicial effect of disclosure upon the NAACP: "There can be no reasonable doubt that a disclosure

[44] *Naim* v. *Naim*, 197 Va. 80, 90, 87 S.E. 2d 749, 756 (1955).

[45] *Loving* v. *Commonwealth of Virginia*, 206 Va. 924, 929, 147 S.E. 2d 78, 82 (1966).

[46] Wadlington, pp. 1212–13. The *Loving* decision was overturned by the United States Supreme Court on June 12, 1967, *Loving* v. *Virginia*, 388 U.S. 1 (1967).

of the names of those who support the activities of the appellants could have no result other than to injuriously affect the effort of appellants to obtain financial support in promoting their aims and purposes."[47] Five years earlier the Virginia court had upheld the right of the committee to require such a disclosure.[48] The change was clearly attributable to recent decisions by the nation's highest court. The opinions in some of those decisions were quoted in the opinion of the state court. One quoted passage demonstrated judicial acceptance of a stinging indictment of the state political establishment: "We cannot close our eyes to the fact that the militant Negro civil rights movement has engendered the intense resentment and opposition of the politically dominant white community of Virginia; litigation assisted by the NAACP has been bitterly fought."[49]

The Virginia Supreme Court's record in race relations cases from 1954 through 1963 is a mixed one. Most of the decisions favorable to blacks can be traced to related action by the federal courts. Nevertheless, as Vines observed with respect to state supreme courts, the "record is more favorable to Negro claimants than is any other part of the state political system."[50] At a time when blacks had no representation in the executive or legislative branches and were actually the object of antagonistic state legislation, they occasionally found relief in the form of decisions by the Virginia Supreme Court.

## Appeals from Lower Courts

In comparison with other state supreme courts, the Virginia court has perhaps the lowest rate of affirming lower court decisions. One sampling of cases from all of the states' highest courts revealed the percentage of cases affirmed by the Virginia court as the lowest

[47] *NAACP Legal Defense and Educational Fund* v. *Committee on Offenses against the Administration of Justice*, 204 Va. 693, 698, 133 S.E. 2d 540, 544 (1963).

[48] *NAACP* v. *Committee on Offenses against the Administration of Justice*, 199 Va. 665, 101 S.E. 2d 631 (1958).

[49] *NAACP* v. *Button*, 371 U.S. 415, 435 (1963), as quoted in *NAACP* v. *Committee*, 204 Va. 693, 698, 133 S.E. 2d 540, 544 (1963).

[50] Vines, p. 17.

rate.[51] Table 7 shows that from October 1961 to September 1966, only 51.2 percent of appeals from lower state courts were affirmed. This rate has prevailed in spite of the many factors operating to encourage affirmance of lower court opinions. For example, not only is there a tendency for the appellate justice to accept the judgment of the trial judge, but the judicial selection process ensures basically compatible judicial philosophies among judges at all levels. Furthermore, trial judges are generally predisposed to follow the precedent established by appellate justices.

The low affirmance rate of the Supreme Court is the result of one overriding factor: the Virginia court does not review lower court cases as a matter of right; those decisions which, in the judgment of at least three justices, are plainly right are not accepted for review. Automatic appeals tend to have a low potentiality for reversal. Those cases accepted for review by the state's highest court, however, are highly susceptible to reversal. In this respect the Virginia court is more like the United States Supreme Court than most state supreme courts.[52]

Table 10 provides data indicating the types of litigation that are frequently reversed by the Virginia Supreme Court. One-fourth of the reversals concern automobile injuries, and almost one-fifth involve criminal offenses. Significantly, more of these cases were reversed in favor of the defendant than were reversed in favor of the plaintiff. A similar pattern in favor of the defendant is also apparent in nonautomobile negligence cases.

On the other hand, the reversal rate for cases of taxation (26.1 percent) and the rate for cases of constitutional law (8.6 percent) are well below the average for all cases (45 percent). These figures seem to indicate that the conflicting judgments of the justices and trial judges are not a result of incompatible judicial philosophies. In fact, the lack of reversals in constitutional law decisions favoring the state suggests adherence to precedent and philosophical consistency on the part of the trial judges. The major differences are clearly related to factual and procedural determinations in criminal prosecutions and torts.

[51] Bradley C. Canon and Dean Jones, "State Supreme Courts–Some Comparative Data," *State Government* 42 (Autumn 1969):264.

[52] Richard J. Richardson and Kenneth N. Vines, "Review, Dissent and the Appellate Process: A Political Interpretation," *Journal of Politics* 29 (1967):605.

*Table 10.* The Virginia Supreme Court's reversals of lower court decisions, Oct. 1961–Sept. 1966

| | No. (and % of total cases in category)[a] | % of total reversed cases | For plaintiff, or state No. | For plaintiff, or state %[b] | For defendant, or antistate No. | For defendant, or antistate %[c] |
|---|---|---|---|---|---|---|
| Automobile injury | 62 (60.8) | 25.0 | 26 | 53.0 | 36 | 67.9 |
| Criminal offense | 46 (52.3) | 18.5 | 10 | 20.4 | 36 | 92.3 |
| Nonautomobile negligence | 26 (59.1) | 10.5 | 9 | 52.9 | 17 | 63.0 |
| Insurance | 15 (35.7) | 6.0 | | | | |
| Pleading and Practice | 13 (63.0) | 5.2 | | | | |
| Contracts | 17 (47.2) | 6.8 | | | | |
| Constitutional law | 3 (8.6) | 1.2 | — | — | 3 | 50.0 |
| Domestic relations | 10 (34.5) | 4.0 | | | | |
| Real property | 9 (33.3) | 3.6 | | | | |
| Taxation | 6 (26.1) | 2.4 | — | — | 6 | 35.3 |
| Eminent domain | 8 (36.4) | 3.2 | | | | |
| Administrative law | 4 (22.2) | 1.6 | | | | |
| Workmen's compensation | 1 (8.3) | .4 | | | | |
| Wills, trusts, estates | 2 (16.7) | .8 | | | | |
| Real estate | 7 (58.3) | 2.8 | | | | |
| Municipal corporations | 3 (33.3) | 1.2 | | | | |
| Business associations | 1 (12.5) | .4 | | | | |
| Sales | 4 (57.1) | 1.6 | | | | |
| Landlord-tenant | 3 (50.0) | 1.2 | | | | |
| Annexation | — — | — | | | | |
| Labor-related matters | 1 (33.3) | .4 | | | | |
| Miscellaneous | 8 (29.6) | 3.2 | | | | |
| Total | 249 — | 100.0 | | | | |

[a] Total given in Table 8.
[b] Of total no. of decisions in favor of plaintiff given in Table 8.
[c] Of total no. of decisions in favor of defendant given in Table 8.

## Appeals to the United States Supreme Court

The decisions of the Virginia Supreme Court are of course subject to review and reversal by the nation's highest court. If a federal question is identified, the petition for certiorari may be accepted and the state Supreme Court decision reversed. Of the 607 cases considered in this study, 29 were appealed to the federal Supreme Court. The decision of the Virginia Supreme Court was reversed in 6 cases and upheld in 1 case; the petition for review was denied in 20 cases and dismissed for lack of a substantial federal question in 2 cases.

The types of cases appealed from the Virginia court were largely in the area of constitutional law and criminal prosecutions (22 cases). There was also 1 case of taxation, 2 of pleading and practice, 2 of eminent domain, and 2 of labor-related matters. On appeal, however, the due process aspects of the cases were stressed. The 6 cases in which the Virginia court was reversed involved the reopening of the Prince Edward County public schools, the constitutionality of Virginia's miscegenation statute, a conviction for unlawful picketing, two Fourth Amendment search and seizure cases, and a contempt of court action.[53]

The Virginia Supreme Court has generally acquiesced in mandates from the United States Supreme Court. Even though in fundamental disagreement with the ruling of the nation's highest court, the Virginia justices have resisted the temptation to resurrect challenges to the high court's authority in the tradition of Judge Spencer Roane. On occasion, however, the Virginia court has exhibited its disapproval of higher court decisions. An example of this attitude can be seen in the opinion interpreting the mandate relating to the Brotherhood of Railroad Trainmen:

> Our duty to obey the mandate of the Supreme Court is clear. In rendering a decision today, we cannot alter our course because of disagreement with Mr. Justice Black's characterization of the Brotherhood's practice of securing employment of union-selected counsel as an exercise of benevolence for the protection of union members and their families. . . . Nor can we alter our course because of agreement with the prediction in Mr. Justice Clark's dissenting opinion: "The potential for evil in the union's system is enormous and . . . will bring disrepute to the legal profession."[54]

Another example is to be found in the majority opinion invalidating the major provisions of Virginia's massive resistance program:

[53] 377 U.S. 218; 388 U.S. 1; *Waxman* v. *Virginia*, 371 U.S. 4 (1962); *Riggan* v. *Virginia*, 384 U.S. 152 (1966); *Clinton* v. *Virginia*, 377 U.S. 158 (1964); *Holt* v. *Virginia*, 381 U.S. 131 (1965).

[54] 207 Va. 182, 186, 149 S.E. 2d 265, 268 (1966).

> Having reached the conclusion that certain provisions of the acts with which we are concerned violate the provisions of the Constitution of Virginia . . . it is not necessary that we consider the question whether these acts likewise violate the provisions of the fourteenth amendment to the Federal Constitution as interpreted by the recent decisions of the Supreme Court of the United States [*Brown* v. *Board of Education*, 347 U.S. 483 and *Cooper* v. *Aaron*, 358 U.S. 1]. . . . There is no occasion for us to discuss these decisions other than to say we deplore the lack of judicial restraint evinced by that court in trespassing on the sovereign rights of this Commonwealth reserved to it in the Constitution of the United States. It was an understandable effort to diminish the evils expected from the decision in the *Brown* case that prompted the enactment of the statutes now under review.[55]

In classifying southern state supreme courts, Kenneth Vines defined "compromiser courts" as "sometimes reluctantly accepting the authority of the national courts and at other times referring to local judicial process and state problems as the basis for making decisions."[56] The Virginia court clearly falls within this category. It has normally accepted national authority, although at times it has invoked its own rules as grounds for not carrying out a mandate of the nation's highest court.

The 1955 constitutional challenge to Virginia's miscegenation law was not a criminal prosecution but a suit for annulment.[57] The litigants, a white person domiciled in Virginia and a nonresident Chinese, left the state to be married in North Carolina, whereupon they immediately returned to Norfolk to live together as husband and wife. The out-of-state marriage was viewed by the court as an effort to evade Virginia's policy against interracial marriage.

The United States Supreme Court vacated the judgment on the ground the record was inadequate and remanded the case to the Virginia court in order for it to be returned to the trial court.[58] The state Supreme Court, however, reaffirmed its earlier decision and noted that it had "no provision either under the rules of practice and procedure of this court or under the statute law of this Commonwealth by which this court may send the cause back to the

[55] 200 Va. 439, 453, 106 S.E. 2d 636, 647.

[56] Vines, p. 14.

[57] 197 Va. 80, 87 S.E. 2d 749.

[58] *Naim* v. *Naim*, 350 U.S. 891 (1955).

Circuit Court."[59] According to the state court, such a remand would have been contrary to existing practice and procedural rules. When the case was returned to the United States Supreme Court, it was dismissed for lack of a properly presented federal question.[60]

Again in 1968 the state Supreme Court refused to comply with a mandate from the United States Supreme Court in a case involving alleged discrimination against a black family in the use of a community swimming pool. The state court rejected the petition for appeal because of failure to perfect the appeal in accordance with the Rules of the Court. Opposing counsel had not been given reasonable written notice of the time and place of tendering the transcript, or a reasonable opportunity to examine the original or a true copy of it. The United States Supreme Court vacated the Virginia judgment and remanded the case for reconsideration in light of a housing discrimination case decided the same day.[61] The Virginia court adamantly maintained its earlier position: "Only this court may say when it does and when it does not have jurisdiction under its Rules. We had no jurisdiction in the cases when they were here before, and we have no jurisdiction now. We adhere to our orders refusing the appeals in these cases."[62]

## Administration of the Virginia Court System

The chief justice of the Virginia Supreme Court has primary responsibility for the administration of Virginia's judicial system. This role, which had been carried out for many years by the occupants of that position, was given formal constitutional status in 1971. Acting as the administrative head of the state judicial system, the chief justice "may temporarily assign any judge of a court of record to any other court of record except the Supreme Court and

59 *Naim* v. *Naim*, 197 Va. 734, 735, 90 S.E. 2d 849, 850 (1956).

60 *Naim* v. *Naim*, 350 U.S. 985 (1956).

61 *Sullivan* v. *Little Hunting Park*, 392 U.S. 657 (1968); *Jones* v. *Alfred H. Mayer Co.*, 392 U.S. 409 (1968).

62 *Sullivan* v. *Little Hunting Park*, 209 Va. 279, 281, 163 S.E. 2d 588, 589 (1968). For a critical discussion of the position taken by the Virginia Supreme Court in this case, see W. Taylor Reveley III, "Practice and Pleading, 1969–1970 Annual Survey of Virginia Law," *Virginia Law Review* 56 (1970): 1525–30.

may assign a retired judge of a court of record, with his consent, to any court of record except the Supreme Court."[63] This power permits the chief justice to supply one remedy, if only a temporary one, for the problem of congested dockets that characterizes the judicial process throughout the country.

The efficacy of judicial leadership by the chief justice was demonstrated by Edward W. Hudgins during his service as the presiding officer of the Supreme Court. Shortly after becoming chief justice in late 1947, Hudgins undertook to revitalize the ineffective Judicial Council (of which the chief justice serves as presiding officer) and to reform court procedure and practice. His ten-year service as chief justice was marked by continued activity and achievement on the part of the Judicial Council. The chief justice was considered the moving force behind the 1950 revision of the Rules of the Court and the creation of the office of executive secretary of the court.[64]

The Judicial Council had been established by the General Assembly in 1928. Although active in its first few years, the council had become almost dormant before it was revitalized under the leadership of Chief Justice Hudgins in 1947. Throughout most of its existence, the Virginia Judicial Council has been composed of three circuit judges, two judges from other courts of record, and four attorneys, with the chief justice serving as presiding officer. A 1972 amendment increased the membership of the council by two members. The chairman of the Committee for Courts of Justice of the Senate and his counterpart on the House committee were made members as were two judges of courts not of record. The number of attorney members was reduced from four to two.[65]

The council meets at Richmond during October on the call of the chief justice and at such other time or place as the presiding officer may designate. Its fundamental responsibility is to "make a continuous study of the organization and the rules and methods of procedure and practice of the judicial system of the Common-

[63] Con., 1971, art. VI, sec. 4.

[64] C. Vernon Spratley, "Edward Wren Hudgins, 1882–1958," *Proceedings of the Virginia State Bar Association* 69 (1958): 175; Allen E. Ragan, "Virginia's Judicial System: Organization and Improvement," *University of Virginia News Letter* 39 (Apr. 15, 1963):30.

[65] Va. Code, sec. 17-222 (1974 suppl.).

wealth, the work accomplished and the results produced by the system and its various parts."[66] The periodic reports of the council to the General Assembly include statistics on the business of the courts of record.

In 1950 the General Assembly established the Judicial Conference, with an active membership composed of all the justices and judges of courts of record. The conference meets annually and is also attended by such honorary members as the attorney general, law school deans, bar association leaders, and the chairmen of the Courts of Justice committees of the General Assembly. The stated purpose of the conference is to discuss and consider "means and methods of improving the administration of justice in this State." In 1962 a similar conference was established for judges of the courts not of record. The chief justice is designated by statute as president of both conferences.[67]

The chief justice is assisted in his administration of the state judiciary by the executive secretary to the Supreme Court. The office of executive secretary was created in 1952 on the recommendation of the Judicial Council. In addition to serving as the secretary of the Judicial Council and the Judicial Conference, the executive secretary collects and tabulates judicial statistics for the purpose of advising the chief justice as to the status of lower court dockets.

## Rule-making Power

Since early in this century the Virginia Supreme Court has assumed general rule-making authority over the practice and procedures used in state courts, legislation granting this authority having been passed in 1916 and 1928. But before 1950 judicial exercise of the power was infrequent. At the urging of the Virginia State Bar Association (presently known as the Virginia Bar Association) and under the guidance of Chief Justice Hudgins, new rules of procedure were drawn up by the Judicial Council and

[66] Va. Code, sec. 17-225 (1974 suppl.).

[67] Va. Code, secs. 16.1-218–16.1-221, 17-228–17-231 (1974 suppl.); Hubert D. Bennett, "Recent Developments in Virginia's Judicial System: Trial Courts of Record," *University of Virginia News Letter* 42 (Sept. 15, 1965):1–4.

submitted to the Supreme Court. These were adopted October 13, 1949, to become effective February 1, 1950.

The Supreme Court is currently operating under the 1950 rules as they have been amended intermittently since then. The justices make changes in the Rules of the Court as it appears necessary to facilitate judicial business or upon the recommendation of the Virginia Judicial Council. The six-part rules govern pretrial procedures and appellate proceedings, as well as admission to the bar. They also specify separate practice and procedure for cases in law and equity.

The initiative in rule-making is considered a logical function of the Virginia Supreme Court because of its unique position as the highest branch of the judiciary. For a time it was not clear who had ultimate authority in the area of rules and practice—the Supreme Court or the General Assembly. In 1935, the court held that court rules could not prevail over statutory provisions.[68] However, in 1950 the preamble of a bill empowering the court to adopt and promulgate rules of practice and procedure acknowledged the inherent rule-making power of the appellate court. Although the preamble of the bill was not carried into the Code of 1950, the preamble stipulated that the rules were to supersede conflicting statutes and was so interpreted by the Supreme Court.[69] While there is no question that the Supreme Court should have the major responsibility for making the rules of practice and procedure, the 1971 Constitution anticipates a possible conflict between the legislature and the Supreme Court. Article VI, section 5, asserts the ultimate authority of the General Assembly by stipulating that the "rules shall not be in conflict with the general law as the same shall, from time to time, be established by the General Assembly."

## Disbarment Proceedings

The courts of record in Virginia have long been conceded the inherent power to suspend or annul the license of an attorney prac-

[68] *Virginia Home for Incurables v. Coleman*, 164 Va. 230, 241–42, 178 S.E. 908, 912 (1935).

[69] *Seaboard Air Line Railroad Co.* v. *Board of Supervisors*, 197 Va. 130, 87 S.E. 2d 799 (1955). See also Aubrey R. Bowles, Jr., "The Court of Law Reform in Virginia," *Virginia Law Review* 38 (1952):696.

ticing in the particular court that pronounces the sentence of disbarment.[70] By statute, procedures have been established whereby any revocation or suspension of license becomes effective in all courts of the comonwealth. If any court of record observes or receives a verified complaint of any malpractice or dishonest or unprofessional conduct on the part of any attorney, it may require the attorney to show cause why his license to practice law should not be revoked or suspended. The issuance of an order to show cause must be certified by the lower court to the chief justice of the Supreme Court, who is to designate two judges of courts of record to hear and decide the case in conjunction with the judge issuing the rule.[71]

In disbarment proceedings in Virginia, an appeal from the judgment of the court to the state Supreme Court is assured by statute as a matter of right. The state Supreme Court ruled in 1970 that such appeal does not apply to the action of the single judge initially issuing or refusing to issue rule to show cause, but only to the judgment of the three-judge court.[72] In response to this decision a 1972 amendment to the disbarment statutes directed courts of record to issue a rule to show cause, regardless of whether they deemed the case a proper one for such action, if the complaint was made by a District Committee of the Virginia State Bar.[73]

The Supreme Court has almost always affirmed the decision of the three-judge court in disbarment proceedings. Nevertheless, the guarantee of an appeal as a matter of right preserves the significance of the high court opinions. In a 1971 case Justice Harrison succinctly stated the principles governing disbarment proceedings:

> A proceeding to discipline an attorney is not a criminal proceeding and the purpose is not to punish him but to protect the public. It is a special proceeding, civil and disciplinary in nature, and of a summary character. It is in the nature of an inquest or inquiry as to the conduct of the attorney. Being an informal proceeding it is only necessary that the attorney be informed of the nature of the charge preferred against him and be given an opportunity to answer. While liberality of construction is the rule, reasonable strictness of proof is necessary before guilt should

[70] *Legal Club* v. *Light*, 137 Va. 249, 119 S.E. 55 (1923).

[71] Va. Code, sec. 54-74 (1972 repl. vol.).

[72] *DeFoe* v. *Friedlander*, 211 Va. 121, 176 S.E. 2d 448 (1970).

[73] Va. Code, sec. 54-74 (1974 suppl.).

be held to have been established—not proof beyond a reasonable doubt, but clear proof.[74]

In a rare incident of disagreement with the lower court decision, the Supreme Court reversed the trial court's dismissal of Bar Committee evidence and remanded the case with directions that the lower court reconvene for the purpose of hearing further evidence.

[74] *Seventh District Committee of the Virginia State Bar* v. *E. Eugene Gunter,* 212 Va. 278, 284, 183 S.E. 2d 713, 717 (1971).

# V *The Court and Political Questions*

THROUGH its opinions, the Supreme Court provides a regularized commentary on the nature and structure of Virginia government. Inherent in this process is the court's periodic reassessment and declaration of its own role in the governmental system. The court must weigh its judicial function against external and self-imposed limitations. In reaching its decisions, the court must decide which issues are "political" and hence more properly handled by the so-called political branches of government.

## The Judicial Role

A perennial issue on the American scene has been the proper role of the nation's courts. Is it one of adjudicator or one of policymaker? Stated in another manner, are judges law-interpreters or lawmakers? A third position, for those judges who refuse to commit themselves to either view, has been described in the legal literature as a pragmatist orientation. When Virginia justices were asked to define their perception of the proper judicial role in terms of one of these labels, they unanimously chose the traditional one of law-interpreter.[1] For them the duty of the judiciary is to construe the law and decide cases. Furthermore, Virginia justices tend to view with disfavor the behavior of judges on other courts, par-

[1] John T. Wold, "Internal Procedures, Role Perceptions and Judicial Behavior: A Study of Four State Courts of Last Resort" (Ph.D. diss., Johns Hopkins University, 1972), pp. 215–16. For evidence that the traditionalist law-interpreter view predominates on selected state supreme courts, see Henry Robert Glick, *Supreme Courts in State Politics: An Investigation of the Judicial Role* (New York: Basic Books, 1971), pp. 38–42. However, only 14.3 percent of the members of the highest court in New Jersey perceived themselvs as law-interpreters, whereas 57.1 percent adopted the lawmaker role and 28.6 percent embraced the pragmatist or more eclectic perception of the judicial role (p. 41).

ticularly justices of the United States Supreme Court, who act on the basis of the lawmaker orientation.

Courts in general renounce any intention of becoming involved in political questions, but the Virginia Supreme Court, like all such judicial tribunals, is sometimes called upon to adjudicate controversies that are highly political in nature. The policy of judicial self-restraint dictates that the justices not concern themselves with considerations more appropriately left to the avowedly political departments. The "political questions" doctrine has been invoked when the courts have wanted to disclaim all authority over a question and to accept the decision of the other departments of government.

Attempts to fashion a clear, well-defined doctrine for this matter from opinions of the United States Supreme Court confirm its imprecise nature.[2] It has been suggested that political questions are simply those the court refuses to decide.[3] And yet the issues that the court does decide may change from one period to another, as evidenced by the handling of reapportionment matters. The rationale for invoking the "political questions" doctrine is varied, but it can probably be narrowed to either separation of powers or expedience: either it is a conflict that must be resolved by the political branches of government, or it is inexpedient or impractical for the judiciary to fashion a remedy.[4]

Political questions are most easily classified according to subject matter: international relations, Indian affairs, republican form of government, legislative enactment, and the process of constitutional amendment. Nevertheless, generalization of the "political questions" doctrine at the national level remains virtually impossible. For example, the United States Supreme Court refused to rule whether a time limit on state ratification of constitutional amendments was necessary or not[5] even though it had decided

[2] Charles G. Post, *The Supreme Court and Political Questions* (Baltimore: Johns Hopkins Press, 1936); Martin Shapiro, *Law and Politics in the Supreme Court* (New York: Free Press, 1964), pp. 174–92, 195–215; Fritz W. Scharpf, "Judicial Review and the Political Question: A Functional Analysis," *Yale Law Journal* 75 (1966): 517–97.

[3] Jack W. Peltason, *Federal Courts in the Political Process* (Garden City, N.Y.: Doubleday, 1955), p. 10.

[4] Shapiro, pp. 182–85.

[5] *Coleman* v. *Miller*, 307 U.S. 433 (1939).

numerous cases relating to the amending process in the past. Albeit all earlier decisions had been permissive toward Congress, the Court had ruled that "the President does not participate in the proposal of an amendment; . . . the states may not submit the ratification decision to a popular referendum; . . . proposal by two thirds of both Houses of Congress requires only the assent of two thirds of the members present as long as these constitute a quorum to do business; . . . the state cannot exclude or restrict the power of their legislatures to ratify amendments to the federal constitution."[6]

Generalization of the "political questions" doctrine is equally difficult at the state level. There is no clear touchstone for determining what is and what is not a political question. The court has generally invoked the doctrine of separation of powers to avoid intervening in matters that have been or could be resolved by other governmental agencies. Nevertheless, the doctrine of political questions yields at best a patchwork picture of the court's function in the political system. Constitutional change may or may not be a proper question for the court to resolve, depending on how and when the issue is presented. On the other hand, the court has shown reluctance to cope with reapportionment issues since rendering a precedent-setting decision in 1932. What is clear is that the Virginia Supreme Court has occasionally chosen not to be completely detached from so-called political entanglements.

## Constitutional Change

The people of Virginia have the right to alter or revise any part or all of the state constitution. The 1870 Constitution, the first to include explicit provision for constitutional change, prescribed two methods for such change: by amendment or by convention. Popular approval of amendments was required; in the event a new constitution was to be drawn up, action by the people was necessary only to approve the calling of a constitutional convention. Under article XII of the 1971 Constitution ratification by the people is required regardless of whether the amending process or a convention is utilized.

The constitutions of 1776 and 1902 were proclaimed by the

[6] Scharpf, p. 588, n. 247.

drafting conventions and were never submitted to the people for approval. On both occasions there was vociferous criticism of such action. When confronted with the legality of the new documents, the Virginia courts served the purpose of legitimization by accepting the constitutions as expressions of the people of the commonwealth. The members of Virginia's first constitutional convention had not even been elected for the express purpose of drafting a constitution. The delegates were members of the governmental body authorized to carry on the business of the commonwealth following the termination of British rule in the colony. Thomas Jefferson was among those Virginians who questioned the status of the constitution in the absence of popular approval. It had no more force than an act of the legislature, argued Jefferson, since it had not been submitted to the people.[7] Virginia judges, on the other hand, viewed the assent of the people as an indication of the constitution's validity: "The people have received this as a Constitution. The magistrates and officers down to a constable (for even the mode of his appointment is directed) have been appointed under it. The people have felt its operation and acquiesced."[8]

The issue of proclamation or submission to the people evoked sharp divisions among the delegates to the Convention of 1901–2. The final proposal in favor of proclamation was passed by a vote of fifty-three to forty-four, including six pairs. Anticipating efforts to annul the work of the convention, the delegates sought to facilitate recognition of the new document by specifying a timetable for legislative, judicial, and executive personnel to swear allegiance to the constitution. Shortly after the convention adjourned, Gov. Andrew Jackson Montague, all executive officials with offices at the seat of government, and all judges of courts of record took an oath to support the new constitution. Later, the legislature added its weight of approval when all but one member took the oath of allegiance.[9]

The decision to proclaim the constitution was an expediency designed to avoid the possibility of rejection by the people. The

[7] Va., Commission on Constitutional Revision, *The Constitution of Virginia: Report of the Commission on Constitutional Revision* (Charlottesville, Va.: Michie, 1969), p. 326.

[8] *Kamper* v. *Hawkins*, 1 Va. Cases 20, 28 (1793).

[9] Ralph Clipman McDanel, *The Virginia Constitutional Convention of 1901–1902* (Baltimore: Johns Hopkins Press, 1928), chap. 5, esp. pp. 121, 130–31.

new document effectively disenfranchised large segments of the citizenry, its precise target being the Negro. Moreover, the vote on calling a constitutional convention had elicited little voter interest. Twice in the preceding fifteen years a referendum on a convention proposal had been negative, and in 1900 the vote in favor of the proposal had been only 77,362 to 60,375. Republican opposition was a virtual certainty in view of the fact that only two of the twelve Republican delegates had voted for proclamation. Those who opposed submitting the constitution to the people saw the Negroes, Republicans, and disaffected Democrats as imperiling its passage.[10] In short, the controversy over the propriety of proclamation was a power struggle of the first magnitude.

The Virginia Supreme Court was confronted with the issue of the constitution's validity in *Taylor* v. *Commonwealth*.[11] A black, John Taylor, pleaded guilty to a charge of housebreaking and, without his consent, was tried without the benefit of jury trial. He was found guilty and was sentenced to the state penitentiary for one year. On a writ of error to the Supreme Court, Taylor's attorney insisted that the authority under which his client was tried (article I, section 8, of the 1902 Constitution) was invalid and without force since the convention had not submitted the document to the people of the commonwealth for ratification or rejection.

The court did not rule on the power of the convention to promulgate the organic law of the state. Instead, the unanimous opinion read that since the work of the Convention of 1901–2 had "been recognized, accepted, and acted upon as the only valid Constitution of the State by the Governor, . . . by the Legislature, . . . by the judiciary, . . . and by the people in their primary capacity . . . and there being no government in existence under the Constitution of 1869 opposing or denying its validity, we have no difficulty in holding that the Constitution in question . . . is the only rightful, valid, and existing Constitution of this State."[12] The court had been confronted with a fait accompli. By the time the justices handed down their opinion, almost a year had passed since all major officials in the state had sworn allegiance to the constitution.

The federal courts subsequently confirmed the decision of Vir-

[10] Ibid., pp. 9–10, 16, 125–29.

[11] 101 Va. 829, 44 S.E. 754 (1903).

[12] 101 Va. 831, 44 S.E. 755.

ginia's highest tribunal. The United States Supreme Court dismissed challenges to the election of Virginia congressmen under the new constitution on the ground that it was a moot question since the House of Representatives, as the sole judge of the qualifications of its members, had seated the Virginia delegation. "Any adjudication which this court might make," wrote Justice David J. Brewer, "would be only an ineffectual decision of the question whether or not these petitioners were wronged by what has been fully accomplished."[13] Several years later the United States District Court for the Eastern District of Virginia handed down a decision based on *Taylor* v. *Commonwealth*: "Whether or not the people of the state of Virginia have duly adopted the Constitution in controversy in this case is a political question, not to be disposed of by this court, but by the legislative and executive departments of the government of that state."[14] In summary, the role of the courts in the controversy over proclamation was forecast by a leading member of the 1901–2 Convention in commenting on the work of that body: "No court in the world's history has ever undone the ordained Constitution of a State, and no one need apprehend that the Constitution of Virginia will ever be undone save by the sovereign act of her own people, who may rescind and remould it by their own free will."[15]

In 1945 the Virginia Supreme Court again found itself drawn into a political controversy involving a constitutional change. The 1944 regular session of the General Assembly enacted legislation to provide for extending the vote in Virginia to citizens in the armed services. The legislative scheme for the registration and payment of poll taxes by service personnel was invalidated by the court as a circumvention of the constitutional requirement that such acts be performed personally by the voter. In the view of a unanimous court, the "altruistic motives" of the legislators did not render their action any less offensive to the constitution.[16] Stunned by this decision, Gov. Colgate Darden and a majority of the legislators concluded that the only way to extend the vote to the mem-

13 *Jones* v. *Montague*, 194 U.S. 147, 153 (1904); *Selden* v. *Montague*, 194 U.S. 153 (1904).

14 *Brickhouse* v. *Brooks*, 165 F.R. 546 (1908).

15 John W. Daniel, "The Work of the Constitutional Convention," *Proceedings of the Virginia State Bar Association* 15 (1902):293.

16 *Staples* v. *Gilmer*, 183 Va. 338, 32 S.E. 2d 129 (1944).

bers of the armed services in time for the 1945 Democratic primaries was to call a constitutional convention. There was not time to alter the constitution by the normal amending process, which required a majority approval of two General Assembly sessions with an intervening general election, followed by a majority approval of the voters.

Governor Darden called a special session of the legislature to convene on December 14, 1944. The General Assembly voted to submit to the voters a proposal calling for a constitutional convention restricted to the question of exempting members of the armed forces from certain registration and poll tax requirements. In accordance with the 1902 Constitution the statute provided that the following question was to be submitted to the voters, "Shall there be a convention to revise the Constitution and amend the same?" In addition, however, an "informatory statement" citing the restrictions on the convention was to be a part of the ballot.[17]

A small group of legislators had provided brief but vigorous opposition to the action of the General Assembly. A storm of criticism was added to their protest by most of the state's major newspapers, the state's Republican party, labor groups, and electoral reform groups. This loose combination of reformist elements wished to abolish the poll tax as a prerequisite for voting and to effect the simplification of registration procedures. The Democratic organization, on the other hand, had a vested interest in not disturbing those provisions that contributed to a restricted electorate in Virginia and hence to the organization's dominance in state politics.

The inevitability of a legal challenge to the statute's validity prompted the attorney general to bring a friendly suit against the state comptroller and the state treasurer. The American Legion filed a memorandum with the state Supreme Court on January 8, 1945, urging it to dispose of the case "with all reasonable speed and dispatch."[18] The cooperation of the court was forthcoming, as evidenced by its promptness in handing down a decision on January 18, the day after oral arguments were heard. Although formal opinions were not handed down until over a month later, the court

[17] Francis Howard Heller, *Virginia's State Government during the Second World War: Its Constitutional, Legislative, and Administrative Adaptations, 1942–1945* (Richmond: Virginia State Library, 1949), chap. 2.

[18] Ibid., p. 24. For more information on friendly suits, see pp. 132–36 below.

announced its decision to uphold the validity of the referendum statute by a six-to-one vote; Chief Justice Preston W. Campbell filed a vigorous dissenting opinion.[19]

The majority opinion relied on the absence of a specific provision in the constitution prohibiting the legislature from restricting the actions of a constitutional convention. "If they [the people] vote in favor of such a convention," read the per curiam majority opinion, "they and not the legislature, will limit the work of the convention and its scope."[20] This argument, which was reiterated several times in the opinion, was dismissed as "a sticking in the bark" by the chief justice. He pointed out that the voters had only one choice—vote no or vote for a restricted convention. "How can a legislature," queried the chief justice, "restrict a constitutional right?"[21] The constitution-making authority is plainly vested in the people. The chief justice, who had been the youngest member of the 1901–2 Constitutional Convention, included pertinent portions of the debates of that convention in his opinion. These excerpts illustrated the strong defeat of a proposal that would have permitted calling a convention whose powers would be restricted by the legislature. The political implications of the case were evident in the dissenting opinion. While disavowing any intention to discuss the political aspects of the question, the chief justice nevertheless felt it necessary to deny that his dissent was politically motivated: "As one of two State officers who for fifty years has been affiliated with what is known in Virginia as 'the Organization,' I have no apprehension of being charged with being an 'organization baiter.' "[22] The chief justice perceived the issue to be whether expediency or legality would prevail; he viewed the majority opinion as sanctioning the former. The majority opinion leaned heavily on the argument of the state's attorney general. The court did not confine itself to a consideration of the power of the General Assembly; it anticipated future action by commenting on the authority of a constitutional convention were one to be approved. On the basis of what one scholarly commentator termed "a striking double

[19] *Staples* v. *Gilmer*, 183 Va. 613, 33 S.E. 2d 49 (1945).

[20] 183 Va. 261, 33 S.E. 2d 52. Unlike the 1902 Constitution, the 1971 Constitution expressly permits the legislature to propose a limited convention to the voters. Con., 1971, art. XII, sec. 2.

[21] 183 Va. 633–34, 33 S.E. 2d 58.

[22] 183 Va. 632, 33 S.E. 2d 57.

hypothesis,"[23] the court warned that if the voters approved the call for a restricted convention, and if the delegates amended or revised any part of the constitution in any way not specifically provided for by the General Assembly, the action would be illegal.

## Reapportionment

Until 1962 one of the most important fields in which the federal courts invoked the "political questions" doctrine was legislative apportionment. Justice Felix Frankfurter had warned the courts against entering "this political thicket." "The one stark fact that emerges from a study of the history of Congressional apportionment," wrote Frankfurter, "is its embroilment in politics, in the sense of party contests and party interests."[24] In 1962, in the landmark case of *Baker* v. *Carr*, the United States Supreme Court, ignoring Frankfurter's warning, ruled that malapportionment was a justiciable issue when properly presented to the federal courts.[25] In 1884 the Virginia Supreme Court had indicated that the reapportionment of congressional districts was a political matter: "The laying off and defining the congressional districts is the exercise of a political and discretionary power of the legislature, for which they are amenable to the people, whose representatives they are."[26] However, in *Brown v. Saunders*, thirty years before *Baker* v. *Carr*, the Virginia court had invalidated the legislative act redrawing the state's congressional districts.[27]

The 1930 census revealed that Virginia's representation in the House of Representatives was to be reduced from ten to nine. In order to disturb the composition of as few districts as possible, the General Assembly simply incorporated the old Tenth District—with the exception of three counties assigned to the Sixth District—into the Seventh District. No changes were made in other districts. The effect of the redistricting plan was not only to dilute the vote of several counties that had demonstrated new Republican

[23] Robert Kent Gooch, "The Recent Limited Constitutional Convention in Virginia," *Virginia Law Review* 31 (1945):713.

[24] *Colegrove* v. *Green*, 328 U.S. 549, 554, 556 (1946).

[25] 369 U.S. 186 (1962).

[26] *Wise* v. *Bigger*, 79 Va. 269, 282 (1884).

[27] 159 Va. 28, 166 S.E. 105 (1932).

strength, but also to create an obvious discrepancy in size among the nine congressional districts:[28]

| District | Population | Variation from ideal size |
|---|---|---|
| 1 | 239,835 | −29,257 |
| 2 | 302,715 | +33,623 |
| 3 | 288,939 | +19,847 |
| 4 | 212,952 | −56,140 |
| 5 | 251,090 | −18,002 |
| 6 | 280,708 | +11,616 |
| 7 | 336,654 | +67,562 |
| 8 | 183,934 | −85,158 |
| 9 | 325,024 | +55,932 |

In considering the validity of the redistricting act, the Virginia court took note of the view expressed in 1884, that congressional reapportionment was a political matter. Writing for a unanimous court, Justice Edward W. Hudgins concluded that the nineteenth-century case had been decided primarily on the issue of whether the apportionment bill had received the two-thirds vote of the Senate, as required by the constitution. No serious consideration had been given to the constitutional provision substantially similar to the one in the 1902 Constitution governing the 1932 case—namely, the requirement that congressional districts "be composed of contiguous and compact territory containing as nearly as practicable, an equal number of inhabitants."

The principle of equality in the apportionment of congressional districts had first been given constitutional status in 1830. In a footnote to its decision the court traced the practical application of the equality principle to Virginia congressional representation since the Civil War. On the basis of this tabulation, which indicated the variation of each district from the ideal unit of representation, the court set forth, in *Brown* v. *Saunders*, its understanding of the constitutional standard for congressional reapportionment: "Mathematical exactness, either in compactness of territory or in equality of population, cannot be attained, nor was it contemplated in the provisions of section 55. . . . No small or trivial deviation

[28] The following figures are from 159 Va. 28, 32, 166 S.E. 105, 106. Ideal population per district = 269, 092.

from equality of population would justify or warrant an application to a court for redress. It must be a grave, palpable and unreasonable deviation from the principles fixed by the Constitution."[29] Applying this standard to the 1932 Apportionment Act, the inequality was found to be "obvious, indisputable and excessive."[30] The invalidation of the redistricting act less than thirty days before the scheduled elections meant the entire membership in the House of Representatives from Virginia would be elected at large for the first time in 144 years. In *Colegrove* v. *Green* Justice Frankfurter suggested that a remedy requiring the statewide election of congressmen might be worse than malapportioned districts.[31] The justices of the Virginia court were unaffected by similar arguments: "However this may be, it is our duty . . . to obey the mandate of the fundamental law."[32]

The immediate impact of the court decision was to assure the election of nine Democratic congressmen. In a predominantly one-party state, the Democratic victory was total. The death of Rep. Harry St. George Tucker in the summer of 1932 and the decision of Rep. John W. Fishburne not to seek reelection left only eight incumbents in the race. All seven of the Democratic incumbents were reelected. Rep. Menalcus Lankford of Norfolk, who had been the only Republican congressman from the South, was defeated. The two new Democratic congressmen, neither of whom had been certain of success prior to the court decision, were destined to become key political figures in Virginia: Colgate W. Darden, Jr. (governor of Virginia, 1942–46), who, before the court decision, had been pitted against Representative Lankford, and A. Willis Robertson (United States senator, 1946–67), who had been running against a former Republican congressman for the seat vacated by Representative Fishburne.

Not until 1965, after the United States Supreme Court had handed down landmark decisions requiring that state legislative

[29] 159 Va. 43–44, 166 S.E. 110.

[30] 159 Va. 45, 166 S.E. 111.

[31] 328 U.S. 553.

[32] 159 Va. 48, 166 S.E. 111. Significantly, the simple and effective remedy of at-large elections utilized by the Virginia court and several other state courts was cited as a precedent for advocates of federal court intervention in legislative apportionment. Anthony Lewis, "Legislative Apportionment and the Federal Courts," *Harvard Law Review* 71 (1958):1087–88.

as well as congressional districts be as equal in population as practicable,[33] did the Virginia court again rule on the validity of a redistricting act. In view of the fact that there was no change in the number of congressional seats allotted to Virginia following the 1960 census, the legislature did not redistrict the state's ten congressional districts. However, there had been significant shifts in population during the 1950s. As a result of the General Assembly's failure to adjust the district lines in acordance with the shifts in population, the disparities in absolute population size among the districts being reviewed by the court were greater than those invalidated in 1932.[34]

The 1932 decision in *Brown* v. *Saunders* was controlling in the 1965 case.[35] A unanimous court was unimpressed by arguments that the cases were distinguishable because of the favorable testimony of population experts, congressmen, and other citizens on behalf of the later redistricting plan. The justices were also unconvinced that military personnel should be excluded from the state census. Hence the districts were invalid as a violation of the Virginia Constitution. The court further concluded that the congressional districts violated the Federal Constitution as well.

Once again the Virginia court required that at-large elections be held if the congressional districts were not properly apportioned. A special session of the General Assembly in 1965 drew up new congressional districts in accordance with constitutional requirements that they be compact and contiguous, as well as substantially equal in population. The immediate political impact of the decision was again decisive. In the first elections held under the new redistricting plan, Rep. Howard W. Smith, a veteran of thirty-six years in Congress and chairman of the powerful House Rules Committee, was defeated by George C. Rawlings, Jr., in the Eighth District Democratic primary. The Eighth District had been profoundly changed with the addition of 100,000 Fairfax residents. Although Smith's age and the aggressive campaign waged by his opponent contributed to the outcome, a noted political analyst concluded that "redistricting must be credited with the ultimate

[33] *Wesberry* v. *Saunders*, 376 U.S. 1 (1964); *Reynolds* v. *Sims*, 377 U.S. 533 (1964).

[34] Ralph Eisenberg, "Legislative Reapportionment and Congressional Redistricting in Virginia," *Washington and Lee Law Review* 23 (1966):319–20.

[35] *Wilkens* v. *Davis*, 205 Va. 803, 139 S.E. 2d 849 (1965).

responsibility for Smith's defeat."[36] In the general election, Republican William L. Scott handily defeated Rawlings with the aid of a large number of Democrats loyal to Smith. The Republicans gained another congressman in the Ninth District, where William C. Wampler defeated incumbent Democratic congressman W. Pat Jennings. The 1965 redistricting plan had added Wythe County to the Ninth District. Although Wampler carried the county by 625 votes, its addition to the district was not a determining factor in the election.

The 1971 congressional redistricting was also challenged before the Virginia Supreme Court. O'Wrighton Delk Simpson, chairman of the Isle of Wight Democratic party, alleged that the Fourth Congressional District had been illegally gerrymandered to preserve the seat of the Democratic incumbent, Watkins M. Abbitt. The petitioner argued that the Fourth District did not consist of compact and contiguous territory, as required by the constitutions of the United States and the state of Virginia.[37] The county of Amelia served as a bridge connecting four other counties, including the incumbent's home county, to the remaining territory of the district.[38]

The Virginia Supreme Court had been asked by Simpson to order at-large statewide congressional elections for November 1972 if the alleged defects in the plan were not corrected. In a brief per curiam opinion, the court rejected the petitioner's request by citing a 1967 federal statute requiring the election of congressmen from districts. The absence of the traditional remedy for dealing with congressional redistricting was utilized by Virginia's high court to dismiss the suit on technical grounds rather than rule on the merits of the case.[39]

Although the Virginia Constitution included provisions applying to the redistricting of congressional districts, it did not mention the standards to be used in reapportioning state legislative districts.[40]

[36] Ralph Eisenberg, "1966 Politics in Virginia: The Elections for U.S. Representatives," *University of Virginia News Letter* 43 (June 15, 1967):38.

[37] *Simpson* v. *Mahan*, 212 Va. 416, 185 S.E. 2d 47 (1971).

[38] A map of the congressional redistricting plan of 1971 can be found in Robert J. Austin, "Congressional Redistricting in Virginia: Political Implications of One-Man-One-Vote," *University of Virginia News Letter* 48 (July 15, 1972):43.

[39] The plan was eventually invalidated by a federal district court because of population disparities. See Austin.

[40] The 1971 Constitution establishes a common standard for the decennial appor-

The constitutional requirement to reapportion two years after a decennial census, however, implied that a population standard was to be used. The legislature had regularly reapportioned legislative districts under the Constitution of 1902. Failure to reflect the full measure of urban growth in the 1962 redistricting act resulted in legal challenges in both federal and state courts. The circuit court judge for the city of Richmond discounted the small disparities in Virginia districts as reasonable and favorable when compared with those of other states. This decision upholding the act's validity was appealed to the Virginia Supreme Court, but no action had been taken when the United States Supreme Court confirmed the judgment of a three-judge federal district court that the act was unconstitutional.[41]

In another case the state Supreme Court was presented with the issue of local reapportionment.[42] In 1963 the city of Virginia Beach had consolidated with Princess Anne County. Under the city charter amended by the General Assembly, the new city council was to consist of eleven members, each to be elected at large. Seven of the council members were to be elected from different boroughs, and four others were to be elected without regard to residence. Under this Seven-Four Plan, the combined population of two boroughs was greater than the combined population of the remaining five. Petitioners from the heavily populated boroughs sought a writ of mandamus compelling the council to reapportion the city equally on the basis of population.

The court identified the basic question before it as not whether disproportionate representation actually existed, but whether the city council had the authority to remedy the disparities in population. The special charter organizing the new city forbade any reapportionment for five years after the effective date of the charter, but required reapportionment within eight years. However, under general laws requiring a reapportionment of seats on city councils every ten years after 1933, an immediate reapportionment was called for. In rendering its decision, the court followed the familiar

---

tionment of legislative and congressional districts: "Every electoral district shall be composed of contiguous and compact territory and shall be so constituted as to give, as nearly as is practicable, representation in proportion to the population of the district." Con., 1971, art. II, sec. 6.

41 Eisenberg, "Legislative Reapportionment," pp. 299–309.

42 *Davis* v. *Dusch*, 205 Va. 676, 139 S.E. 2d 25 (1964).

practice of upholding special legislation when it conflicts with general laws. Other considerations to protect the public interest were also noted:

> Here, we have a new city just emerging from the governmental structures of a former municipality and a former county. We must consider, as the legislature surely did, that that union posed difficult and unique problems which required special provisions in the legislation giving life to the new city—provisions which were essential to meet and surmount objections which might have prevented the consolidation. One would have to be naive, indeed, to believe that if those special provisions had not been granted the formation of the city would notwithstanding, have still resulted.[43]

To order a reapportionment of the city, in the opinion of the court, "might be to strike the blow which would cause the new city to die aborning."[44] Furthermore, as was the case in *Simpson* v. *Mahan* (1971), legislative action, this time in the form of special legislation by the General Assembly, had precluded the requested remedy.[45]

## Elections

Purely partisan disputes over the conduct of elections constitute one area in which the Virginia Supreme Court has for the most part been successful in maintaining its detachment. The Virginia Constitution provides that the General Assembly shall enact laws to regulate elections. In pursuance of this constitutional mandate, and to expedite the speedy resolution of contested elections, the legislature has specifically denied any appeal from a final judgment of a lower court of record. The statutory provisions are controlling in these matters.[46] A 1939 opinion of the state Supreme Court noted that at no time during the existence of the common-

[43] 205 Va. 684, 139 S.E. 2d 30.

[44] 205 Va. 685, 139 S.E. 2d 31.

[45] On appeal to the United States Supreme Court, the Seven-Four Plan was upheld as "a detente between urban and rural communities that may be important in resolving the complex problems of the modern megalopolis in relation to the city, the suburbia, and the rural countryside." *Dusch* v. *Davis*, 387 U.S. 112, 117 (1967).

[46] Con., 1902, art. II, sec. 36; art. IV, sec. 56; Con., 1971, art. II, sec. 4; Va. Code, secs. 24.1-236–24.1-248 (1973 repl. vol.).

wealth had there been a case "in which a court of equity . . . assumed jurisdiction on the sole ground that the question involved was the contest of an election." The court concluded: "In view of the constitutional mandates, the pertinent acts of the legislature and the origin and history of the jurisdiction of courts of equity, it would seem beyond controversy that the public policy of this Commonwealth has been, and is to regard all contests of elections as purely political."[47]

The role of the Supreme Court is confined to issuing a writ of mandamus requiring a hearing on the merits in a lower court. The availability of this procedure is a safeguard against a miscarriage of justice in the judicial settlement of a contested election. For example, the election of local constitutional officers in Lee County on November 3, 1959, was contested, but a three-judge court dismissed the complaint regarding four of the five officers on the ground that the contestants had not properly notified the defendants of the charges against them. A per curiam opinion of the Supreme Court awarded a writ of mandamus to the contestants, instructing the lower court to hear the issues of the contested election on the merits. The effect of the decision, notwithstanding the statute prohibiting an appeal from the lower tribunal in an election contest, was to reverse the three-judge court in order to prevent a failure of justice.[48]

## Executive Appointments

The Virginia Supreme Court's general inclination not to interfere with executive prerogatives was demonstrated in a 1928 case concerning gubernatorial appointments.[49] The adoption of a package of constitutional amendments on June 19, 1928, increased by two the number of judges to sit on the state Supreme Court. The decision of Gov. Harry F. Byrd, Sr., not to make interim appointments, thus leaving initial selection to the 1930 General Assembly, was challenged in an original writ of mandamus. The court was of the opinion that the governor's power to fill vacancies temporarily was

47 *Cundiff* v. *Jeter*, 172 Va. 470, 475, 2 S.E. 2d 436, 438 (1939).
48 *Kirk* v. *Carter*, 202 Va. 335, 117 S.E. 2d 135 (1960).
49 *Allen* v. *The Governor*, 151 Va. 21, 144 S.E. 469 (1928).

a discretionary function rather than merely a ministerial duty.

The power of the executive to fill vacancies is not exclusive, since it is the constitutional duty of the General Assembly to elect persons to sit on the appellate bench. The court acknowledged that Governor Byrd's decision to leave the new seats vacant for another fourteen months had "led to radical differences of opinion as to public policy, and executive and judicial power." Having conceded the situation was "unfortunate," the justices concluded it did not justify "any invasion of the executive department by the judicial department. In the constitutional division of powers, each is and should be independent."[50]

[50] 151 Va. 27, 144 S.E. 470.

# VI *The Court as Public Umpire*

ONE of the basic functions of the Virginia Supreme Court is the surveillance of official action. When state agencies or their representatives disagree as to the ground rules of state politics, or a private person challenges official policy, the court often provides a forum for clarification and sometimes final resolution of the dispute.

## The Legislature

The General Assembly is the supreme lawmaking body within the state. The powers of the state legislature are distinguishable from those of the United States Congress because of the differing natures of the constitutions under which the two were established. A state constitution largely restricts power, whereas the Federal Constitution primarily grants power. The Virginia Constitution specifies what the branches of government may not do rather than what they may do. Consequently, the General Assembly is free to act in any manner not specifically prohibited by the Virginia Constitution or the United States Constitution.

Legislation that is challenged on constitutional grounds is presumed to be valid. The Virginia Supreme Court has held that "all statutes and ordinances are presumed to be constitutional, and if there is any doubt such doubt should be resolved in favor of their constitutionality."[1] With this as its standard test, it is not surprising that in spite of the routine nature of a constitutional challenge, the court rarely finds a statute to be in contravention of a constitutional provision. Margaret V. Nelson reported that in the period from 1789 to 1928, in not more than sixty cases were mea-

[1] *Town of Ashland* v. *Hanover County*, 202 Va. 409, 416, 117 S.E. 2d 679, 684 (1961).

sures declared unconstitutional by the Virginia Supreme Court.[2] Dr. Nelson concluded that the impact of judicial review in Virginia had been negligible: "Indications are that the general trend of legislative enactments would have been the same even in the absence of the practice of judicial review. The courts tended to follow public opinion on vital issues. Rarely did they set the pace, as, indeed they could hardly be expected to do."[3] Nothing has changed in the court's exercise of judicial review since 1928 to alter this assessment in any substantial manner. Although the Virginia Supreme Court has continued to invalidate certain legislative enactments, it has not done so in such a way as to nullify major public policy.

The 1946 case of *Moore* v. *Sutton*, in which the court invalidated a state statute, is remembered more for the influence of the justices' political philosophy on the decision than for the practical effects of their ruling. The case involved the validity of a statute regulating the practice of professional photography. The Virginia court, as was the case in other jurisdictions, found such regulation to exceed the state legislature's power to act in the interest of the public health, morals, safety, and general welfare of the citizenry. The political philosophy of the justices was clearly evident in the last paragraph of the court's opinion: "In this day of bureaucracies multiplied we are constrained to emphasize the virtue of a firm adherence to the philosophy that that state is best governed which is least governed."[4]

## Test Cases

Whenever a major piece of legislative policy has been at stake, the customary practice of the state has been to initiate a friendly suit testing the constitutionality of the act. The attorney general can invoke the court's original jurisdiction by filing a petition for a writ of mandamus directing the state comptroller or the state treasurer, or both, to make payments authorized by the act in question. The

[2] Nelson, *A Study of Judicial Review in Virginia, 1789–1928* (New York: Columbia University Press, 1947), p. 202.

[3] Ibid., p. 222.

[4] 185 Va. 481, 490, 39 S.E. 2d 348, 352 (1946).

court is then obligated by statute to consider and determine all questions raised in the attorney general's petition that pertain to the constitutionality or interpretation of the act regardless of whether the questions have any bearing on the duties of the state comptroller or the state treasurer.[5] In conforming with this procedure, the court has gone one step further by declaring that the court is not limited in its deliberations to the questions raised in the attorney general's petition but may consider other constitutional questions presented to it—by the counsel for the state comptroller, as an example.[6] This procedure was immediately employed to test the constitutionality of the act that had precipitated the passage of the "test case" legislation—namely, the act providing for the registration and payment of poll taxes for members of the armed services. The act was declared unconstitutional.[7] One year later the attorney general filed a petition when the legislature proposed that a constitutional convention be called that would be limited in power to a consideration of amendments designed to rectify the situation.[8]

In 1955, in the case of *Almond* v. *Day*, the legislative proposal to provide tuition grants for the education of war orphans at private institutions was struck down. The court expedited its proceedings so as to adjudicate the issue more quickly. Chief Justice Edward W. Hudgins called a special session of the court to announce the decision three weeks earlier than would have been the case under its regular schedule. The decision confirmed that the system of tuition grants being contemplated by the legislators as an alternative to desegregation of the public schools would not be permissible. Writing for the court, Justice Eggleston offered the following advice to the legislature:

> To sustain the validity of Item 210, in so far as it purports to authorize payments for tuition, institutional fees and other designated expenses of eligible children who attend private schools, in the face of the constitutional provisions which have been discussed, would mean that by like appropriations the General Assembly might divert public funds to the

[5] Va. Code, sec. 8-714 (1957 repl. vol.).

[6] *Almond* v. *Day*, 197 Va. 419, 430, 89 S.E. 2d 851, 858 (1955).

[7] *Staples* v. *Gilmer*, 183 Va. 338, 32 S.E. 2d 129 (1944).

[8] *Staples* v. *Gilmer*, 183 Va. 613, 33 S.E. 2d 49 (1945). See pp. 119–22 above for a full discussion of this case.

support of a system of private schools which the Constitution now forbids. If that be a desirable end, it should be accomplished by amending our Constitution in the manner therein provided. It should not be done by judicial legislation.[9]

Thus, as had been the case in 1944 and 1945 following a ruling of unconstitutionality, the General Assembly, with the cooperation of the governor, promptly acted to provide for amending the Virginia Constitution.

In *Harrison* v. *Day* the General Assembly's 1956 "massive resistance" plan to prevent desegregation in the public schools was also tested in a friendly suit before the state's highest tribunal. The legislation provided for the closing of racially integrated public schools, the cutting off of funds to such schools, and the availability of tuition grants to students choosing to enter private schools. Once again the court expedited the resolution of the issue. The decision of a three-judge federal district court pertaining to the constitutionality of the same legislation was expected on January 19, 1959. The Virginia justices gathered that day to make their decision known in spite of the fact that it was a legal state holiday commemorating the birth of Gen. Robert E. Lee.[10] Arriving at the Supreme Court Building about 8:30 A.M., some of the justices had to knock and identify themselves before gaining entrance to the locked building. Following some minor changes in the text of the opinion during an early morning conference, the justices entered what was by then a packed courtroom to announce their decision several hours in advance of the federal court ruling.

As was expected, the legislation was pronounced invalid by both courts. The Virginia Supreme Court found the legislation to be in violation of the 1902 constitutional mandate requiring the General Assembly to "maintain an efficient system of public free schools throughout the State." As he had in the 1955 war orphans case, Chief Justice Eggleston referred to the amendment alternative: "If it be desirable that all of the provisions dealing with the public school system be stricken from the Constitution, it should be done by proper amendments to the Constitution in the manner therein

[9] 197 Va. 431, 89 S.E. 2d 859.

[10] Benjamin Muse, *Virginia's Massive Resistance* (Bloomington: Indiana University Press, 1961), pp. 122–23.

provided. It should not be done by judicial construction. The aim of judicial construction, and also its limitation, is to determine the meaning of what has been written, not to delete sections from the Constitution on the theory that if conditions had been different they would not have been written."[11] Having found the statutes inconsistent with the state constitution, the court declined to consider whether the Fourteenth Amendment to the United States Consitution had been violated. The opinion of the court further empathized with the General Assembly's reaction to the 1954 school desegregation decision: "It was an understandable effort to diminish the evils explicit from the decision in the Brown case that prompted the enactment of the statutes now under review."[12]

The federal court decision, pronounced on the same day as that of the Virginia court, ensured nullification of the state's "massive resistance" propram. Nevertheless, in spite of the sympathetic tone of the Virginia court's opinion, it had participated in that nullification. The vulnerability of the justices to a political backlash was greater than at any time since the Readjuster court had been replaced in 1894. The initial reaction of Governor Almond, however, suggested that such a reaction was unlikely: "It is not necessary for me to say this, but I wish to make it very clear, I have implicit faith in, and the highest respect for, the capacity and integrity of the Supreme Court of Appeals and for each and every member thereof."[13] The election of Justice I'Anson to the Supreme Court less than two weeks later by a legislative vote of 130 to 0 erased any political vulnerability of the members of the court. Justice I'Anson, who had been serving as an interim appointee to the high bench during the preceding four months, had voted with the majority in the five-to-two decision of the Virginia court.

In ruling that the state could neither close public schools nor cut off funds to avoid racial integration in public schools, the Virginia Supreme Court also struck down the tuition grants. However, the tuition grants were unconstitutional only to the extent that they were tied to the provision withholding appropriations from integrated public schools. In fact, the court indicated there was "no constitutional objection to the prescribed procedure for

[11] 200 Va. 439, 449–50, 106 S.E. 2d 636, 644 (1959).

[12] 200 Va. 453, 106 S.E. 2d 647.

[13] Muse, pp. 123–24.

making tuition grants out of funds properly available for the purpose . . . thus leaving it to the discretion of the General Assembly."[14] The legislature promptly enacted a new tuition grant program that was administered without objection from the state courts until it began encountering difficulty in the federal courts.

In 1972 the conventional test suit was used to settle the validity of the Tuition Assistance Loan Act of 1972.[15] This legislation, which was tested under a new provision of the 1971 Constitution, authorized tuition assistance to Virginia students attending accredited nonsectarian institutions of higher learning in Virginia. By a unanimous vote the justices invalidated the act as providing for conditional grants or gifts rather than loans, as permitted by article VII, section 11 of the Virginia Constitution. The court was not persuaded that the obligation on the student to maintain satisfactory academic progress was substantial enough to satisfy the requirements of a loan. The opinion of the court, however, suggested that an obligation of public service to the commonwealth would render the assistance constitutional. Based on past actions, the response of the legislature was predictable. The 1973 session of the General Assembly enacted new legislation enumerating specific actions beneficial to the commonwealth that would satisfy the obligation of the loan. In a second test case the Virginia Supreme Court upheld the provision of the 1973 law permitting repayment of loans to students attending eligible sectarian and nonsectarian institutions by employment by the commonwealth or by any of its political subdivisions.[16] Meanwhile, the 1973 and 1974 legislative sessions approved an amendment to article VIII, section 11 of the constitution permitting the General Assembly to provide grants as well as loans to students attending nonprofit institutions of higher education. The amendment was adopted by the voters in November 1974.

Many of the test cases brought before the Virginia Supreme Court since the 1940s involved section 185 of the 1902 Constitution, which prohibited the state and its subdivisions from granting credit or aid to any person, association, or corporation. In most of the cases brought before the court the action of the legislature was

[14] 200 Va. 452–53, 106 S.E. 2d 647.
[15] *Miller* v. *Ayres*, 213 Va. 251, 191 S.E. 2d 261 (1972).
[16] *Miller* v. *Ayres*, 214 Va. 171, 198 S.E. 2d 634 (1973).

sustained. An exception was the 1968 case reviewing the power of the Virginia Industrial Building Authority, acting as a political subdivision of the state, to guarantee loans for industrial projects. By a five-to-two margin the court found this exercise of governmental power constitutionally impermissible, but took favorable notice of a proposed constitutional amendment, passed at the same session of the General Assembly as the act in question, authorizing loan guarantees by a public authority in order to finance industrial development.[17] The essence of that proposed amendment was made a part of article X, section 10 of the 1971 Constitution.

Test cases are also initiated at the local government level. A 1958 case raised the issue of constitutionality for a state statute permitting property qualifications for county voters on bond issues.[18] The voters of Arlington County had decided in a general election that bond issues should be subject to the approval of a majority of the voters who were freeholders as well as a majority of the voters voting in bond elections. The Electoral Board of Arlington County initiated the litigation by filing for a writ of mandamus directing the commonwealth's attorney of that county to certify a voucher for payment of services rendered by an employee of the board who prepared an official list of the voters in the county who were freeholders. Upon review of the statute authorizing a property restriction on the right to vote, the court found it in violation of the "qualified voters" provisions of the Virginia Constitution.

Another such local case was designed to test an urban county's power to adopt a general sales tax under the Code of Virginia.[19] Following the lead of the city of Norfolk, the city of Richmond adopted a sales tax to go into effect on July 1, 1965. Meanwhile, Henrico County had enacted a similar sales tax ordinance. The issue was brought before the state Supreme Court as a result of an original petition by the Board of Supervisors of Henrico County requesting that the county director of finance be compelled to administer the ordinance.

The county argued that as a county adjoining a large city, it was granted the same taxing authority by the code as was the city of

17 *Button* v. *Day*, 208 Va. 494, 505, 158 S.E. 2d 735, 742 (1968).

18 *Carlisle* v. *Hassan*, 199 Va. 771, 102 S.E. 2d 273 (1958).

19 *Board of Supervisors of Henrico County* v. *Corbett*, 206 Va. 167, 142 S.E. 2d 504 (1965).

Richmond. In a technical interpretation of the relevant statutes, the court found the county without statutory power to enact such a tax ordinance. With the decision being handed down less than a month before the effective date of the Richmond sales tax, the city postponed the effective date to January 1, 1966, since Henrico County would not be allowed to levy the tax simultaneously. The effect of the decision was to deny urban counties an important tax source that was being tapped by large cities. By April 1966, seventeen cities had adopted local sales taxes.[20] The plight of urban counties was one of many factors contributing to the 1966 General Assembly's authorization of a state sales tax with an optional 1-percent local levy.

## Vagueness and Uncertainty

When the court has been faced with criminal statutes that are vague or that do not define the offense with sufficient certainty, it has generally not attempted to save them through interpretation. The justices have applied the due process doctrine of certainty in such instances. "It is elementary that an act creating a statutory offense, to be valid, must specify with reasonable certainty and definiteness the conduct which is commanded or prohibited, that is, what must be done or avoided, so that a person of ordinary intelligence may know what is thereby required of him. . . . Unless an act creating a statutory offense satisfies this requirement of certainty and definiteness it violates the Due Process Clause of the Fourteenth Amendment and of the Virginia Constitution."[21] If such deficiencies are found in legislation, the court invalidates the statutes and reverses the convictions. The burden then falls on the legislature to rewrite the statutes. "It is the function of the judiciary to interpret statutes. Rewriting them is the function of the legislature."[22]

In 1971 the court invalidated vague or indefinite statutes in four

[20] Michael S. Deel and Stuart W. Connock, "Virginia's Sales Tax: Its Origin and Administration," *University of Virginia News Letter* 46 (Apr. 15, 1970):29. See also T. J. Reed, "A City Sales Tax: Norfolk's First Year," ibid. 42 (Nov. 15, 1965):9–12.

[21] *Caldwell* v. *Commonwealth*, 198 Va. 454, 458, 94 S.E. 2d 537, 540 (1956).

[22] 198 Va. 459, 94 S.E. 2d 540.

cases.[23] Prior to that year provisions of several major enactments had fallen before the court's doctrine of certainy. The hit-and-run statute, which obligated the driver of a motor vehicle involved in an accident to give assistance and information, was invalidated because of its failure to specify when and to whom the information was to be furnished."[24] A provision of the Uniform Narcotic Drug Act met a similar fate before the court.[25] Section 54-504 of the act required that the date of selling be recorded for all narcotics sold or dispensed of in any manner. Shortly after making a sale to an addict, the defendant was arrested for failure to make a timely record. Following his release on bail the same day, the defendant returned to his store and entered the date of the sale in his record. His conviction was reversed on the ground the statute did not specify any time when or within which the record was to be made. In a 1955 case, a provision of the Alcoholic Beverage Control Act was declared unconstitutionally vague and indefinite.[26] The defendant had been held to be an "improper person" and had therefore been prohibited from purchasing or possessing alcoholic beverages. The court, however, was of the opinion that the phrase "improper person" admitted of such arbitrary interpretation as to violate the doctrine of certainty.

In the 1971 case of *Owens* v. *Virginia* the definition of "unlawful assembly" as contained in Virginia's antiriot statute was found unconstitutional. Unlawful assembly had been defined by the act as follows: "whenever three or more persons assemble with the common intent or with means and preparations to do an unlawful act which would be riot if actually comitted, but do not act toward the commission thereof, or whenever three or more persons assemble without authority of law and for the purpose of disturbing the peace or exciting public alarm or disorder."[27] The defendants had been charged with the offense of remaining at the place of a riot or an unlawful assembly. Since the trial court had not specified

[23] *Owens* v. *Virginia*, 211 Va. 633, 179 S.E. 2d 477 (1971); *Hanock* v. *Brown*, 212 Va. 215, 183 S.E. 2d 149 (1971); *Kohlberg* v. *Virginia Real Estate Commission*, 212 Va. 237, 183 S.E. 2d 170 (1971); *Nicolls* v. *Commonwealth*, 212 Va. 255, 183 S.E. 2d 734 (1971).

[24] *Caldwell* v. *Commonwealth*, 198 Va. 454, 94 S.E. 2d 537 (1956).

[25] *Peacock* v. *Commonwealth*, 200 Va. 464, 106 S.E. 2d 659 (1959).

[26] *Booth v. Commonwealth*, 197 Va. 177, 88 S.E. 2d 916 (1955).

[27] 211 Va. 633, 179 S.E. 2d 477 (1971).

which offense had resulted in the convictions, the Supreme Court reversed the lower court on the ground that the convictions may have been based on unlawful assembly, which was a constitutionally impermissible definition. The General Assembly responded to this decision as it had in the criminal statute cases mentioned above. In the first session of the legislature following the court's invalidation of the criminal provision, the General Assembly rewrote the definition of unlawful assembly in such a way as to incorporate the standard of clear and present danger of violent conduct, which the court had expressly indicated was necessary: "whenever three or more persons assembled share the common intent to advance some lawful or unlawful purpose by the commission of an act or acts of unlawful force or violence likely seriously to jeopardize public safety, peace or order, and the assembly actually tends to inspire persons of ordinary courage with well-grounded fear of serious and immediate breaches of public safety, peace or order."[28]

## The Executive

The Virginia Supreme Court is rarely called on to review the actions of the state's chief executive, and so judicial rulings against Virginia governors are rare. It is necessary to go back to the administration of Gov. James H. Price (1938–42) to find a major decision against executive authority. Two state Supreme Court cases resulted from conflicts between Attorney General Abram P. Staples and Governor Price. The attorney general, a loyal member of the Byrd organization, successfully challenged the governor's authority on two separate occasions.

Governor Price, who had been elected without Senator Byrd's endorsement, was faced with an antagonistic legislature throughout his term of office. The differences between the two branches of government were manifest in the governor's nine item vetoes of the 1940–42 appropriation bill. As attorney general, Staples held invalid seven of the nine vetoes on the ground that a governor could not legally veto an item affecting some other item that he approves. The attorney general argued his own case before the

[28] Va. Acts, 1971, ch. 251.

Supreme Court against a team of lawyers with strong antiorganization connections who were representing the chief executive. With one justice dissenting on the ground that two of the vetoes were valid, the court upheld Staples's position.[29]

On another occasion Governor Price increased the annual salary of the secretary of the commonwealth from $4,000 to $5,000. Once again the attorney general rendered an opinion denying the governor any constitutional or statutory power to authorize such an increase. A unanimous Supreme Court subscribed to the view of Attorney General Staples.[30]

## State Regulatory Commissions

Virginia has three major regulatory commissions whose decisions are reviewed by the state Supreme Court: the State Corporation Commission (SCC), the Industrial Commission of Virginia and the State Milk Commission. Decisions of the SCC may be appealed to the court as a matter of right by the commonwealth or any party in interest or aggrieved party. Since appeal as a matter of right does not exist for decisions of the Industrial and Milk commissions, the volume of appeals from the SCC is greater than that from the other two commissions combined. As pointed out in Chapter IV, between October 1961 and September 1966 the rate of affirmation for orders of the state comissions (66.7 percent) was higher than that for lower court decisions (51.2 percent). This figure is indicative of the court's proclivity to leave undisturbed the decisions of administrative agencies created by the legislature to carry out specialized functions. In examining those instances in which the court does provide a check on administrative decision-making, it is well to remember that the court has devoted the bulk of its energies simply to giving legal approval to the decisions of the state commissions. With this in mind, it must also be emphasized that there are differentials in the rate of approval from one commission to another, and even for the same commission from one period to another.

The SCC and the Industrial Commission are each composed of

29 *Commonwealth* v. *Dodson*, 176 Va. 281, 11 S.E. 2d 120 (1940).

30 *Jackson v. Hodges*, 176 Va. 89, 10 S.E. 2d 566 (1940).

three members elected by the General Assembly for fixed six-year terms. The members devote full time to their duties, and there are no limits on the number of terms a commissioner can serve. Until 1966 the Milk Commission was composed of three members who were appointed by the governor to serve at his pleasure. Since that time the membership of the commission has been increased twice to the present size of a nonvoting administrator and seven members. The administrator serves at the pleasure of the governor and devotes full time to the duties of the office. The other members, who are also appointed by the governor, can serve for no more than two terms of four years. The legislature also sets certain requirements for the composition of the commissions. At least one member of the SCC must meet the qualifications prescribed for judges of courts of record. Conflicts of interest are avoided by denying an SCC seat to any person holding a position with or having a financial interest in any corporation subject to regulation by the commission. Not more than one member of the Industrial Commission can be a person classified as a representative of employers, and not more than one can be someone similarly associated with employees. Of the members of the Milk Commission, two are required by statute to be producers of milk, one must be a processor-distributor, and four are to be consumers without any financial interest in the production or distribution of milk.[31]

## State Corporation Commission

The oldest and most important of the three commissions is the State Corporation Commission. It was created by the Constitutional Convention of 1901–2 with a unique status, combining legislative, executive, and judicial functions. The creation of the commission was prompted by the need to curb the activities of the railroads without unfairly discriminating against them. In line with this purpose, the commission was originally assigned the functions of regulating the rates and services of the railroads and issuing corporate charters. The function of the commission was defined by Judge Stafford G. Whittle in an early case: "In this

[31] Va. Code, secs. 12.1-6–12.1-11, 65.1-10 (1973 repl. vol.); secs. 3.1-426–3.1-426.1 (1974 suppl.).

Commonwealth, the State Corporation Commission, created by constitutional authority, is the instrumentality through which the State exercises its governmental powers for the regulation and control of public service corporations."[32]

The hybrid nature of the powers assigned to the regulatory commission meant the partial relaxation of the venerable doctrine of separation of powers. Some mingling and overlapping of powers has been tolerated by the court as inevitable. In this regard, the position of the Virginia court is consistent with that of federal and other state courts:

> It is undoubtedly true that a sound and wise policy should keep these great departments of the government as separate and distinct from each other as practicable. But it is equally true that experience has shown that no government could be administered where an absolute and unqualified adherence to that maxim was enforced. The universal construction of this maxim in practice has been that the whole power of one of these departments should not be exercised by the same hands which possess the whole power of either of the other departments, but that either department may exercise the powers of another to a limited extent.[33]

The SCC has no inherent power, but only that conferred on it by the constitution or the General Assembly. The Virginia Supreme Court, however, has broadly construed the authority of the legislature to impose additional duties on the SCC.[34] As a result, the powers of the commission have become broad in scope and varied in nature. Unlike its counterparts at the federal level and in other states, the SCC possesses the powers of a court of record, allowing it to enforce its own orders. Furthermore, it is vested with extensive executive authority by virtue of its duty to administer all laws relating to the regulation and control of corporations.

Article IX, section 4 of the 1971 Virginia Constitution expressly vests the sole power of reviewing the final orders and judgments of the SCC in the state Supreme Court. No other court of the common-

[32] *Norfolk and Portsmouth Belt Line Railroad Co.* v. *Commonwealth*, 103 Va. 289, 294, 49 S.E. 39, 41 (1904).

[33] *Winchester and Strasburg Railroad Co. et al.* v. *Commonwealth*, 106 Va. 264, 268, 55 S.E. 692, 693 (1906).

[34] *Lewis Trucking Corporation* v. *Commonwealth*, 207 Va. 23, 28–29, 147 S.E. 2d 747, 751 (1966).

wealth may even enjoin action by the commission, much less reverse or modify its decisions. Historically, the Supreme Court has exhibited a strong tendency to accept the decisions of the SCC. In the first twenty years of the commission's existence, more than one-third of the court's affirmances actually adopted the opinion of the commissioners, virtually in its entirety, as the opinion of the court.[35] Considering the large number of cases heard by the SCC and the right of absolute appeal from its decisions to the state Supreme Court, the rate of appeals is nominal. From the formation of the SCC until June 1972, 209 of its orders have been reviewed by the Virginia court, and 57 of these have been reversed or vacated.[36] During the first thirty-one years of the commission's work, 77 cases were appealed, with 27 being reversed or remanded.[37] During the next forty years there were 132 appeals but only 30 reversals, the rate of reversal dropping to less than one-fourth of the cases appealed. Not only did this comparatively low rate of reversal suggest general approval of the SCC by the Virginia Supreme Court; but the fact that the reversed cases accounted for less than 1 percent of the total number of cases heard by the SCC also indicated general satisfaction with the commission.

The SCC became the object of growing criticism within the commonwealth during the last half of the 1960s. Concern over rising prices for the consumers utilizing the services of the regulated corporations and an average age of over seventy-five years for the commissioners prompted the criticism. A sizable group of General Assembly members, joined by Governor Holton, supported an increase in the commission's membership from three to five, as well as a study of the SCC.[38] These moves were blunted by a complete turnover in the commission's personnel with the seating of two new members in April 1972 and a third in 1973. Before these personnel changes, the review of the SCC by the state Supreme Court had mirrored the criticism within the state.

From June 1967 through June 1972, nineteen cases concerning

[35] Armistead M. Dobie, "Judicial Review of Administrative Action in Virginia," *Virginia Law Revew* 8 (1922):570–71.

[36] Figures for the period before 1962 were taken from Ralph T. Catterall, "The State Corporation Commission of Virginia," *Virginia Law Review* 48 (1962):139–51.

[37] Lewis F. Powell, Jr., "The Relation between the Virginia Court of Appeals and the State Corporation Commission," *Virginia Law Review* 19 (1933):589–93.

[38] *Roanoke Times*, Dec. 5, 1971; *Richmond Times-Dispatch*, Mar. 31, 1972.

actions of the SCC reached the Supreme Court, with ten decisions, including two involving the same case, going against it. One of the reversals pertained to a disclaimer by the SCC of any authority to grant or refuse a license for an airport except as a ministerial duty. In holding that the SCC had not been denied such statutory power, the court made this observation: "Otherwise, it is conceivable that, in the advanced and advancing era of air travel, the State Corporation Commission could be required to issue a permit to operate an airport immediately adjacent to an airport, or in an extensively developed area, with the result that confusion and peril to the general public would be greatly increased."[39] In another jurisdictional case, the court held that the SCC should have referred the issue before it to the Interstate Commerce Commission.[40] The SCC was also reversed for altering its tax assessment techniques and for improperly computing rates for automobile liability insurance.[41] Another decision of the Virginia Supreme Court overturned the refusal of the SCC to grant a request for a branch bank.[42] Other than a case involving the interpretation of the statutory term *contiguous*,[43] the remaining reversals were primarily procedural. The commission was reversed for failing to hold full hearings on a telephone rate increase application[44] and for denying the request of a subsidiary, short line railroad to file a separate tax report.[45] It was also reversed for refusing to grant a continuance in VEPCO rate increase proceedings, as requested by Lt. Gov. Henry E. Howell, Jr., who, as an officer of the General Assembly, was entitled to the continuance under the Code of Virginia.[46]

The large number of reversals was attributable at least in part to the increased number of appeals. However, it is clear that the Virginia Supreme Court availed itself of the numerous oppor-

39 *Lillard* v. *Fairfax County Airport Authority*, 208 Va. 8, 13–14, 155 S.E. 2d 338, 342 (1967).

40 *Agricultural Services* v. *Commonwealth*, 210 Va. 506, 171 S.E. 2d 840 (1970).

41 *Norfolk and Western Railroad Co.* v. *Commonwealth*, 208 Va. 77, 155 S.E. 2d 315 (1967); *Howell* v. *Commonwealth*, 209 Va. 776, 167 S.E. 2d 322 (1969).

42 *Mutual Savings* v. *Commonwealth*, 212 Va. 557, 186 S.E. 2d 13 (1972).

43 *First Virginia Bank* v. *Commonwealth*, 212 Va. 654, 187 S.E. 2d 186 (1972).

44 *Fairfax County* v. *Chesapeake and Potomac Telephone Co.*, 212 Va. 57, 182 S.E. 2d 30 (1971); *Arlington County* v. *Chesapeake and Potomac Telephone Co.*, 212 Va. 64, 182 S.E. 2d 34 (1971).

45 *Southern Railway Co.* v. *Commonwealth*, 211 Va. 210, 176 S.E. 2d 578 (1970).

46 *Howell* v. *Catterall, Dillon, and Hooker*, 212 Va. 525, 186 S.E. 2d 28 (1972).

tunities for review by closely scrutinizing the operations of the SCC. Pure questions of law, such as jurisdiction and statutory interpretation, have long been the subject of appeals to the state Supreme Court. While these matters continue to be a source of reversals, the court's attention to procedural issues was primarily responsible for the rise in the reversal rate of the SCC decisions between June 1967 and June 1972.

## Industrial Commission of Virginia

The second largest number of appeals from state commissions to the Virginia Supreme Court emanates from the decisions of the Industrial Commission. The creation of an Industrial Commission for the commonwealth was authorized by the 1918 Virginia Workmen's Compensation Act. The purpose of the act was to substitute for the unsatisfactory and often unavailable common law remedies a speedier and more equitable form of relief for personal injuries sustained by workers. The Industrial Commission was charged with administering the provisions of the act, and hearing and determining cases arising from injury, death, or occupational diseases of workers.

The first two rulings of the commission to come before the court for review served to clarify the role of the state's high court. In one of the cases the Supreme Court held that it was without jurisdiction to hear appeals from the commission unless a constitutional issue was raised or unless there had been some attempt to exceed the jurisdiction conferred, which would justify the exercise of the court's original jurisdiction to issue a writ of prohibition.[47] A 1922 amendment by the legislature promptly vested the Supreme Court with the power to hear appeals from decisions of the Industrial Commission.[48] The legislature stipulated that cases so appealed to the Supreme Court from the commission were to be placed on the privileged docket of the court and heard at the next ensuing term, a requirement that continues today. The other of the first two rulings of the commission to be reviewed by the court was heard in accord with the certification alternative. (Until 1972 it

[47] *Richmond Cedar Works* v. *Harper*, 129 Va. 481, 106 S.E. 516 (1921).
[48] Va. Acts, 1922, ch. 425.

was possible for the commission to certify questions of law to the Supreme Court for its decision.) In reversing the commission's holding that a policeman was an employee as defined by the Workmen's Compensation Act, the court concluded that "if any such offices are to be included within the provisions of the statute, the amendment should be made by the legislature and not by the tribunals called upon to construe and enforce the law."[49]

In the first decade of review by the Supreme Court the major issue was the extent to which the court was bound by the statutory directive that the findings of fact made by the commission were conclusive and binding. After initially accepting the finality of administrative findings of fact, the court began to qualify its position.[50] "To adopt this contention literally," acknowledged the court in 1925, "would mean that there could never be an appeal from an award made by the Commission." Not only must there be an absence of fraud, prejudice, and bias on the part of the commissioners, but the court "will not accept as finding of fact by the Commission that which it judicially knows is not a fact." The court must be satisfied that the evidence is credible, and that it is properly interpreted and applied to the circumstances. While these qualifications are important for defining the role of the court, they do not remove primary responsibility for findings of fact from the commission.

The court has tended to affirm about two-thirds of the decisions appealed from the Industrial Commission. From 1921 to 1941, the court heard eighty direct appeals, of which fifty-three were affirmed and twenty-seven reversed.[51] A majority of the reversals were in favor of the claimant. Furthermore, with few exceptions the decisions of the court have directed the Industrial Commission toward a liberal interpretation of the Workmen's Compensation Act: "The workmen's compensation act . . . , although in derogation of the common law, is highly remedial, and should be liberally construed in favor of the workman."[52] One observer of practice before the commission, writing in 1942, found the court's stance "hard to believe, especially for one who did not expect to

[49] *Mann* v. *Lynchburg*, 129 Va. 453, 465, 106 S.E. 371, 375 (1921).

[50] For citations and discussion of relevant cases, see James Ernest Pate, "Practice before the Industrial Commission," *Virginia Law Review* 29 (1942):372–74.

[51] Ibid., p. 375, n. 72.

[52] *Gobble* v. *Clinch Valley Lumber Co.*, 141 Va. 303, 127 S.E. 175 (1925).

find a common law court interpreting a statute expressing a broad, humane, social policy in a more liberal way than the administrative agency established to enforce it."[53]

An examination of commission decisions reviewed by the state Supreme Court from October 1961 through September 1972 suggests only a slight modification of the earlier trend. Of the twenty-four cases heard by the high court, fourteen were affirmed and ten were reversed. These statistics represent a modest increase in the percentage of appeals in which decisions of the commission were reversed. Exactly half of the reversals operated to the advantage of the claimant. Three of the cases reversed, including two decided against the claimant, were concerned with one of the most troublesome questions faced in the administration of the Workmen's Compensation Act: Can the injury or disease in question be classified as one "arising out of and in the course of the employment . . . ?" Although the words of the statute have been liberally construed to carry out the humane and beneficent purpose of the act, the burden of proof is on the claimant. In the view of the court, "The words cannot be liberalized by judicial interpretation for the purpose of allowing compensation on every claim asserted."[54] The complexity of the issue is illustrated by a recent Virginia Supreme Court decision construing the scope of employment to include the voluntary errand of an employee for his employer. "To bar an employee from the protection of Workmen's Compensation benefits because he voluntarily acted in his employer's interest," argued the court, "would be to discourage constructive initiative, which is not a desirable result."[55] An impartial observer, however, saw in the court's decision "implications for an unwarranted expansion of employer liability."[56] Other reversals by the court suggest a continuation of its liberal interpretation of the Workmen's Compensation Act. In *Barker* v. *Appalachian Power Co.*,[57] the court liberally construed the act to allow the claimant the fullest possible recovery. Two additional reversals favored the worker in the application of the statutory requirement

[53] Pate, p. 375.

[54] *Conner* v. *Bragg*, 203 Va. 204, 208, 123 S.E. 2d 393, 396 (1962).

[55] *Lucas* v. *Lucas*, 212 Va. 561, 564, 186 S.E. 2d 63, 65 (1972).

[56] "Workmen's Compensation, Annual Survey of Virginia Law," *Virginia Law Review* 58 (1972):1378.

[57] 209 Va. 162, 163 S.E. 2d 311 (1968).

that notice of the accident be given to the employer within thirty days by the employee or his representative.[58]

## State Milk Commission

The State Milk Commission was organized in May 1934 after the passage of the Milk Control Act earlier that year. The legislation empowered the commission to regulate Virginia's milk industry. Six months after its formation the commission was out of business, at least temporarily, as the result of a four-to-two vote of the Virginia justices invalidating the state statute. In April 1935, almost one year after the organization of the Milk Commission, it was once again regulating the milk business in the commonwealth, because the state Supreme Court, after granting a rehearing of the case, reversed itself.[59] By a vote of four to three the justices decided the Milk Control Act was constitutional after all. The unusual reversal of the court over such a short period can be explained primarily in terms of a change in personnel. Justice John Eggleston held for the validity of the act, whereas the jurist whom he had succeeded, Louis S. Epes, had held against it in the original hearing. Justice George L. Browning, who had not sat on the case when it was first heard, also voted in the rehearing to sustain the constitutionality of the statute. The three justices whose earlier views were rejected in the rehearing used their original opinion in disagreeing with the new majority.

As a background to the struggle was the fact that shortly before the Virginia Milk Commission was organized, the United States Supreme Court, in the celebrated case of *Nebbia* v. *New York* (1934), had upheld by a five-to-four vote the establishment of a similar regulatory body in New York. Since *Nebbia* controlled the constitutionality of such regulation under the Federal Constitution, the issue before the Virginia court was whether the milk control statute contravened the state constitution. Due to the divided nature of the decision by the United States Supreme Court, the dissenting Virginia justices discounted the effect of that

58 *Lucas* v. *Research Analysis Corporation*, 209 Va. 583, 166 S.E. 2d 294 (1969); *Dowdy* v. *Giant of Virginia*, 210 Va. 408, 171 S.E. 2d 254 (1969).

59 *Reynolds* v. *Milk Commission*, 163 Va. 957, 179 S.E. 507 (1935).

decision, saying that "its persuasive influence by virtue of its judgment alone is not strong." The distaste of the dissenters for this regulatory legislation could not be concealed:

> Courts should not travel beyond the record, but they should not affect to be ignorant where the matter is one of common knowledge. We know that producers have participated in organized blockades of centers of consumption, and in the prosecution of their purpose milk trucks have been overturned and their contents wasted. It has not been suggested that this was done to protect the health or morals of the city. Plainly it was an economic struggle. This struggle, happily divested of lawlessness in Virginia, is voiced in the act in judgment. What the legislature undertook was to make the dairy business profitable, and this it sought to accomplish by fixing the price of its products.[60]

The new majority on the Virginia court were of the opinion that the challenged provisions of the Federal Constitution and the state constitution were so similar that if the statute did not violate one, it would not violate the other. The majority opinion also argued that the General Assembly "is better qualified than the court to determine the necessity, character and degree of regulation of an industry, which new and perplexing conditions may require."[61]

Over ten years later the justices of the Virginia Supreme Court were still divided in their attitudes toward the Milk Commission. Following an investigation of the milk market in Suffolk, the commission refused to issue a producer-distributor license to an applicant on the ground that there was already an adequate supply of pure wholesome milk for distribution in the area. In an appeal of this ruling, the Milk Commission took the position that the Supreme Court was bound by the commission's findings of fact. The court rejected this reasoning when it pointed out that "the evidence must sustain the decision which, in turn, must not be arbitrary or capricious." The court further found that "any presumption of the correctness of the findings is much weakened when the arbiter, as in this case, is a party to the controversy. It [the commission] would be less than human if it were not interested in up-

[60] 163 Va. 980, 989, 179 S.E. 516, 519.
[61] 163 Va. 967, 179 S.E. 510.

holding its own action."[62] By a five-to-two vote, the court reversed the ruling and remanded the case with directions that the license be issued.

In a 1944 decision the court had also ruled against the Milk Commission. The court found the commission to have exceeded its statutory power by fixing price differentials for the same grade of milk based on the type of container in which it was sold. Justice Browning, one of the four justices who had voted in 1935 to sustain the validity of the Milk Control Act, filed a strongly dissenting opinion in which he suggested that the decision crippled the authority of the Milk Commission by "judicial fiat": "I cannot escape the conviction that the majority opinion is a grave blow to the usefulness of the Milk Commission. It is a constricted interpretation of a statute that is based upon humane principles designed to promote and conserve the public well-being. It sterilizes a legislative effort which was conceived in a desire to thwart a growing economic evil. I fear that it is about to go the way that many critics of liberal government wish all bureaus and boards and commissions to go."[63]

A series of decisions in the 1950s interpreting the statutory power of the commission did not confirm Justice Browning's worst fears, although some of the decisions did limit the discretion of the commission. The power of the commission to fix prices was construed to mean that it must fix both maximum and minimum prices, not minimum prices alone.[64] The commission was also denied the power to fix the price paid to Virginia producers for milk sold and processed in Virginia for distribution outside the state.[65] Nevertheless, by 1957 a study of state milk regulation in the Southeast concluded that "the Virginia courts have not been unduly restrictive in interpreting the authority vested in the regulatory agency by the lawmakers."[66]

62 *Roundtree* v. *State Milk Commission,* 184 Va. 777, 787, 36 S.E. 2d 613, 617 (1946).

63 *Lucerne Cream and Butter Co.* v. *Milk Commission,* 182 Va. 490, 511, 29 S.E. 2d 397, 406 (1944).

64 *Safeway Stores* v. *Milk Commission,* 197 Va. 69, 87 S.E. 2d 769 (1955).

65 *Pet Dairy Products* v. *State Milk Commission,* 195 Va. 396, 78 S.E. 2d 645 (1953).

66 Clyde C. Carter, "State Regulation of Milk in the Southeast," *Southern Economic Journal* 24 (July 1957):69.

Only four decisions of the State Milk Commission were appealed to the Supreme Court from 1959 through June 1973; during the last eight years of that period no rulings were reviewed. All four of the decisions appealed concerned the issuance of a license, and the ruling of the commission was reversed in each instance. In one case the court held that no license was necessary, and in the other three it reversed the commission's ruling and indicated that the license was to be issued.[67] Rising milk prices and consumer criticism led the 1973 General Assembly to create a study commission to review the State Milk Commission. As a result of the study, the number of consumer representatives was increased from two to four and a processor-distributor member was provided for. The power of the Milk Commission to establish minimum retail prices was also restricted. Furthermore, the 1974 legislature continued the Milk Commission Study Commission so that the members could observe the effects of their recommendations and make additional recommendations if necessary.[68]

## Relations among Political Subdivisions

Although conflicts between Virginia political subdivisions come to the state Supreme Court in a variety of forms, disputes arising out of annexation proceedings are the ones that reach the court most frequently. Prior to the 1902 Constitution the legislature was responsible for altering municipal boundaries. Then, in 1904 the General Assembly declared that annexation should be a judicial function. The Virginia Supreme Court upheld the constitutionality of the 1904 statute[69] and, ever since, has played an important role in annexation.

The Supreme Court has consistently presumed the correctness of the annexation court, whose size and composition have under-

[67] *Richmond Food Stores* v. *Milk Commission,* 204 Va. 46, 129 S.E. 2d 35 (1963); *Roller et al.* v. *Milk Commission,* 204 Va. 536, 132 S.E. 2d 427 (1963); *Brown* v. *Milk Commission,* 205 Va. 18, 135 S.E. 2d 98 (1964); *Clover Creamery* v. *Milk Commission,* 205 Va. 763, 139 S.E. 2d 922 (1965).

[68] Va. Acts, 1974, ch. 467; Va. Acts, 1974, Senate Joint Resolution no. 19, p. 1514.

[69] *Henrico County* v. *Richmond,* 106 Va. 282, 55 S.E. 683 (1906); see also William L. Martin and J.E. Buchholtz, "Annexation–Virginia's Dilemma," *Washington and Lee Law Review* 24 (1967):243–44.

gone several changes since 1904,[70] on all questions of fact and will not disturb an annexation decision unless it is plainly wrong or is without credible evidence to support it.[71] Rulings on points of law have generally been the subject of annexation cases before the Supreme Court. On occasion the state Supreme Court will hand down a final order in an annexation proceeding. As Chester Bain points out, the section of the statute stipulating the order to be entered by the Supreme Court in annexation cases has remained substantially unchanged since 1904: "If the judgment of the circuit court be reversed on appeal, or if the judgment be modified, the Supreme Court of Appeals shall enter such order as the circuit court should have entered and such order shall be final."[72]

Many of the annexation cases presented to the Supreme Court for review involve points of disagreement about the institution of the proceedings, the pretrial conference, hearing preliminaries, and posttrial considerations. The decisions of the Supreme Court on the points of law incident to an annexation trial are helpful in clarifying the proper procedures for future annexation proceedings. For example, in one case the faulty newspaper publication of a map and aerial photograph of the area proposed for annexation by a city was held not to be ground for dismissal of the city's suit.[73] The Supreme Court was satisfied that republication of the material could cure this technical defect. On the other hand, the failure of a published map to designate the existing uses of land proposed for annexation, as required by statute, properly resulted in a dismissal of the proceeding. According to the Supreme Court, "The defect is not a procedural defect in the notice, pleadings, or trial. It is a defect in the annexation ordinance itself, that is, in the legislative act of the city council."[74]

The statutory standard for the annexation courts has been the "necessity for and expediency of annexation, considering the best interests of the county and the city or town, the best interests,

[70] Chester Bain, *Annexation in Virginia: The Use of the Judicial Process for Readjusting City-County Boundaries* (Charlottesville: Published for the Institute of Government, University of Virginia, by the University Press of Virginia, 1966), pp. 66–72.

[71] *Henrico* v. *City of Richmond*, 177 Va. 754, 15 S.E. 2d 309 (1941).

[72] Va. Code, sec. 15.1-1050 (1973 repl. vol.); Bain, pp. 204–5.

[73] *Portsmouth* v. *Norfolk County*, 198 Va. 247, 93 S.E. 2d 296 (1956).

[74] *Martinsville* v. *Henry County*, 204 Va. 757, 761–62, 133 S.E. 2d 287, 290 (1963).

services to be rendered and needs of the area proposed to be annexed, and the best interests of the remaining portion of the county."[75] This standard, obviously, vests broad discretion in the annexation courts. Whereas the proper procedures in annexation proceedings can become relatively standardized through Supreme Court decisions, exact formulas for determining what factors should justify the expansion of a city's boundaries are impossible. The courts must decide not only which factors are relevant to their decision but also which factors should be given additional weight.

The Virginia Supreme Court has conceded that annexation courts "exercise, to a degree, legislative as well as judicial functions."[76] It has further acknowledged that no single factor controls in determining the necessity for and expediency of annexation.[77] As a result, annexation courts must exercise value judgments as to what evidence is relevant to a determination of the best interests of all parties involved. A policy decision must be made by the courts on the basis of local factors such as population density, growth rates, governmental service performance, existing community of interest, and financial impact.

If the mass of evidence is conflicting, the Supreme Court normally defers to the firsthand judgment of the annexation court, which is often strengthened by the lower court judges' inspection of the area proposed for annexation. "The annexation court judges visited and studied the areas affected. They saw the physical properties under the control of the city and had an opportunity to observe and study the services rendered by the municipality. They observed and studied the services that were being rendered by the county and the needs of the area sought to be annexed."[78]

Notwithstanding this presumption of correctness for decisions of annexation courts, the Supreme Court must also make certain policy determinations in reviewing the application of annexation standards to specific cases. In the 1959 case of *Rockingham* v. *Town of Timberville*, the court was faced with the necessity and

[75] Va. Code, sec. 15.1–1041 (1973 repl. vol.).

[76] *Falls Church* v. *Fairfax County*, 193 Va. 112, 115, 68 S.E. 2d 96, 98 (1951).

[77] *County of Fairfax* v. *Town of Fairfax*, 201 Va. 362, 368, 111 S.E. 2d 428, 433 (1959).

[78] *Johnston* v. *County of Fairfax*, 211 Va. 378, 384, 177 S.E. 2d 606, 610 (1970); see also *Chesterfield County* v. *Berberich*, 199 Va. 500, 100 S.E. 2d 781 (1957).

expediency of the annexation granted by the lower court. The annexation of territory four times the size of the town and with a population more than double that of the town was not justified by the evidence, in the opinion of the high court. The population of the town had not grown in nearly fifty years other than through annexation, and the services that could be provided by the town already existed in more adequate form in the territory sought. "The only material benefit that would accrue to any of the parties," according to the court, "would be additional taxes made available to the town." The judgment of the annexation court was reversed because it must not "consider only the preservation of the town, but must also consider the best interests of the area sought to be annexed."[79]

In other cases the Supreme Court has modified the decision of an annexation court and has included territory that had been excluded in the lower court's final order. The exclusion of part of the property of a railroad company was rectified on the basis of evidence demonstrating not only the railroad company's need for compact territory but also the need for public municipal industrial development.[80] A largely undeveloped subdivision was added to an annexation order on the ground that the evidence showed the area was closest to the heart of the city and, according to all city experts testifying, should have been included.[81]

Financial issues not related to annexation constitute the second largest category of conflicts between Virginia political subdivisions reaching the Supreme Court. In *Town of Ashland* v. *Board of Supervisors for Hanover County*[82] the county challenged the authority of the town to impose an automobile license tax separate from a similar county ordinance. The League of Virginia Municipalities filed a brief amicus curiae on behalf of Ashland, and the League of Virginia Counties supported Hanover's arguments. The high court's decision in favor of Ashland upheld the General Assembly's power to classify a town within a county as a separate taxing district for the purpose of levying license taxes on motor vehicles owned by the town's residents. Although revenue raised

[79] 201 Va. 303, 309–10, 110 S.E. 2d 390, 395 (1959).

[80] *Town of Narrows* v. *Giles County*, 184 Va. 628, 35 S.E. 2d 808 (1945).

[81] *County of York* v. *Williamsburg*, 204 Va. 732, 740, 133 S.E. 2d 520, 525 (1963).

[82] 202 Va. 409, 117 S.E. 2d 679 (1961).

by the county ordinance was used partly for the benefit of the town's residents, the court noted that town services such as street maintenance and fire protection would also benefit residents outside of the town.

Contract disputes between political subdivisions are sometimes not resolved before the state Supreme Court has handed down its ruling. When the city of Roanoke succeeded to the property rights and franchise of a public service corporation that had been furnishing water to the town of Vinton, the city maintained that it was not bound to continue furnishing water at the stated rate.[83] The court held the contract as not perpetual but terminable by either party. The higher rate charged by the city for its services was sustained, and the town was ordered to pay the rate retroactive to its initial effective date.

Financial obligations of a city to a county arising out of the former's transition from town to city status have been the subject of several cases before the state Supreme Court. In *Colonial Heights* v. *Chesterfield*,[84] the court acknowledged the impossibility of prescribing a fixed formula of debt adjustment in every case. In asserting that the city must be credited with that same proportion of the county assets as it must assume of the county debt, the court upheld the city's claim to the county elementary school within its limits. But a 1956 case afforded the court an opportunity to assert that before a city may take title to county school property within its new boundaries, proper compensation must be made to the county.[85] In a sequel to this case, the court was confronted with determining the proper amount that the city must pay to the county.[86] The lower court decision was modified to provide that the amount of compensation due by the city to the county should be based on property valuation as of the date of transition rather than the present date.

[83] *Town of Vinton* v. *City of Roanoke*, 195 Va. 881, 80 S.E. 2d 608 (1954).
[84] 196 Va. 155, 82 S.E. 2d 566 (1954).
[85] *Alleghany County* v. *City of Covington*, 197 Va. 845, 91 S.E. 2d 654 (1956).
[86] *City of Covington* v. *Alleghany County*, 200 Va. 587, 106 S.E. 2d 655 (1959).

# VII *The Court in Political Perspective*

THE Virginia Supreme Court occupies a position of low visibility within the state's political system. The selection of its personnel, changes in its operation, and announcement of its decisions are accompanied by minimal interest and news coverage when compared with the activities of other branches of government, or even those of the State Corporation Commission, sometimes referred to as the fourth branch of Virginia government. The names of the court's members and the contents of its opinions are by and large unknown to the general public. Nevertheless, the attentive public, including the bar, certain categories of litigants, and key state officials, are appreciative of the court's multifunctional role within the political system.

As an actor in the political system, the court fulfills a variety of functions and is subject to the political, economic, and social influences of its environment. The interaction of the court with the executive and legislative branches has been extensive and pervasive. Indeed, the role of the court can be understood only in the context of these manifold political relationships. Characteristically, the Supreme Court has been the more passive actor. The influence of the legislative and the executive branches, through selection of the court's members, consideration of its financial and organizational matters, and reaction to its policy decisions, has been continuous and enduring.

## Output and Impact

Historically, much of the authority and structure of the Virginia Supreme Court as a political institution evolved as a result of power struggles among political individuals and institutions. Although the origins of the court are found in the powerful General Court of the colonial era, the full potential of the highest judicial tribunal within Virginia became apparent only with the formation of the state Supreme Court, under the 1776 Constitution. Composed of some of the most eminent citizens of the commonwealth, the court developed into a separate and integral part of the state's political system. The court quickly established itself as a coordinate branch of Virginia government by asserting and defending its independent status and the power of judicial review. While the court earned a reputation of caution and restraint in dealing with the other governmental agencies—a reputation that continues even today—it left no doubt that it was a politicolegal institution to be dealt with in its own right.

Chief Justice Edward Hudgins, the presiding justice of the Virginia Supreme Court for eleven years, described its members as the "peaceful arbiters of disputes which have arisen between man and man, and man and the state."[1] The court has also been described as the final arbiter on questions of state law and the state constitution. The image of the court as an objective and rational body makes it appealing as a forum for settling disputes; but by the nature of the political system, it is only one such forum. In commenting on the political functions of state supreme courts, Kenneth N. Vines remarked: "Supreme Court decisions often occur at or near the end of the political process. . . . Thus a Court decision may end a long and troublesome argument that has developed in the political system or may point the way to a settlement of a serious grievance."[2]

In the area of public law the latter function is clearly the one most often performed by the Virginia Supreme Court. The court has pointed the way to the resolution of issues by defining the constitutional boundaries of the legislative and executive branches. As the final interpreter of the state constitution, it has articulated the rules of the game. But rarely has the court thwarted legislative policy. The conventional test suit has been utilized to clarify alternative methods of reaching certain ends, and not as a forum for finally resolving public policy issues. Decisions in these test cases take on the character of advisory opinions. Appropriate action can then be taken by the legislature in accordance with the opinion of

[1] *Richmond Times-Dispatch*, Dec. 7, 1958.

[2] Vines, "Political Functions of a State Supreme Court," *Tulane Studies in Political Science* 8 (1962):56.

the Supreme Court. By the same measure, statutes pronounced overly broad or vague can be rewritten to eliminate the cause of the judicial objection without abandoning the original goal of the legislation.

Perhaps the most politically significant role of the state Supreme Court is to confer legitimacy on the public policy decisions of other government agencies. It has for the most part not been an initiator or nullifier of public policy. The public policies of the dominant political alliance have generally been strengthened by the formal support of the state's highest judicial tribunal.[3] Margaret V. Nelson concluded her study of judicial review in Virginia with a similar observation: "The Courts tended to follow public opinion on vital issues. Rarely did they set the pace, as, indeed they could hardly be expected to do. But rarely, too did the courts retard it; and that is a healthy sign in a democracy."[4] The court has not ventured far from public opinion—if public opinion is defined in terms of a majority vote of the legislature—in its decisions. In a few cases during the 1930s and 1940s, the court expressed its dissatisfaction with certain pieces of regulatory legislation passed by the Virginia General Assembly, but it generally upheld the prerogatives of the legislature, thus adding its weight of approval to the changes in public policy.

On occasion the court, far from retarding progress, has actually prodded public opinion. The Virginia court's general acceptance of pronouncements by the nation's high court has propelled it, although reluctantly, into a position of leadership with respect to state policy. As already demonstrated in Chapter IV, a few race relations cases, primarily in the early 1960s, afforded the court an opportunity to carry out this function. On the other hand, the court's opposition to decisions of the nation's highest court has at various times complemented the general temper of state politics.

[3] Notwithstanding the popular image of the United States Supreme Court, a similar argument has been made with respect to that tribunal by Robert Dahl, "Decision-Making in a Democracy: The Supreme Court as a National Policy-Maker," *Journal of Public Law* 6 (1958):279–95; an updated version of this article appears under the title "The Supreme Court's Role in National Policy-making," in Thomas P. Jahnige and Sheldon Goldman, eds., *The Federal Judicial System: Readings in Process and Behavior* (New York: Holt, Rinehart and Winston, Inc., 1968), pp. 358–63.

[4] Nelson, *A Study of Judicial Review in Virginia, 1789–1928* (New York: Columbia University Press, 1947), p. 222.

The dual role of the court as both enforcer and resister of United States Supreme Court opinions was illustrated in the 1959 school desegregation case, *Harrison* v. *Day*.[5] The court invalidated Virginia's massive resistance legislation on the basis of the Virginia Constitution while simultaneously expressing disapproval of the initiation of race relations policy by the United States Supreme Court. It is partly because of this dual role, manifest in the court's handling of race relations cases, that the success of the NAACP in particular and blacks in general in certain key cases did not encourage that group to increase the volume of its litigation before the court.

The court has performed a supervisory role for the state regulatory commissions by reviewing their decisions and interpreting their statutory powers. After initially sustaining the legislation empowering these commissions, the court has proceeded to review the regulatory bodies. It has provided an important check on the powerful State Corporation Commission and has directed the Industrial Commission of Virginia toward a liberal interpretation of the significant workmen's compensation statutes. Decisions of the annexation courts have likewise been subjected to scrutiny. By and large the court has legitimized the decisions of these bodies, thereby intensifying their impact on the political scene. The area of relations among political subdivisions has also presented the court with occasional opportunities to end certain disputes as it mediates the legal battles between cities and counties. Moreover, the court's initiation of a liberal construction of tax exemptions had a profound impact on the local fiscal structure. As in the past, however, recourse for this court policy was found in the insertion of constitutional language requiring a strict construction of exempt property.

## Virginia's Political Culture

The political culture of Virginia has been fundamentally conservative throughout the twentieth century. Although political change is prevalent in Virginia at this time, many of the political values, traditions, and styles of the past remain. It is the contention of this study that the Supreme Court, like other Virginia agencies, is both

[5] 200 Va. 439, 106 S.E. 2d 636 (1959).

product and creator of the state's political culture, past and present. At times the impact of partisan politics has been direct and all-encompassing, as was the case with Spencer Roane and during the Readjuster era. While it is true that partisan identification with the dominant Democratic organization has been decisive in the selection of twentieth-century justices, the personnel of the court have been consumed by Virginia's political culture in a much more fundamental way. The organization leaders have been characterized as "a group of like-minded men"; their style has been described as "that of the soft-spoken, calm, reserved, reasonable, attractive, and patrician-looking conservative lawyer or businessman."[6] Consensus rather than dissent has marked the actions of Virginia's political elite. Once a decision has been made, public disagreement is frowned upon. What is revealing about this portrait of the organization's leaders and their style of operation is that the same can be said of the state Supreme Court and its members. Granted the legal subculture influences judicial codes of behavior and operation, but the impact of the political culture cannot be discounted. Virginia justices have acted in a manner in which the small but politically sophisticated electorate expected their political leaders to behave. The habit of consensus allowed the justices, just as it had the Democratic organization, to present a forceful face to the rest of its political environment.

During the dominance of the politically conservative Byrd organization the selection process was stabilized. Appointments by organization governors were readily elected by the General Assembly. As a result of this harmonious procedure, the characteristics and behavior patterns of the justices were strikingly similar. With Virginia in the throes of political change, however, it might be expected that the selection process will become less predictable. The tremendous growth in the size of Virginia's electorate has been paralleled by the impressive successes of the Republican party and marked increases in black and urban voting. With the opening up of the electoral process to a great diversity of participants, it is safe to assume that groups not yet represented on the court will be considered. The appointment of Justice Poff in 1972 marked the

[6] Ralph Eisenberg, "Virginia: The Emergence of Two-Party Politics," in *The Changing Politics of the South*, ed. William C. Havard (Baton Rouge: Louisiana State University Press, 1972), pp. 44, 46.

opening of the court to Republicans for the first time in this century. Traditional patterns as to sex, race, religion, and national origin may also be occasionally violated in the future given the changing political complexion of the state.

Other recent breakthroughs in the selection process are likely to be continued. A factor mitigating against continuation of the twentieth-century trend to select justices from among persons with exclusively legal-judicial backgrounds is the demand initiated by the Virginia Bar Association for a balance between members of the bench and members of the bar. As evidenced by the composition of the present court, the effect of this demand will probably mean the selection of more persons who have held only legislative or executive elective positions. In the history of the court the selection of persons who have held no public office has been a rare occurrence.

It is difficult to predict what impact a changing political culture will have on the output and roles of the state Supreme Court. Many of the political changes in Virginia are irreversible, but it remains to be seen what form and style the new Virginia politics will take. As long as the political transition within the state is gradual, the court can be expected to accommodate itself to political realignment. The inclusion of new groups in Virginia politics will probably result in a more diverse membership for the court. Only a rapid or drastic shift of political power would challenge the place of the court in the Virginia political system. By its very nature as a judicial institution and as a result of the lengthy tenure of its members, the court is slow to change. Nevertheless, action to relieve the court's docket, either from within or by the legislature, might accelerate changes in the operation of the court. As a creature of its political environment, the court, in terms of its membership as well as its organization and policy, is subject to changing political realities.

Appendixes
Selected Bibliography
Index

Appendix A

# Justices of the Virginia Supreme Court, 1779-1974

Edmund Pendleton, 1779–1803
George Wythe,[a] 1779–1788
Robert Carter Nicholas,[a] 1779–1780
John Blair, 1779–1789
Paul Carrington, 1779–1807
Peter Lyons, 1779–1809
Bartholomew Dandridge,[a] 1779–1785
Benjamin Waller,[a] 1779–1785
William Roscoe Wilson Curle,[a] 1779
Richard Cary,[a] 1779–1788
James Henry,[a] 1779–1788
William Fleming, 1780–1824
James Mercer, 1781–1788, 1789–1793
Henry Tazewell, 1785–1788, 1793–1794
John Tyler,[a] 1785–1788
Richard Parker,[a] 1788
St. George Tucker, 1788, 1804–1811
Spencer Roane, 1795–1822
Francis Taliaferro Brooke, 1811–1851
James Pleasants, 1811 (Jan.–Feb.)
William H. Cabell, 1811–1852
John Coalter, 1811–1831
John Williams Green, 1822–1834
Dabney Carr, 1824–1837
Henry St. George Tucker, 1831–1841
William Brockenbrough, 1834–1838
Richard Elliott Parker, 1837–1840
Robert Stanard, 1839–1846
John James Allen, 1840–1865
Briscoe Gerard Baldwin, 1842–1852
William Daniel, 1846–1865

[a] Member of the first Supreme Court only by virtue of having served on the High Court of Chancery, Court of Admiralty, or General Court at some time between 1779 and 1788.

Richard Cassius Lee Moncure, 1851–1865, 1866–1882
Green Berry Samuels, 1852–1861
George Hay Lee, 1852–1861
William Joseph Robertson, 1859–1865
William T. Joynes, 1866–1869, 1870–1872
Lucas P. Thompson, 1866
Alexander Rives, 1866–1869
Joseph Christian, 1870–1882
Waller R. Staples, 1870–1882
Francis Thomas Anderson, 1870–1882
Wood Bouldin, 1872–1876
Edward Calohill Burks, 1876–1882
Lunsford Lomax Lewis, 1883–1894
Benjamin Watkins Lacy, 1883–1894
Thomas R. Fauntleroy, 1883–1894
Robert A. Richardson, 1883–1894
Drury A. Hinton, 1883–1894
John William Ricly, 1895–1900
Richard Henry Cardwell, 1895–1916
James Keith, 1895–1916
John Alexander Buchanan, 1895–1915
George Moffett Harrison, 1895–1917
Archer Allen Phlegar, 1900–1901
Stafford Gorman Whittle, 1901–1919
Joseph Luther Kelly, 1915–1924, 1925
Frederick Wilmer Sims, 1916–1925
Robert Riddick Prentis, 1916–1931
Martin Parks Burks, 1917–1928
Edward Watts Saunders, 1920–1921
Jesse Felix West, 1922–1929
Preston White Campbell, 1924–1946
Richard Henry Lee Chichester, 1925–1930
Henry Winston Holt, 1928–1947
Louis Spencer Epes, 1929–1935
Edward Wren Hudgins, 1930–1958
Herbert Bailey Gregory, 1930–1951
George Landon Browning, 1930–1947
Joseph William Chinn, 1931–1936
John William Eggleston, 1935–1969
Claude Vernon Spratley, 1936–1967
Archibald Chapman Buchanan, 1946–1969
Abram Penn Staples, 1947–1951
Willis Dance Miller, 1947–1960

Lemuel Franklin Smith, 1951–1956
Kennon Caithness Whittle, 1951–1965
Harold Fleming Snead, 1957–1974
Lawrence Warren I'Anson, 1958–
Harry Lee Carrico, 1961–
Thomas Christian Gordon, Jr., 1965–1972
Albertis Sydney Harrison, Jr., 1967–
Alexander Marrs Harman, Jr., 1969–
George Moffett Cochran, 1969–
Richard Harding Poff, 1972–
Ashbury Christian Compton, 1974–

# Appendix B

## Succession of Justices of the Virginia Supreme Court, 1789–1974

*The membership of the court has been set at seven since two seats were filled in 1930 in accordance with a 1928 amendment to the 1902 Constitution. Prior to that time the court had generally consisted of five members, although the number was as low as three on two occasions (1809–11, 1866–69). The membership can be increased to as many as twelve under the authority of article VI, section 2 of the 1971 Constitution.*

| | | | | | |
|---|---|---|---|---|---|
| 1789 | Pendleton | Blair | Lyons | Carrington | Fleming |
| 1789–1793 | Pendleton | Mercer | Lyons | Carrington | Fleming |
| 1793–1794 | Pendleton | Tazewell | Lyons | Carrington | Fleming |
| 1795–1803 | Pendleton | Roane | Lyons | Carrington | Fleming |
| 1804–1806 | S. Tucker | Roane | Lyons | Carrington | Fleming |
| 1807–1809 | S. Tucker | Roane | Lyons | — | Fleming |
| 1809–1811 | S. Tucker | Roane | — | — | Fleming |
| 1811–1822 | Coalter | Roane | Brooke | Cabell[a] | Fleming |
| 1822–1824 | Coalter | Green | Brooke | Cabell | Fleming |
| 1824–1831 | Coalter | Green | Brooke | Cabell | Carr |
| 1831–1834 | H. Tucker | Green | Brooke | Cabell | Carr |
| 1834–1837 | H. Tucker | Brockenbrough | Brooke | Cabell | Carr |
| 1837–1838 | H. Tucker | Brockenbrough | Brooke | Cabell | Parker |
| 1839–1840 | H. Tucker | Stanard | Brooke | Cabell | Parker |
| 1840–1841 | H. Tucker | Stanard | Brooke | Cabell | Allen |
| 1842–1846 | Baldwin | Stanard | Brooke | Cabell | Allen |
| 1847–1851 | Baldwin | Daniel | Brooke | Cabell | Allen |
| 1851–1852 | Baldwin | Daniel | Moncure | Cabell | Allen |
| 1852–1859 | Samuels | Daniel | Moncure | Lee | Allen |
| 1859–1861 | Robertson | Daniel | Moncure | Lee[b] | Allen |
| 1861–1866 | Robertson | Daniel | Moncure | — | Allen |
| 1866–1869[c] | Joynes | Rives[d] | Moncure | — | — |
| 1870–1872 | Joynes | Christian | Moncure | W. Staples | Anderson |
| 1872–1876 | Bouldin | Christian | Moncure | W. Staples | Anderson |
| 1876–1882 | E. Burks | Christian | Moncure | W. Staples | Anderson |
| 1882 | E. Burks | Christian | Lewis | W. Staples | Anderson |
| 1883–1894 | Hinton | Lacy | Lewis | Richardson | Fauntleroy |

| | | | | | | | |
|---|---|---|---|---|---|---|---|
| 1895–1900 | Riely | Cardwell | Keith | J. Buchanan | | | |
| 1900–1901 | Phlegar | Cardwell | Keith | J. Buchanan | G. Harrison | | |
| 1901–1915 | S. Whittle | Cardwell | Keith | J. Buchanan | G. Harrison | | |
| 1915–1916 | S. Whittle | Cardwell | Keith | Kelly | G. Harrison | | |
| 1916–1917 | S. Whittle | Prentis | Sims | Kelly | G. Harrison | | |
| 1917–1919 | S. Whittle | Prentis | Sims | Kelly | M. Burks | | |
| 1920–1921 | Saunders | Prentis | Sims | Kelly | M. Burks | | |
| 1922–1924 | West | Prentis | Sims | Kelly | M. Burks | | |
| 1924–1925 | West | Prentis | Sims | Campbell | M. Burks | | |
| 1925 | West | Prentis | Kelly[e] | Campbell | M. Burks | | |
| 1925–1928 | West | Prentis | Chichester | Campbell | M. Burks | | |
| 1928–1929 | West | Prentis | Chichester | Campbell | Holt | | |
| 1929–1930 | Epes | Prentis | Chichester | Campbell | Holt | | |
| 1930–1931 | Epes | Prentis | Browning | Campbell | Holt | Hudgins | Gregory |
| 1931–1935 | Epes | Chinn | Browning | Campbell | Holt | Hudgins | Gregory |
| 1935–1936 | Eggleston | Chinn | Browning | Campbell | Holt | Hudgins | Gregory |
| 1936–1946 | Eggleston | Spratley | Browning | Campbell | Holt | Hudgins | Gregory |
| 1946–1947 | Eggleston | Spratley | Browning | A. Buchanan | Holt | Hudgins | Gregory |
| 1947–1951 | Eggleston | Spratley | A. Staples | A. Buchanan | Miller | Hudgins | Gregory |
| 1951–1956 | Eggleston | Spratley | Smith | A. Buchanan | Miller | Hudgins | K. Whittle |
| 1957–1958 | Eggleston | Spratley | Snead | A. Buchanan | Miller | Hudgins | K. Whittle |
| 1958–1960 | Eggleston | Spratley | Snead | A. Buchanan | Miller | I'Anson | K. Whittle |
| 1961–1965 | Eggleston | Spratley | Snead | A. Buchanan | Carrico | I'Anson | K. Whittle |
| 1965–1967 | Eggleston | Spratley | Snead | A. Buchanan | Carrico | I'Anson | Gordon |
| 1967–1969 | Eggleston | A. Harrison | Snead | A. Buchanan | Carrico | I'Anson | Gordon |
| 1969–1972 | Cochran | A. Harrison | Snead | Harman | Carrico | I'Anson | Gordon |
| 1972–1974 | Cochran | A. Harrison | Snead | Harman | Carrico | I'Anson | Poff |
| 1974– | Cochran | A. Harrison | Compton | Harman | Carrico | I'Anson | Poff |

[a] James Pleasants resigned almost immediately and was replaced by Cabell.

[b] Lee did not sit on the court after the April term 1861 because his home was in West Virginia.

[c] Eight decisions of a special military Court of Appeals composed of Horace B. Burnham (president), O. M. Dorman, and W. Willoughby were reported in 60 Va. (19 Grattan) 545–669 (1869, 1870).

[d] Lucas P. Thompson died before taking his seat on the bench, and Rives was appointed to fill the vacancy.

[e] Kelly resigned from the court on Jan. 31, 1924, but was reappointed on Feb. 19, 1925; he served until his death, Apr. 14, 1925.

APPENDIX C

# Presidents and Chief Justices of the Virginia Supreme Court, 1779-1974

*A 1928 amendment to the 1902 Constitution provided that the justice longest in continuous service should be chief justice. Before that time, the presiding officer of the court had been designated as its president; however, for many years the practice had been to elect as president the member who had served for the longest period. Seniority continues to be the method of selecting the chief justice under the 1971 Constitution, although article VI, section 3 authorizes the General Assembly to alter the manner of selection.*

*Presidents*
Edmund Pendleton, 1779–1803
Peter Lyons, 1803–1809
William Fleming, 1809–1824
Francis Taliaferro Brooke, 1824–1831
Henry St. George Tucker, 1831–1841
William H. Cabell, 1842–1851
John James Allen, 1851–1865
Richard Cassius Lee Moncure, 1866–1882
Lunsford Lomax Lewis, 1882–1894
James Keith, 1895–1916
Richard Henry Cardwell, June, 1916–Nov., 1916
George Moffett Harrison, Nov., 1916–March, 1917
Stafford Gorman Whittle, 1917–1919
Joseph Luther Kelly, 1920–1924, March, 1925
Frederick Wilmer Sims, 1924–1925

*Chief Justices*
Robert Riddick Prentis, 1925–1931
Preston White Campbell, 1931–1946
Henry Winston Holt, 1946–1947
Edward Wren Hudgins, 1947–1958
John William Eggleston, 1958–1969
Harold Fleming Snead, 1969–1974
Lawrence Warren I'Anson, 1974–

Appendix D

# Official Reporters of the Virginia Supreme Court, 1820-1974

*Before 1820 the opinions of the justices were collected and printed by private individuals for their own personal profit. In a letter to the speaker of the House of Delegates, the justices complained that the task of publishing the opinions had not been "sufficiently attended to" as a venture in private enterprise. The General Assembly quickly complied with the justices' request for funds to employ an official reporter, and the first reporter was appointed by the court in 1820.*

Francis W. Gilmer, 1820–1821
Peyton Randolph, 1821–1828
Benjamin Watkins Leigh, 1829–1842
Conway Robinson, 1842–1844
Peachy R. Grattan, 1844–1880
James M. Matthews, 1880–1881
George W. Hansbrough, 1881–1894
Martin Parks Burks, 1895–1916
Thomas Johnson Michie, 1916–1937
Addinell Hewson Michie, 1937–1952
Charles Killian Woltz, 1953–1967
Charles Marshall Davison, Jr., 1967–

## Appendix E

# General Summary of Justices of the Virginia Supreme Court, 1789–1974

| | | Legislative-Administrative Experience | | | | Legal-Judicial Experience | | | |
|---|---|---|---|---|---|---|---|---|---|
| Name | Law education * = degree | House of Burgesses and/or Delegates | State Senate | Congress | Executive or regulatory[a] | General and Chancery courts | Courts of record | Courts not of record | Prose-cutor |
| Pendleton | John Robinson | X[b] | | | X | X | | | |
| Blair | Temple, London, Eng. | X | | | | X | | | |
| Carrington | Col. Clement Read | X | X[b] | | X | X | | | |
| Lyons | James Power (uncle) | | | | | X | | | |
| Fleming | — | X | | (Con'tl)X | | X | | | |
| Mercer | John Mercer (father) | X | | (Con'tl)X | X | X | | | |
| Tazewell | John Tazewell (uncle) | X | | | | X | | | |
| Roane | William and Mary (W & M) | X | X | | X | X | | | |
| S. Tucker | W & M | | | | | X | | | |
| Brooke | Robert Brooke (brother) | X | X[b] | | | X | | | X |
| Pleasants | William Fleming | X | | | | | | | |
| Cabell | S. Tucker | X | | | X | X | | | |
| Coalter | S. Tucker | | | | | X | | | X |
| Green | — | | X | | | X | | | |
| Carr | William Wirt | | | | | X | | | X |
| H. Tucker | S. Tucker (father) | X | X | X | | X | | | |
| Brockenbrough | — | X | | | | X | | | |
| Parker | Richard Parker (grandfather) | X | | X | | X | | | |
| Stanard | — | X | | | | | | | |
| Allen | James Allen (father) | | X | X | | | X | | |
| Baldwin | William Daniel | X | | | | | | | |
| Daniel | Univ. of Va. (UVa) | X | | | | | | | |
| Moncure | Private | X | | | | | | | X |
| Samuels | H. Tucker | | | X | | | X | | |
| Lee | H. Tucker | X | | | | X | | | X |
| Robertson | UVa* | | | | | | | | X |

| Name | Occupation at appt. or election | Initially apptd. or elected | Date of appt. or election | Age at appt. or election | Age at end of service | Died (D), retired (R), defeated (Def.), term expired (Exp.) | Length of service |
|---|---|---|---|---|---|---|---|
| Pendleton | Chancery Ct. judge | E | Dec. 24, 1788 | 67 | 82 | D | 14 yrs. 5 mos. |
| Blair | Chancery Ct. judge | E | Dec. 24, 1788 | 56 | 57 | R | 4 mos. |
| Carrington | Gen. Ct. judge | E | Dec. 24, 1788 | 55 | 73 | R | 17 yrs. 7 mos. |
| Lyons | Gen. Ct. judge | E | Dec. 24, 1788 | 54 | 75 | D | 20 yrs. 1 mo. |
| Fleming | Gen. Ct. judge | E | Dec. 24, 1788 | 52 | 87 | D | 34 yrs. 9 mos. |
| Mercer | Gen. Ct. judge | E | Nov. 18, 1789 | 53 | 57 | D | 3 yrs. 11 mos. |
| Tazewell | Gen. Ct. judge | E | Nov. 6, 1793 | 39 | 41 | R | 1 yr. |
| Roane | Gen. Ct. judge | E | Dec. 2, 1794 | 32 | 60 | D | 27 yrs. 5 mos. |
| S. Tucker | Gen. Ct. judge | E | Jan. 6, 1804 | 51 | 59 | R | 7 yrs. |
| Brooke | Gen. Ct. judge | E | Jan. 30, 1811 | 47 | 87 | D | 40 yrs. |
| Pleasants | clerk, House of Delegates | E | Jan. 30, 1811 | 41 | 41 | R | —[c] |
| Cabell | Gen. Ct. judge | A | Mar. 21, 1811 | 38 | 79 | Exp. | 41 yrs. |
| Coalter | Gen. Ct. judge | A | May 11, 1811 | 39 | 59 | R | 19 yrs. 10 mos. |
| Green | dist. chancellor | E | Oct. 4, 1822 | 40 | 52 | D | 11 yrs. 5 mos. |
| Carr | dist. chancellor | E | Feb. 24, 1824 | 50 | 63 | D | 12 yrs. |
| H. Tucker | dist. chancellor | E | Apr. 11, 1831 | 50 | 60 | R | 10 yrs. 4 mos. |
| Brockenbrough | Gen. Ct. judge | E | Feb. 20, 1834 | 55 | 60 | D | 4 yrs. 11 mos. |
| Parker | U.S. senator | E | Feb. 9, 1837 | 53 | 56 | D | 3 yrs. 7 mos. |
| Stanard | attorney | E | Jan. 19, 1839 | 57 | 64 | D | 6 yrs. 5 mos. |
| Allen | circuit judge | E | Dec. 12, 1840 | 43 | 67 | Exp. | 23 yrs. 5 mos. |
| Baldwin | state delegate | E | Jan. 28, 1842 | 53 | 63 | D | 10 yrs. 5 mos. |
| Daniel | attorney | E | Dec. 15, 1846 | 40 | 58 | Exp. | 19 yrs. 3 mos. |
| Moncure | state Const. Conv. delegate | E | Mar. 13, 1851 | 46 | 77 | D | 30 yrs. 5 mos. |
| Samuels | circuit judge | E[d] | May 27, 1852 | 46 | 52 | D | 6 yrs. 6 mos. |
| Lee | Gen. Ct. judge | E[d] | May 27, 1852 | 44 | 53 | R | 9 yrs. |
| Robertson | prosecutor | E[d] | May 1859 | 41 | 48 | Exp. | 5 yrs. 9 mos. |

## APPENDIX E (*Continued*)

| Name | Law education * = degree | Legislative-Administrative Experience | | | | Legal-Judicial Experience | | | |
|---|---|---|---|---|---|---|---|---|---|
| | | House of Burgesses and/or Delegates | State Senate | Congress | Executive or regulatory[a] | General and Chancery courts | Courts of record | Courts not of record | Prose-cutor |
| Joynes | – | X | | | | | X | | X |
| Thompson | – | X | | | | X | | | |
| Rives | UVa | X | X | | | | | | |
| Christian | Private | | X | | | | X | | |
| W. Staples | W & M | X | | (Confed.)X | | | | | |
| Anderson | Fleming B. Miller | X | | | | | | | |
| Bouldin | William Leigh | X | | | | | | | |
| E. Burks | UVa* | X | | | | | | | |
| Lewis | UVa* | | | | | | | | X |
| Lacy | Richard T. Lacy (father) | X[b] | | | | | X | X | |
| Fauntleroy | UVa* | X | | | X | | | | X |
| Richardson | – | X | | | | | | | |
| Hinton | William T. Joynes | | | | | | | | X |
| Riely | Maj. W. S. Barton | | | | | | | | X |
| Cardwell | Samuel C. Redd | X[b] | | | | | | | |
| Keith | UVa | X | | | | | X | | |
| J. Buchanan | UVa | X | | X | | | | | |
| G. Harrison | UVa | | | | | | | | |
| Phlegar | W. Staples | | X | | | | | | X |
| S. Whittle | UVa | | | | | | X | | |
| Kelly | UVa* | | | | | | X | | |
| Sims | – | | X | | | | | X | |
| Prentis | UVa* | | | | X | | X | | |
| M. Burks | UVa* | | | | | | | | |
| Saunders | UVa* | X[b] | | X | | | X | | |
| West | UVa | | | | | | X | X | |

| Name | Occupation at appt. or election | Initially apptd. or elected | Date of appt. or election | Age at appt. or election | Age at end of service | Died (D), retired (R), defeated (Def.), term expired (Exp.) | Length of service |
|---|---|---|---|---|---|---|---|
| Joynes | state delegate | E | Feb. 22, 1866 | 48 | 54 | R | 4 yrs. 5 mos. |
| Thompson | — | E | Feb. 22, 1866 | —[e] | —[e] | D | —[f] |
| Rives | attorney | A | before Oct., 1866 | 59 | 62 | Def. | 3 yrs. 2 mos. |
| Christian | circuit judge | E | Mar. 23, 1870 | 41 | 54 | Def. | 12 yrs. |
| W. Staples | attorney | E | Mar. 23, 1870 | 44 | 56 | Def. | 12 yrs. |
| Anderson | attorney | E | Mar. 23, 1870 | 61 | 74 | Exp. | 12 yrs. |
| Bouldin | attorney | E | Apr. 2, 1872 | 61 | 65 | D | 4 yrs. 2 mos. |
| E. Burks | attorney | E | Dec. 15, 1876 | 55 | 60 | Exp. | 5 yrs. 3 mos. |
| Lewis | fed. dist. attorney | E | Feb. 25, 1882 | 35 | 48 | Exp. | 12 yrs. 5 mos. |
| Lacy | circuit judge | E | Feb. 25, 1882 | 43 | 54 | Exp. | 12 yrs. |
| Fauntleroy | sec. of commonwealth | E | Feb. 25, 1882 | 58 | 71 | Exp. | 12 yrs. |
| Richardson | attorney | E | Feb. 25, 1882 | —[e] | —[e] | Exp. | 12 yrs. |
| Hinton | commonwealth's attorney | E | Feb. 25, 1882 | 42 | 54 | Exp. | 12 yrs. |
| Riely | commonwealth's attorney | E | Jan. 6, 1894 | 54 | 61 | D | 5 yrs. 8 mos. |
| Cardwell | speaker of House of Delegates | E | Jan. 6, 1894 | 48 | 71 | R | 21 yrs. 11 mos. |
| Keith | circuit judge | E | Jan. 6, 1894 | 54 | 76 | R | 21 yrs. 6 mos. |
| J. Buchanan | attorney | E | Jan. 6, 1894 | 50 | 71 | R | 20 yrs. |
| G. Harrison | attorney | E | Jan. 6, 1894 | 47 | 70 | R | 22 yrs. 2 mos. |
| Phlegar | attorney | A | Oct. 1, 1900 | 54 | 54 | Def. | 5 mos. |
| S. Whittle | circuit judge | E | Feb. 1, 1901 | 51 | 70 | R | 18 yrs. 10 mos. |
| Kelly | Corporation Ct. judge | E | Feb. 3, 1914 | 46 | 58 | D | 9 yrs. 2 mos. |
| Sims | attorney | E | Feb. 2, 1916 | 53 | 62 | D | 8 yrs. 8 mos. |
| Prentis | SCC | A | Oct. 25, 1916 | 61 | 76 | D | 14 yrs. 11 mos. |
| M. Burks | dean of law school | A | Feb. 27, 1917 | 66 | 77 | D | 11 yrs. 1 mo. |
| Saunders | U.S. rep. | E | Jan. 16, 1920 | 59 | 61 | D | 1 yr. 11 mos. |
| West | circuit judge | E | Jan. 17, 1922 | 59 | 67 | D | 7 yrs. 9 mos. |

APPENDIX E (*Continued*)

| Name | Law education * = degree | Legislative-Administrative Experience | | | | Legal-Judicial Experience | | | |
|---|---|---|---|---|---|---|---|---|---|
| | | House of Burgesses and/or Delegates | State Senate | Congress | Executive or regulatory[a] | General and Chancery courts | Courts of record | Courts not of record | Prose-cutor |
| Campbell | UVa | | | | | | X | | X |
| Chichester | UVa | | | | | | X | X | X |
| Holt | Washington and Lee (W & L)* | | | | | | X | | |
| Epes | W & L* | | X | | X | | | | |
| Hudgins | University of Richmond (UR)* | X | | | | | X | | |
| Gregory | W & L* | | | | | | X | | |
| Browning | Georgetown Univ.* | X | | | | | X | | |
| Chinn | UVa | | | | X | | X | | X |
| Eggleston | W & L* | | X | | | | | | |
| Spratley | UVa* | | | | | | X | | X |
| A. Buchanan | W & L* | | | | | | X | | |
| A. Staples | W & L* | | X | | X | | | | |
| Miller | UR* | | | | | | X | | X |
| Smith | UVa* | X | | | | | X | | X |
| K. Whittle | W & L* | | | | | | X | | |
| Snead | UR* | | | | | | X | X | |
| I'Anson | UVa* | | | | | | X | | X |
| Carrico | Geo. Washington Univ.* | | | | | | X | X | |
| Gordon | UVa* | | | | | | | | |
| A. Harrison | UVa* | | | | X | | | | X |
| Harman | W & L* | | | | | | X | | |
| Cochran | UVa* | X | X | | | | | | |
| Poff | UVa* | | | X | | | | | |
| Compton | W & L* | | | | | | X | | |

| Name | Occupation at appt. or election | Initially apptd. or elected | Date of appt. or election | Age at appt. or election | Age at end of service | Died (D), retired (R), defeated (Def.), term expired (Exp.) | Length of service |
|---|---|---|---|---|---|---|---|
| Campbell | circuit judge | E | Jan. 29, 1924 | 50 | 72 | R | 21 yrs. 7 mos. |
| Chichester | Special Ct. of Appeals | A | June 1, 1925 | 55 | 59 | D | 4 yrs. 8 mos. |
| Holt | Special Ct. of Appeals | A | Apr. 24, 1928 | 63 | 83 | D | 19 yrs. 5 mos. |
| Epes | SCC | A | Nov. 15, 1929 | 47 | 53 | D | 5 yrs. 4 mos. |
| Hudgins | circuit judge | E | Jan. 20, 1930 | 48 | 76 | D | 28 yrs. 6 mos. |
| Gregory | Law and Chancery Ct. judge | E | Jan. 20, 1930 | 45 | 66 | D | 21 yrs. 1 mo. |
| Browning | circuit judge | E | Feb. 12, 1930 | 62 | 80 | D | 17 yrs. 7 mos. |
| Chinn | Ch. Comm. of Fisheries | A | Dec. 3, 1931 | 65 | 70 | D | 5 yrs. 9 mos. |
| Eggleston | state senator | A | Mar. 2, 1935 | 48 | 83 | R | 34 yrs. 8 mos. |
| Spratley | circuit judge | A | Aug. 27, 1936 | 54 | 85 | R | 31 yrs. 1 mo. |
| A. Buchanan | circuit judge | A | Sept. 12, 1946 | 56 | 79 | R | 23 yrs. 2 mos. |
| A. Staples | attorney general | A | Aug. 28, 1947 | 61 | 65 | R | 3 yrs. 4 mos. |
| Miller | Law & Equity Ct. judge | A | Oct. 17, 1947 | 54 | 67 | D | 13 yrs. 3 mos. |
| Smith | circuit judge | A | Jan. 26, 1951 | 60 | 66 | D | 5 yrs. 10 mos. |
| K. Whittle | circuit judge | A | Mar. 13, 1951 | 59 | 73 | R | 13 yrs. 11 mos. |
| Snead | circuit judge | A | Nov. 21, 1956 | 53 | 71 | R | 17 yrs. 8 mos. |
| I'Anson | hustings ct. judge | A | Aug. 25, 1958 | 51 | — | — | — |
| Carrico | circuit judge | A | Jan. 17, 1961 | 44 | — | — | — |
| Gordon | attorney | A | Feb. 17, 1965 | 49 | 56 | R | 7 yrs. 3 mos. |
| A. Harrison | attorney | A | Oct. 23, 1967 | 60 | — | — | — |
| Harman | circuit judge | A | Aug. 29, 1969 | 49 | — | — | — |
| Cochran | attorney | A | Aug. 29, 1969 | 57 | — | — | — |
| Poff | U.S. rep. | A | Aug. 28, 1972 | 48 | — | — | — |
| Compton | circuit judge | A | Sept. 4, 1974 | 44 | — | — | — |

[a] Includes service on Committee of Safety, Privy Council, and State Corporation Commission, as well as service as secretary of the commonwealth, governor, and attorney general.

[b] Speaker. [c] Resigned without serving. [d] Popularly elected. [e] Unavailable. [f] Died before taking seat.

# *Selected Bibliography*

## General


Abraham, Henry J. *The Judicial Process*, 3d rev. ed. New York: Oxford University Press, 1975.

Beatty, Jerry K. "An Institutional and Behavioral Analysis of the Iowa Supreme Court—1965–1969." Ph.D. dissertation, University of Iowa, 1970.

Brennan, William J. "State Supreme Court Judge versus United States Supreme Court Justice: A Change in Function and Perspective." *University of Florida Law Review* 29 (Fall 1966):225–37.

Brown, Elliott A. "The South Dakota Supreme Court: A Behavioral Introduction." *Public Affairs* (University of South Dakota) 26 (Aug. 15, 1966):1–6.

Canon, Bradley C. "Characteristics and Career Patterns of State Supreme Court Justices." *State Government* 45 (Winter 1972):34–41.

———. "State Supreme Courts—Some Comparative Data." *State Government* 42 (Autumn 1969):260–64.

———, and Dean Jaros. "External Variables, Institutional Structure and Dissent on State Supreme Courts." *Polity* 3 (Winter 1970):175–200.

Crito, Constance R. "American State Supreme Courts and Judges: A Study in Political Development." Ph.D. dissertation, Yale University, 1969.

Dolbeare, Kenneth M. *Trial Courts in Urban Politics: State Court Policy Impact and Functions in a Local Political System.* New York: John Wiley and Sons, 1967.

Fair, Daryle Russell. "The Supreme Court of Pennsylvania, 1933–1963: A Case Study in Judicial Behavior." Ph.D. dissertation, University of Pennsylvania, 1965.

Frye, Robert J. *The Alabama Supreme Court: An Institutional View.* University, Ala.: Bureau of Public Administration, University of Alabama, 1969.

Glick, Henry Robert. *Supreme Courts in State Politics: An Investigation of the Judicial Role.* New York: Basic Books, 1971.

———, and Kenneth N. Vines. *State Court Systems.* Englewood Cliffs, N.J.: Prentice-Hall, 1973.

Henderson, Bancroft C., and T. C. Sinclair. *The Selection of Judges in Texas: An Exploratory Study*. Houston: University of Houston Public Affairs Research Center, 1965.

Herndon, James. "Appointment as a Means of Initial Accession to Elective State Courts of Last Resort." *North Dakota Law Review* 38 (1962):60–73.

Jacob, Herbert. "The Effect of Institutional Differences in the Recruitment Process: The Case of State Judges." *Journal of Public Law* 33 (1964):104–19.

Ledbetter, Calvin Reville, Jr. "The Arkansas Supreme Court: 1958–1959." Ph.D. dissertation, Northwestern University, 1961.

Peltason, Jack W. *Federal Courts in the Political Process*. Garden City, N.Y.: Doubleday, 1955.

Prewitt, Kenneth. *The Recruitment of Political Leaders: A Study of Citizen-Politicians*. Indianapolis: Bobbs-Merrill Co., 1970.

Schmidhauser, John R. "The Justices of the Supreme Court: A Collective Portrait." *Midwest Journal of Political Science* 3 (Feb. 1959): 1–57.

Sickels, Robert J. "The Illusion of Judicial Consensus: Zoning Decisions in the Maryland Court of Appeals." *American Political Science Review* 59 (Mar. 1965):100–104.

Vines, Kenneth N. "Southern State Supreme Courts and Race Relations." *Western Political Quarterly* 18 (1965):5–18.

———, and Herbert Jacob. "Studies in Judicial Politics." *Tulane Studies in Political Science* 8 (1962).

Wood, John W. "State Judicial Selection: Realities vs. Legalities." *State Government* 31 (1958):17–19.

## Virginia

Austin, Robert J. "The Virginia Supreme Court of Appeals: Career Patterns and the Selection Process." *University of Virginia News Letter* 45 (Dec. 15, 1968):13–16.

Bain, Chester W. *Annexation in Virginia: The Use of the Judicial Process for Readjusting City-County Boundaries*. Charlottesville: Published for the Institute of Government, University of Virginia, by the University Press of Virginia, 1966.

Bennett, Hubert D. "Recent Developments in Virginia's Judicial System: Trial Courts of Record." *University of Virginia News Letter* 42 (Sept. 15, 1965):1–4.

Catterall, Ralph T. "The State Corporation Commission of Virginia." *Virginia Law Review* 48 (1962):139–51.

*Dedication of Building of Supreme Court of Appeals of Virginia, Richmond, Virginia, January 6, 1941.* Richmond: Richmond Press, 1941.

Eisenberg, Ralph. "Legislative Reapportionment and Congressional Redistricting in Virginia." *Washington and Lee Law Review* 23 (1966): 295–323.

———. "Virginia: The Emergence of Two-Party Politics." In *The Changing Politics of the South,* edited by William C. Havard. Baton Rouge: Louisiana State University Press, 1972.

Gay, Thomas Edward, Jr. "Creating the Virginia State Corporation Commission." *Virginia Magazine of History and Biography* 78 (Oct. 1970):464–80.

Gooch, Robert Kent. "The Recent Limited Constitutional Convention in Virginia." *Virginia Law Review* 31 (1945):708–26.

Heller, Francis Howard. *Virginia's State Government during the Second World War: Its Constitutional, Legislative, and Administrative Adaptations, 1942–1945.* Richmond: Virginia State Library, 1949.

I'Anson, Lawrence W. "How the Supreme Court of Appeals of Virginia Functions." *Proceedings of the Virginia State Bar Association* 71 (1960):221–29.

Kelly, Joseph L. "An Inside View of the Work of the Virginia Supreme Court." *Proceedings of the Virginia State Bar Association* 35 (1923): 213–25.

Key, V. O., Jr. *Southern Politics in State and Nation.* New York: Knopf, 1949.

Kirtley, Marjorie D. Unpublished compilation of brief biographies of the justices of the Virginia Supreme Court. Richmond: State Law Library, Sept. 1969, rev. Apr. 1973.

Lilly, Graham C., and Antonin Scalia. "Appellate Justice: A Crisis in Virginia?" *Virginia Law Review* 57 (1971):3–64.

Mays, David J. *Edmund Pendleton, 1721–1803, A Biography.* 2 vols. Cambridge: Harvard University Press, 1952.

McDanel, Ralph Clipman. *The Virginia Constitutional Convention of 1901–1902.* Baltimore: Johns Hopkins Press, 1928.

Morris, Thomas R. *Virginia's Lieutenant Governors: The Office and the Person.* Charlottesville: Governmental and Administrative Research Division, Institute of Government, University of Virginia, 1970.

Nelson, Margaret V. *A Study of Judicial Review in Virginia, 1789–1928.* New York: Columbia University Press, 1947.

Powell, Lewis F., Jr. "The Relation between the Virginia Court of Appeals and the State Corporation Commission." *Virginia Law Review* 19 (1933): 433–58, 571–93.

Ragan, Allen E. "Virginia's Judicial System: Organization and Improvement." *University of Virginia News Letter* 39 (Apr. 15, 1963):29–32.

Rankin, Hugh F. *Criminal Trial Proceedings in the General Court of Colonial Virginia.* Charlottesville: University Press of Virginia, 1965.

Sutelan, David K., and Wayne R. Spencer. "The Virginia Special Court of Appeals: Constitutional Relief for an Overburdened Court." *William and Mary Law Review* 8 (1967):244–76.

Tunstall, Robert B. "Why Ignore the Bar? A Study of Accessions to the Supreme Court of Appeals of Virginia." *Virginia Law Review* 38 (1952):1091–1109.

Va., Commission on Constitutional Revision. *The Constitution of Virginia: Report of the Commission on Constitutional Revision.* Charlottesville, Va.: Michie, 1969.

Wadlington, Walter. "The Loving Case: Virginia's Anti-Miscegenation Statute in Historical Perspective." *Virginia Law Review* 52 (1966): 1189–1223.

## Interviews

J. Lindsay Almond, Jr., former Governor of Virginia, Richmond, Feb. 23, 1971.

William G. Broaddus, former Law Clerk, Virginia Supreme Court, Richmond, Jan. 26, 1971.

William R. Broaddus, Jr., Member, Virginia State Bar Association Committee on Nominations to the Virginia Supreme Court, Martinsville, Feb. 3, 1971.

Archibald C. Buchanan, former Justice, Virginia Supreme Court, Tazewell, Oct. 29, 1970.

Harry L. Carrico, Justice, Virginia Supreme Court, Richmond, Oct. 1, 1970; Jan. 26, 1971.

Charles M. Davison, Jr., Reporter, Virginia Supreme Court, Charlottesville, Feb. 1, 1971.

John W. Eggleston, former Chief Justice, Virginia Supreme Court, Norfolk, Aug. 20, 1971.

Mills E. Godwin, Jr., former Governor of Virginia, Suffolk, Feb. 17, 1971.

Thomas C. Gordon, Jr., Justice, Virginia Supreme Court, Richmond, Mar. 14, 1972.

Albertis S. Harrison, Jr., Justice, Virginia Supreme Court, former Governor of Virginia, Lawrenceville, May 18, 1971.

Oliver W. Hill, NAACP attorney, Richmond, Nov. 30, 1972.

Richard H. Poff, Justice, Virginia Supreme Court, Richmond, Sept. 12, 1973.

Harold F. Snead, Chief Justice, Virginia Supreme Court, Richmond, July 13, 1972.
William M. Tuck, former Governor of Virginia, South Boston, Mar. 3, 1971.
S. W. Tucker, NAACP attorney, Richmond, Nov. 30, 1972.
Howard G. Turner, Clerk, Virginia Supreme Court, Richmond, Mar. 19, 1971.
Charles K. Woltz, former Reporter, Virginia Supreme Court, Charlottesville, Jan. 14, 1971.

# Index